My Three Lumps

Surviving Breast Cancer and Divorce
Simultaneously at Age 28

GWEN ROSHA ANDERSON

Barringer Publishing, Naples, Florida
www.barringerpublishing.com
Cover phto by Victoria Ashbrook
Cover, graphics, layout design by Lisa Camp
Editing by Carole Greene

ISBN: 978-0-09882034-6-4

Library of Congress Cataloging-in-Publication Data
My Three Lumps / Gwen Rosha Anderson

Printed in U.S.A.

Dedication

For my family, and most importantly, my mother.
Without them, I wouldn't have made it past July 9, 2008.
I love you with all my heart and soul.

And to Kern and Estella Magda.
You are the "something amazing" I was saved for.

Preface

It is now a year after my diagnosis, and I'm also nearing the end of my year of chemotherapy. I've been putting off rewriting my thoughts until now, until I felt strong enough again to reread the chronicle of all the pain I went through over the past twelve months. When I'd tried doing this earlier, even just rereading my handwritten journals, I was ripping my healing wounds open again, feeling the agony as I had on the day I went through it the first time. Now I am strong, the woman I was a long time ago. I am ready to share my story with other young survivors, showing them that even in the darkest days, you can discover a ray of sunshine somewhere, if you just choose to believe in it.

~G. T. R. A., September 21, 2009

Prologue

If I have to hear, "But you're so young!" one more time, I swear I'm going to vomit on someone. Yes, twenty-eight is young to be getting divorced, especially after only two years of marriage. And sure, twenty-eight IS nearly unheard of within "normal" populations of people to be diagnosed with breast cancer. But you know? It sure can happen. It sure can be a swell pain in the ass. Statistics didn't mean squat for me. This whole experience was beyond what I could have imagined I'd ever have to deal with.

All my life, I just wanted to have curly hair and big boobs. I should have been more careful what I wished for…

Part One:
THE LUMPS ARE DISCOVERED

JUNE 18, 2008

It was just a routine annual physical, just like the ones in all the years prior. The only reason I religiously kept these appointments was to keep up on my birth control. Yeeck—the one thing that truly scared me was being a mom! I was finishing up *In Cold Blood* by Truman Capote while waiting for Dr. Moghaddam (Ma-GOD-um) to come into the room. It was my first appointment with her, having just changed Ob-Gyns when my insurance changed. I really enjoyed my relationship with my last PA/Ob-Gyn whom I'd seen for the past two years; she had a great bedside manner and didn't condescend. Dr. Moghaddam, however, I found just the opposite of that. She rushed through my entire exam, not even introducing herself or asking who I was when she entered. She was so disconnectedly casual about finding the "denseness" in my left breast. Of course, I was "so young" and it "was probably nothing," but "just in case" she referred me to the Breast Center in Coon Rapids.

Okay, then, no big deal.

7

JUNE 25, 2008

I detest finding places located in unfamiliar areas. I know that I should be able to find things in Coon Rapids, especially since I work there. How embarrassing that I didn't even know where the Northtown Mall was. I went to the Breast Center of Suburban Imaging much earlier than my scheduled 3:30 appointment. I was done with summer school at 11:15, and no way was I wasting gas at $4 a gallon to drive home to Maple Grove first. I had my new book, *Memoirs of a Geisha*, to keep me busy. (I'm so content now that I've rediscovered my love of reading.) Fortunately, the Breast Center was able to sneak me in early.

I undressed completely from the waist-up and put on my pretty pink robe, many extra sizes bigger than my 115-pound frame—bigger than most women's frames! I probably could have wrapped it around myself a few times. I sat with my book in the second waiting room, now feeling awkward. You'd think I would be worried about sitting in public with a robe that wasn't close to closing securely. However, looking around the waiting room, I became painfully aware of how young I was compared to the other patients. I felt bad for these older women being diagnosed with cancer, being "tortured" with all their treatments. Thank God I'm young, I thought, and don't have to deal with all of that.

I was bizarrely fascinated with my ultrasound when I was called in. Dr. Moghaddam hadn't specified in her notes to the Breast Center which breast was dense and where the denseness was, so they poked around both of them. They reviewed where my skin was, where the breast tissue was, where my muscle was ("There's a lot of muscle in there, actually," was what the ultrasound tech told me, which made me feel stronger than Hulk Hogan), and where my ribs were. I thought about asking the tech to check my abdomen too, you know, just in case. I figured that wasn't quite the time, which was too bad. It would have been cool to see my guts.

As the tech moved from the right breast to the left, she methodically moved in her clockwise positions around the areola. At one-o-clock on my left breast, she casually mentioned that there was a cyst. She took several pictures and measurements before finishing up. My clumsiness blessed me when we were finished, by splattering the blue ultrasound goo all over my face and chest. I cleaned up and went back to waiting room #3 in my pretty pink robe.

The nurse came back to get me and told me the doctor reviewing my ultrasounds wanted to be safe and get a mammogram of my left breast before I left. HOW UNCOMFORTABLE was that whole experience! They squished my small A-cup boob in between these two plates, the top one clear, so I could see myself squished and contorted for the photo. I felt like a little kid during the whole thing, not being able to hold still in the "right way." Move my hand there, chin *up*, don't breathe, put my arm back down, hold still, chin up, etcetera. After the forty-five-degree angle shot, I was finally free to get dressed again and wait in the nurse's office.

Now, of all the nurses I've seen so far, I remembered Marlene better than most. Right away, she was concerned about my well-being. She checked on me after waiting alone for a long, silent while in the office. She eventually came in to explain the next steps for me, how I'd have to come back for a cyst aspiration on an upcoming Tuesday or Thursday. She left me armed with a fistful of information on benign lesions and less-common benign breast lumps. She said that they would drain the cyst like a blister unless it didn't drain or drained an opaque, non-white color.

The next Tuesday or Thursday I had open was July 8 or 10. Better just get the good or bad news out of the way, even if it was my birthday. No biggie, just a breast-blister draining and not a biopsy. My birthday could handle that.

JUNE 30, 2008

Over the weekend, my husband Andy and I had quite a few discussions about life and our lives. Well, not so much discussions as fights. I was glad I would be going to D.C. that week for the NEA Conference, to give us a chance to do our own thing for a few days. I loved him so much, but sometimes I felt like I didn't give my opinions a chance to be heard anymore. I tried so hard to do only what he wanted that I got resentful when my thoughts got left behind. Why should I ever leave behind what makes *me* happy? Often, I was the only one who cared about what makes me happy.

I needed to focus more on what made me happy, and being happier would bring peace to our relationship.

JULY 3, 2008

I called Andy tonight from D.C. after the convention had ended for the day. Andy told me that he got his second DUI yesterday while bringing an old coworker home. At first, I was furious. What was he thinking?! Was he thinking about how it would affect him or us? Then I realized that no amount of yelling would help the situation. I'd just rather sort everything out when I got home on Sunday. Thank God the convention would keep me busy for the next few days. No aspirin for my headache now; no blood thinners until after the aspiration on Tuesday.

JULY 6, 2008

I got in about ten P.M. Andy was silently waiting by luggage carousel 2. I still didn't want to talk. I had just finished *Tuesdays with Morrie* on the plane, and I was choosing to be happy. Morrie was a sociology professor who had such a positive life outlook after being diagnosed with Lou Gehrig's disease. In his teachings, he spoke of non-attachment. The Buddhists would recognize what feelings they held and then let them go. I recognized my sadness, anger, and frustration with Andy, and I chose to just let it go. Finally, I was choosing to be happy.

Calmly, on the way home, I asked him to decide whether or not he wanted to be married anymore. He wasn't acting like I mattered to him with his recent decisions, so I told him my decision to "move" to the guest room…to give him time to think. But I didn't have to. He told me he'd decided to sleep at work because he'd realized he didn't want to be married anymore.

I spent a long night alone, unpacking, cleaning, and researching marriage counselors on the Internet. What a long trip, long day, and long morning ahead. But at least I was choosing to be happy.

JULY 7, 2008

Andy decided that he wasn't strong enough to be married. He wanted to have time to be immature with his bar friends and not worry about how a married man "should act." (His words, not mine.) How awful to find out that your husband would choose his friends over you. How even more awful to beg—literally beg—your husband to stay with you and make your marriage work. Even though the pain of this situation was excruciating, I still chose to be happy.

JULY 8, 2008

Happy Birthday to me. Vic's right; it's difficult to imagine me as twenty-eight. Even twenty-eight-year-olds keep busy on their birthdays. I started with TaeBo in my bedroom (as Andy was sleeping on the living room couch). At least he remembered it was my birthday and wished me a happy one. I'd feared he'd forget that. I brought cookies to celebrate at summer school. People without summer birthdays never know how excluding it feels not to celebrate at school with everyone else.

My Breast Center appointment was at 1:00 P.M. with Dr. Shah, but Dr. Crook came to greet me. I dressed yet again in my pretty pink robe and waited for the aspiration to begin. Dr. Crook said that, to her, the lump on my ultrasound didn't look like a cyst, that they would go straight to biopsy. Instantly, tears sprang to my eyes. Honestly, what next?

I'd been fighting with Andy for days, my marriage was ending, and now my cyst wasn't a cyst anymore. Didn't *anyone* care that it was my birthday?! I was supposed to be showered with cards, calls, happiness, and it would end with blowing the candles out. I felt bad for Dr. Crook and her nurse for having to deal with my erratic behavior. Of course, to them I was just upset about my new non-cyst. Dr. Crook held my hand to reassure me that things would be all right. Then we proceeded to biopsy.

They numbed my lump area with Novocain then told me about the biopsy "gun." It would sound like a staple gun discharging. Sure, *try* not to jump when you hear that going off! They took four "good" samples of the lump and sent them to pathology. Steri-Strips in place, they also gave me a small icepack for the biopsy area. Wish I had asked for another ice pack for the right side; I loved the added girth to my bust line! They said they'd call tomorrow with the results. Again, no big deal. They gave me information only on the benign lumps. If there were a chance at malignancy, I figured, they'd have given me some info on it.

I decided to stop at my house before heading up to St. Cloud for dinner with my mom, just to freshen up my eyes and makeup. Just my luck, Andy was home. He wanted time to himself, and being there was not what I was ready for. Not wanting to intrude, I tried to busy myself and stay out of his way. He joined me for a cigarette on the deck, and then asked me about my appointment. I tried to stay casually aloof, not wanting him to worry or feel bad for me. I mentioned my thoughts of my benign-only diagnoses, but it didn't seem to calm him. I stayed impressively calm throughout the whole conversation. With tears in his eyes, he asked me something about finding out "the worst." It felt good that he still worried about me, even if he didn't want to be married to me anymore.

I was keeping my fingers crossed for us, but I still feared the worst. If someone needs time to figure out what he wants, and one of those choices is you, shouldn't that be a hint to me? Shouldn't I let go of hope for ever having "us" back? I couldn't let even the glimmer of hope go. I'd meant it when I vowed "for good times and in bad," even if he didn't. I left for Mom and Dad's after a hug from him and the offer to go see *Wall-E* when I got back. Hope was still vaguely alive!

When I got to Mom's, I went straight to her for a hug. Nothing feels as good as Mom's arms comforting me. I got all weepy telling my story to her, then to Kathryn, then to Vic. What a crappy birthday; my husband was leaving me and I had a questionable lump in my breast. Honestly, if it weren't for my family, I would have lost it today. They all sat patiently and listened to all of my rambling, not to tell me they understood how I felt, but that they supported me. My family didn't offer up much advice on anything, just patiently listened and reflected right alongside of me. Kath whipped out the sloe gin and 7-Up quickly, just like the ultrasound team told me to do earlier. Vic brought my favorite cookies—coconut chocolate chip—and I rationed them out to preserve their celestial goodness. Kathryn was the strong one, telling me to insist that Andy move out, and I began to see that she was right. It would be better for both of us if he just took the time he needed away from me. Mom said, after Kath left, that I shouldn't make any quick decisions, to give the situation the time it needed and things would work out.

As much as I was torn in the direction of staying strong and independent, I longed for the feeling of love and contentment with Andy.

Dinner at the Mexican Village that night was wonderful: family, fun, laughter, food, and fried ice cream. Even after getting the quick reference to my biopsy out of the way (to catch everyone up on what was going on), it was a perfect evening of feeling "normal." We got a great laugh out of racing my wind-up sushi toys from Amanda around the table. We all enjoyed the fried ice cream by just passing it counter-clockwise among us— me, Alison, Amanda, Mom, Brit, and Sydney my niece, though Syd didn't partake in its cool Mexican deliciousness.

I was back in Maple Grove by nine P.M. to pick up Andy and head to the movie. Changing at home before leaving worked to my advantage; my short skirt held his attention the whole time! The power of TaeBo-strong legs. We spent the movie carefully keeping each other's attention, the flirting frustration overcoming me. How awkward to not know how to act around your husband, to be a stranger in his presence. I cried at the end of the Pixar love story, trying not to think of my own crumbling love story I now lived. I went to bed alone, eagerly looking forward to tomorrow.

Part Two:
LIFE (AS I KNEW IT)
COMPLETELY CHANGES

JULY 9, 2008

The day started as usual with summer school in the A.M. I talked briefly with Garnet, my summer school co-teacher, about how impressed I was with the Breast Center and how concerned they were about my well-being. Marlene had called around 11:00 A.M. to check how I was doing. I didn't have a chance to answer, since my cell was in my classroom and I was enjoying the sunshine of bus duty. It felt wonderful to be so cared for, especially thinking about how Dr. Moghaddam brushed me off.

Garnet understood what I felt. She shared with me that ten years earlier she herself was diagnosed with malignant melanoma. She had gone to her doctor out of complete vanity; she had a black dot on her fair-skinned back and wanted it removed. The doctor removed the dot, along with a strip of her back four inches long, one inch wide, and one inch deep. She'd been in remission for ten years. She also never told her parents anything about the entire process. I couldn't imagine going through that alone, even if it kept painful news from loved ones. I was glad I had Garnet to share in my fears, even if they weren't warranted.

I went home that day to wait for my results. I filled the moments talking to Tracy, a surgical nurse friend of mine. Tracy was always so upbeat and optimistic, a perfect person to have in your corner. I ended our conversation when the other line beeped in. I told her I'd let her know what the prognosis was, though I had a sinking feeling of what it was when I saw the caller I.D. It was Marlene from the Breast Center again. She told me the doctor was at the hospital, but she wanted her to call me with the results. Instant butterflies sprang into my stomach as I waited, breathless, for her response.

"Gwen, it's cancer."

Instant hysterics and disbelief hit me like a Mack truck. Not only did I not believe her, I was now crying hysterically and near hyperventilation. She said how sorry she was while I couldn't do anything but sob. Though it was only seconds, my world stopped for what seemed like days. I don't know how I snapped out of it, but an instant calm washed over me. I sniffled my nose and asked her what kind it was. Somehow, I found a pen and my planner and wrote, as she spelled it for me: "infiltrating ductal carcinoma." She could've made up a disease for all I knew then about types of breast cancer.

I thanked her and asked her what my next steps were. She said I'd need to see a surgeon ASAP and that she'd call with an appointment for me. I was embarrassed, in hind-sight, thinking of my first reaction to the thought of her making an appointment for me—*Ooh, I have to work this around my school teaching schedule.* Now was NOT the time to put work before my health. I agreed, thanked her again then accepted another "I'm so sorry."

Yeah, me too.

I was instantly on the phone again, calling Tracy back. Again in hysterics, I told her I had cancer. She impressed me with her cool, calm medical demeanor. She asked me what I knew, what my next steps were, and told me that I'd beat this. "If you ever need anything…" she added. What do you even ask for when people offer that? I humbly accepted with a "Thank you" and I called my mom. Before the call even started, my pacing began; I couldn't stand still anymore. When Mom answered the phone, I tried to stay calm. The last thing I wanted to do was to freak her out, though everything I was about to say would do just that.

"Mom, I got the results."

"Okay…" (She took a deep breath.)

"I have cancer."

Here's where I can't remember what I said anymore. I know for certain there was a lot of crying from both of us, mostly me. I told her what it was exactly. There was a ton of denial, only mine. Even though the rational part of me had already taken in and processed the news, especially now talking to Mom, nothing felt real. How could I have cancer? Everyone kept telling me how young I was, that this was supposed to be nothing.

I'd had so many random thoughts, and I'd gone over the whole series of bad news. First, I couldn't believe it, no matter what my brain said. Everyone kept reassuring me, giving me only benign information, telling me I was so young and healthy. Then I was angry; why did the nurses and techs lie to me? Yes, I was young. Yes, I was healthy. Sure, it may have been nothing. BUT IT WASN'T. Maybe just believing it was a cyst made it easier to live my life for two weeks, but now it hit me right in the gut. They were trying to be helpful, but they had lied to me.

Marlene called me back and told me that I had an appointment with a good doctor on Friday at 2:00 P.M.— Rodney Lovett at Mercy Hospital in Coon Rapids. I updated Mom on the appointment, and she asked if I'd like her to come with me. Without hesitation I said yes. I needed my mom with me. The whole time I was on the phone with her, I knew my voice was shrill, my heart was palpitating, and my manner was frantic. The second I got off the phone with her, I intended to keep moving by vacuuming the house. But sadness hit me.

I closed my phone and went to my knees behind the couch in the living room, to pray. I was not a religious person by any stretch of the imagination—hadn't believed in God since I was seventeen—but now I realized that I needed any and all support I could get. I prayed that He would guide me and be with me through all that was to come. My exact words weren't "Why me?" but "Okay, God, what do I do now?" I sat there on my knees for a while, but finally I got up and tried to act normal again.

After talking to Mom, I knew that I didn't want to tell Andy *anything*. The last thing I wanted was for him to feel bad for me, to stay with me just because I was sick. If he chose to stay, I'd tell him then. If he chose to leave, he'd never have to know. Just the thought of *not* telling him was already eating me alive, and it had only been an hour of knowing.

I still had no intention of telling him until I talked to my friend Carrie that evening. I told her about what I'd found out (bad things always come in threes—Andy's DUI, him leaving me, and now cancer) and she'd maintained that he'd come to his senses. I also told her that I didn't want to tell him about my illness; I didn't want it to be the reason he stayed with me. She convinced me to tell him. She argued that he needed to know so if he chose to stay, he'd need to know that things would be even harder. Over our beef "pitzas" I'd made, I decided that she was right. She went home and I decided to wait for Andy…to talk. I sat at home, waiting with my newly-acquired cancer self-help books from the library. I'd always been the good student, so of course the first place I'd go after a diagnosis was to the library.

I got through about two pages of the first book, rereading the same pages more than a couple of times, before Andy got home. When I saw him come around the corner of the stairs, I asked him if we could talk. He agreed and sat next to me on the couch. I took a deep breath and felt my heart beating out of my chest. I put his hand over my heart, hoping he'd feel how important this was to me. I laid everything I knew (so limited yet) out there and solemnly added, "This is not to make you stay. I don't want this to be the reason you stay with me. I can handle this alone, but I can't handle knowing that this is the reason you stayed."

He told me that during the day, he had a long talk with himself in a park. He asked himself if he were single, what would he want to do that night? He said that he'd want to be with me. He decided he wanted to be with me and make things work.

I asked him repeatedly, "Are you sure? I want you to take the time you need for *you*. This seems quick—are you sure?"

He became upset after a few times and asked me to stop asking—he was sure.

I cried and held tightly to him. This was what I needed: my best friend here to support me, to hold me, to love me. I spent the rest of the night never far from his side. This was where I wanted to be.

JULY 10, 2008

The next morning I happily went to work, wearing my wedding ring again. I didn't feel scared anymore, knowing Andy was staying by my side. Garnet asked me what the doctor said, and I shared the news with her. It was comforting to share with someone who understood. At dinner that night at the Crystal Bistro, I shared my news with Jason and Jessica, great friends from college. It's hard being honest with the ones you love. Jason was visibly upset, but both of them were so caring and supportive. It's amazing to know such great friends will never leave you.

I made it home by 8:00 P.M. to meet my sisters, Rachel (the future pharmacist and my new oncology specialist), Sheila, and Alison—all members of my newly-formed extra-support team.

Everyone brought incredible desserts and a desire for fun. Sure, we snuck in some shop-talk about what I needed to ask and talk about with my surgeon. We did laugh until we cried at Rachel's toe cramp, at all the sweets we ate, and at everyone feeling me up while I lay topless on the floor. Just when you need a camera! At the end of the night, I was ready to face Dr. Lovett.

JULY 11, 2008

Mom came at 1:00 P.M. to bring me to my first official appointment as a cancer patient. I felt awful being short with her when she was trying to read to me the information on the prayer blanket she brought for me. What's an extra minute to just *listen* to the woman who's given you everything she has? That prayer blanket spent the day with me, though. We braved the July humidity and heat, along with awful MapQuest directions, to make our trek to Mercy Hospital's Professional Building, Suite 104. We made it with literally minutes to spare. I found Dr. Lovett's card in the waiting room and freaked out. He looked older than the hills! What if the man died in surgery? Could he still *see?*

Grief, Gwen.

In the exam room, I felt no embarrassment getting topless again, this time in front of my mom. She had to bathe me after my car accident in 2002; I was hoping she wouldn't find it weird to see my naked body again. She was talking nervously with Dr. Lovett as we waited for "The Plan." His plan for me included a surgery for the upcoming Tuesday, July 15. All of a sudden, I had no time to freak out about my cancer. Surgery was right around the corner. During the whole while we were in his "care," Dr. Lovett made me feel important, like I wasn't just a patient but a *person*. He asked me if I was married and when I said yes, he wondered aloud where my husband was that day. I didn't have the guts to tell him my marriage was so uncertain that I didn't know if I'd still be married by today.

Mom and I left with more information than ever. Now I'd have to do genetic testing after surgery to see if the cancer ran in my family. God help me, if I can prevent one of my sisters from going through this too. Speaking of the lovelies, Kathryn was coming to visit that night. She recommended quesadillas, and I enjoyed the cooking distraction from thinking. I enjoyed the time having cocktails and a dinner of appetizers with two of the strongest women I know. When Andy came home, the dynamic between the three of us completely changed. We engaged in awkward small talk, probably due to my birthday and what happened between the two of us the day before.

Mom and Kath left soon afterward, and Andy and I spent a quiet, eventless evening at home. I was more than sick of cancer talk, but it was all I could think about. I was now struggling with my choice to be happy, just as I'd promised both of us only a few days prior.

JULY 12, 2008

I'd e-mailed my friend Jenni A. the day before to say hi and to tell her my news. I had a feeling I knew it was her calling that morning; I knew she'd read it. I also knew she was a good person who would understand; she was diagnosed with multiple sclerosis in 2001. She was great to vent to. She'd seen worse than this. I was so blessed to have treasured her as my friend through all these years.

Tracy and I popped into Barnes and Noble before Amanda came down at five P.M. She brought me a set of wind-up sushi to complete the collection she'd started for me on my birthday, a relaxing lotion, and a fragrance fan. She's great at knowing things—like the sushi—to cheer me up. For the first time in days, I spent the day feeling like a person again. We didn't talk about the cancer, but about books, foods we like (and how asparagus makes urine smell funny), and her tough time with her pregnancy. It was good to hear about her struggles, how she put on her happy face through her pain. I saw how it could be done. I admired her for that, seeing how hard it was just trying to live your life and hide who you are and how you feel.

What an incredible woman, and I'm so proud of her strength, her *fuerza*.

JULY 13, 2008

A relatively quiet day. Andy and I decided to walk to Weaver Lake just to get out of the house. While we were strolling there, he told me of his plans to meet up with some guys from work to watch the new Batman movie early that week. Normally that would never bother me in the least, but my surgery was scheduled for Tuesday, only two days away. I started to feel he was avoiding spending time with me, since he was making zero plans to be with me. I knew this was hard on him too, so I tried to choose happiness yet again and just be happy he had plans with friends. Still, it was hard to feel so alone. On our way home, I mentioned that I was looking for a counselor for us. He said it wouldn't be a bad idea, but again that was all he said about my suggestion we get counseling.

JULY 14, 2008

One day to S-Day (surgery). I started super early in the morning with an MRI, chest x-ray, and another mammogram (this time on the right breast, to make sure I was clear of cancer on that side.) It was hard to sit and get all these tests, scared that they would show something more. I tried to make the most of the "last day of freedom" and ran some errands. I stopped at a massage place and got a gift certificate for Andy for an hour-long massage plus gratuity, just to let him know how much I appreciated his future support in the upcoming days. I wanted to have something for him to take care of himself too. I got Mom another gas gift card to defray all the costs of so many Twin Cities visits. That night, I caved early and gave Andy his gift, wanting to show him how much I appreciated him. We had a great night of Guitar Hero, drinks, and a good night of intimacy. I felt so happy and content, but at the same time, scared out of my mind for tomorrow.

JULY 15, 2008

S-Day. I squeezed in my last workout, trying desperately to hang on to my last normal moments. My mother-in-law Diane came up from southern Minnesota to be there for my surgery, an act that was surprising to me. I was sure she wanted to support Andy through it. Mom came early too, armed with treats—fresh veggies, broccoli-and-cauliflower soup, and a potted plant for the shepherd's hook she'd placed in my front yard. Andy was worried about leaving early because of traffic, and I upset him by wanting to wait for my teeth whitening strips to be done. He got pretty irritated, and nothing I said seemed to calm him. We all seemed nervous.

I drove us to the Breast Center for my wire tumor locator and then to the MRI room for my radioactive injection. It felt so awkward to have a wire sticking out of my breast, even though it was covered by tape. I couldn't understand why I needed the wire inserted at the Breast Center before driving to the hospital. The radioactive injection was to locate my sentinel node with a Geiger meter in surgery, the kind of meter that will beep when it goes over what it is looking for—just like looking for hidden treasures. It really stung, even with my breast being numbed. I had a feeling that the pain would soon be worse. I felt awful that my three-member support team sat in that waiting room for three hours for this whole process to be over. When I came out, Mom smiled and the other two were very somber and sedate. Andy drove us to Mercy, I was admitted, and immediately I was whisked through admissions and into surgery. They had a cancellation and Lovett moved me up from 2:30 to 1:00. I watched a television monitor that looked like a flight schedule showing when people were finished with surgery, knowing that list would soon include me.

I went with a nurse to a small room to change into my stylish hospital robes, tights, and anti-slip socks, topped off with a hairnet. Later on, when my family came to say good-bye before surgery began, I felt immediate pain, isolation, and intense fear. To hug away my loved ones before marching to surgery felt like I'd never see them again. I had never felt as scared as I did then, actually feeling now like I was saying my final goodbyes. I clearly remember hugging Andy last and thanking him for loving me so much.

I lay on the gurney, still unable to stop sobbing. I was wheeled to a pre-surgery holding room full of curtains and other pre-surgery patients. Two nurses came to ask me what surgery I was having and more random check-in questions. The anesthesiologist checked in as well, a good-looking German doctor whom I didn't quite understand (though with that face, I didn't care what he was saying). Finally, Dr. Lovett came. I felt relief to see a familiar face. He drew a mark ("an *L* for Lovett") above my left breast, and soon he was gone too. I stared at the spotted ceiling tiles, trying to remember this exact moment to write it in my journal. I cried again. Then two more nurses came in and one gave me the "relaxation medication." I was trying to figure out: *Is this the good stuff, or just the relaxing medicine?* That was the last thing I remembered.

I woke up later in pain, but not awful pain. Then it got worse. The recovery nurse gave me some medicine, but it didn't really help. I tried to eat a graham cracker, but I had such awful cotton mouth that all I could do was sip water. After not eating all day, I was starving, but I couldn't eat a thing. Mom, Andy, and Diane came to say hello, and Andy was allowed to stay. So quietly, he helped me put my street clothes back on. Soon I felt like I was going to pass out, and I had to lie down again. Finally, after a lifetime, we got me dressed. I was pushed to the car in a wheelchair, feeling so much like a cancer patient then.

I remember Andy driving too fast through the parking lot or hitting the brakes too quickly, and I asked him to slow down, and that really angered him. I noticed, and I tried to help my awful mood by thanking him for driving us home. I don't remember the drive, but I remember sitting on the old couch in my living room, in awful pain. Diane headed home soon after we got back. After Andy filled my Vicodin prescription, I took one and tried to eat crackers, which made me nauseous again. I painfully fell asleep on the couch, Andy upstairs and Mom downstairs with me on the other couch.

My surgery was over.

JULY 16, 2008

The next morning, I woke up with Mom still next to me on the couch. She didn't want me to wake up alone downstairs. I managed to take a Vicodin to help the pain. I spent the morning watching movies with Mom while Andy slept until 11:00. He got up and started work stuff immediately. He did eventually sit with me on the couch, but I felt he was too distant, not really there. I told him if he wanted to go to work to just go. He left at 5:00 P.M. to help train the new bartender. I felt my heart being ripped out, seeing him leave, but I knew he was dealing with a lot too. Mom and I made beef barley soup, even though I couldn't do much with my gimpy left side. It hurt that before Andy left he didn't bother to help us cook, even though he could see I was obviously having so many problems chopping.

Mom helped me take a bath that night, my first since the surgery. It didn't feel weird getting naked in front of her yet again, but taking off the Ace bandage "corset" was heart-wrenching. To see my body so covered in iodine from surgery, and then seeing my smaller breast shriveled and mashed was too much for me. I cried for all the hurt, the surprise, the fear, the pain, for what I had lost. Not yet could I see what I had courageously done to save my life; that didn't matter. I looked awful. All I could see were Steri-strips and a scar under my left arm from the lymph node removal. Mom and I spent a lot of time—and a lot of cotton balls and rubbing alcohol—to start removing all the iodine. All the while, I sat naked—and exposed in so many ways—in front of my mom.

We stayed up late that night watching *In Her Shoes* and *P.S. I Love You.* She wanted to stay with me until Andy got home. She left at 6:00 the next morning when he finally did come home. I sat up all night reading cancer books and taking notes. Andy didn't say much to me and eventually went to sleep.

JULY 17, 2008

Mom left, and I was still awake. When Andy went to work later that morning, I felt so alone that my chest hurt. I sat and cried by myself until Mom called and said she was coming back again. My heart swelled with so much love and happiness to be with her again. We watched *Mad Money* and she, Brit, Rachel, and Dan came to eat a new Indian recipe I tried that night. We talked about Brit's relationship issues with her boyfriend Brandon, and I saw how hard it was for Mom to try to let Brit be an adult and make her own decisions.

I now see clearly how difficult it is for a mother to watch her children grow up and not need her as much, but how we will always be her babies. Her being there and keeping me feeling better was an incredible gift and blessing. She again stayed with me until Andy got home. She had to work that day in St. Cloud and left at 6:45 A.M. I began to fear the time when she had to leave. She became my new best friend through all of this, and I became dependent on her hugs to keep me alive.

JULY 18, 2008

Andy went to work in the morning, so I decided to try walking to Weaver Lake for exercise. I wrote in my journal while taking in the sunshine and cool lake breeze. It felt peaceful to reflect there. I read a book about one woman's spiritual journey through her breast cancer. There was a connection between the woman and me. I began to understand the difficult and incredible journey ahead of me. Surgery, chemo, radiation—it all started to make more sense. It didn't make my thoughts easier but painful and real. Then Dr. Lovett called with my surgery report.

They had removed the stage 1b tumor and had free margins around it (no cancer spreading to the nearby tissue). My sentinel node also tested negative for cancer; thank God! However, there was more bad news. They found stage 0 DCIS (ductal carcinoma in situ)—precancerous cells—nearby the tumor area. I needed another surgery to remove it.

I called Andy and Mom, neither of them surprised, but happy the rest went so well. My best news of the day was getting my car fixed for $20 rather than the hundreds I'd feared. I thanked the mechanic for the best news I'd heard all week, and I meant it, even if they thought I was crazy for being so elated. I had a near normal night at home with Andy, ordering pizza and watching *Entourage*. I needed a night of "normal."

JULY 19, 2008

Andy left for work early in the morning after I'd made him a batch of his favorite blueberry muffins. We seemed so happy, and it felt so darn nice. Rachel came at 10:00 A.M. to go to the Farmers' Market in Minneapolis and to run errands with me. What a great sister! At the market, we bought quite the spread and spent the afternoon preparing pesto with our fresh basil stash. We also were so idyllically proud of the fresh strawberry sauce we'd made, not knowing what the heck we were doing. I started to overwork myself that night—cleaning the house— just because it felt great to be mobile again. When I talked to Andy before he went behind the bar, I was like a kid sharing all my fun activities of the day with him. Though he was right there on the phone, I knew something was off.

JULY 20, 2008

Andy and I woke up relatively early, and I tried my Power Shaping video, just to slowly work back into "real" exercise. It was awkward and slow, but I hadn't felt that good from working out in a long time. It was exhilarating, feeling as if I was physically beating the cancer myself just then, and not vice versa. Success was mine! I even called my summer school substitute teacher Pam, to thank her for her help during the week and to let her know that I could go back to work tomorrow. I was feeling closer to normal all the time. Andy and I had even made plans for that afternoon to grill out with our friends Tracy and Jason. We even had a pretty hot moment in the kitchen. What a great start to the day!

We took a shower, and while we were washing up, I saw the big mole on his back again. To me, it looked like melanoma. After all my recent events, I wanted to help him, save him from a cancer ordeal. I asked him if he cared about his health at all would he please get it checked out. Only two weeks prior, I'd asked him about getting it checked out. He wanted to deal with my cancer first, and I accepted it then. Now, in light of recent events, I asked again. He said he would, but he'd said that before with no results, so I pressed a little harder. As I can be a tad dramatic, I said something about not wanting him to die. In hindsight, I was just so concerned about him and I wanted him to be concerned too. He became quiet, and we got out of the shower in silence. He seemed angry with me, and after we dressed and sat on the couch, there was still silence between us.

I asked him what was up with him, that he seemed so far away. He told me that he didn't know how to say it, but that he couldn't do it anymore; he couldn't be with me. I calmly absorbed it; I'd had a feeling this was coming. I could sense things had been off ever since he'd decided to stay with me. He cried, and I actually was the calm one for once. I went outside to call Mom, to tell her, and that I would need her help with the treatments. She was also calm, not knowing what to say either. She said she'd be there for my next surgery and the day after to take care of me. She ended the call telling me how much she loved me.

I then called Tracy to tell her we couldn't make it but that I still wanted to come see her myself. She sensed something off, told me she had a bottle of wine, and to come on over. I packed up the dinner I was planning to make and said goodbye to Andy. He said he might head to his parents' house but he didn't know for sure where he'd be.

I drove to Tracy's and dropped the bomb. She hugged me and listened as a true friend would. I cried in honest disbelief and shock, pain for everything that was happening to me. She said he was a jerk, that I was better off. Everything a good friend would want her good friend in need to hear. While talking, I realized that Andy hadn't deposited any money in our joint account for over a month. I panicked, fearing he'd try to take more of the money from us, and I flew home to take care of the accounts.

Unfortunately, he was still there when I got back, but I ignored him. I found the savings account information and took his name off of the account, the account that held our $60k in savings. Oddly, he still said nothing to me as I rifled through my file holder filled with account information. He'd packed a bag and said he might be back later on, but that he still didn't know where he'd be. I had no idea what to say to him anymore.

After he'd left, I enacted what I call the "panic calls" mode, calling Carrie, Tracy again, Sheila, Jason, and Kathryn. Everyone was also shocked and angry. Most were ready to hunt him down and "take care of him" for me, especially Jason (bless his heart; that man would do anything for me). My heart was now splintered. I was alone, emotionally and physically, though I was surrounded by my family and friends. My entire desire to fight was officially gone.

JULY 21, 2008

Che (Jason) gave me a family law attorney's name. I called and waited for her reply but none came. Life became a flurry of phone calls—doctor referrals, calls to friends, Comcast, XCel Energy, CenterPoint Energy, two mortgage companies, coworkers, counselors, and two airlines about our Ireland trip in August. Through all the chaos, Dr. Lovett gave me a new surgery date: August 8. He asked who I was going to Ireland with, and my voice started to quiver when I said I didn't know. I told him that Andy had left, and even he shed a tear with me.

I also called Andy to see what he wanted to do (with us), and he shocked me by saying he'd looked up divorce papers. He never took initiative unless he really wanted something. It was official—he wanted a divorce, but he didn't want to start paperwork yet. Umm, what?! What was I supposed to do now? Where was I going to go?

Sheila and Ali came over that night, thank goodness. I was a wreck. Sheila literally held my hand and told me what a beautiful person I was. Thank God for sisters. We shared *Under the Tuscan Sun,* more tears from me, and many hours together that night. Sheila also slept in my bed with me and continued to ease my pain with her caring and supportive words. Again, thank God for sisters.

JULY 22, 2008

Another whirlwind day. First was summer school, and I shared with Garnet all the crap, and she offered advice on housing, money, and love. She said to keep the house, buy Andy out, and reminded me how she'd got screwed the same way eight years ago. What a feeling to know I wasn't alone, though I always knew I wasn't. After more account changes, I went to Wells Fargo to figure out accounts, and then I spent an hour on the phone with airlines. Aer Lingus said they would change the name on Andy's ticket for $90, so I worked it out with Northwest to cancel Andy's flight to New York and put my sister Alison on it. Then Aer Lingus told me that since it was a dual airline flight, I couldn't change the name on the reservation. *@&#%^@%!! Now I'd spent $560 on a flight for my sister and I was still stuck with Andy's name on the other flights. I ended up making Alison feel bad for not being able to bring her to Ireland as I'd asked her to, and I was still left going to Ireland by myself.

When I finally got to my parents' house that day, two-and-a-half hours late, I went right to Vic's arms and cried. I held her tightly; I didn't know how to deal with any more *anythings.* I had no idea what to do with my life. We had lunch. I cried some more and gave more hugs. I called a real estate attorney to see how to get the house, and he told me to file a quitclaim deed, but I needed a family law attorney to file it for me. More phone calls to make.

Later that night, I went to my friend Cindy's to talk about life. She listened sympathetically over many glasses of wine, and she told me more of what good friends tell their friends in need. She even said that when I'd visited her weeks earlier I'd seemed upset and needed to get out of my unhappy life. She also gave me the name of a good divorce attorney in St. Cloud to call (hers). I felt so good leaving her house, feeling empowered and stronger. She gave me the courage I needed to face another day.

JULY 23, 2008

Shel, Ali, and Brit came over to do some shopping and errands. I felt like such a jerk for returning Andy's massage gift certificate when they'd clearly never done anything like that before. I swiped the "I'm getting divorced" card for the first time, and they took pity on me and made it happen. I was already sick of explaining to people that I was getting divorced. Andy and I decided to try to talk things out that night, so I went into a frenzy cleaning up the house and trying to pack up all of his stuff. Poor Shel and Ali helped me clean the house for hours. Since Shawn, Andy's father, was in town, Mom told me to ask him to come too. I respected Shawn and his values/thoughts so much that I'd honestly thought he'd help me reason with Andy. I also asked Mom if she would come too, but she had kids to watch at her house. Andy called at 9:00 P.M. to say they were on their way, and Mom showed up right after he called! I started to cry—again—when I saw her car pulling into the driveway and ran down to hug her. She brought Kath, because Mom's "such a marshmallow," and suddenly I had five people there to support me.

Andy and I sat down at the dining room table to talk, and Shawn and Mom sat in the living room, not more than a few feet away. We started to talk about the house and I told him I wanted to stay. He was hesitant just to sign things over to me though, saying I'd have a property and he'd have nothing. I was scared to take on all the bills myself. Then he told me he'd split the savings 50-50. With my medical bills, I didn't want to do that. I wanted to offer him $10k to just walk away from everything. Then he wanted to divide the furniture 50-50. Wait a minute! I wasn't the one who walked away here, and suddenly I was losing half of everything. I got emotional in front of them, everyone, and it didn't get me any sympathy from the opposition. Shawn called Mom out into the hallway to chat while Andy and I continued to talk things over. Shawn came back in to ask what kind of mortgage we had. He was afraid when our ARM was up that I'd have to refinance and I might not have the money to afford it.

We settled nothing that night except Kath telling me to use LendingTree to refinance the house. Andy and I divided the DVDs (what an odd place to start; wasn't there a more valuable place to start, like the house??) My wonderful family had to take off soon after that. How could I ever thank them enough for what they'd done for me tonight?

Andy and his dad started to pack his things into their cars, and afterwards, Shawn came up to give me a hug. He said he loved me and asked me if it would be okay for Diane to keep up on my health info, and of course I said sure and thanked him for coming.

Before he left, I asked Andy to share a cigarette with me. We shared mostly small talk until I asked him, "Do you think that counseling would have helped?"

"Maybe a year ago," was the reply I got.

Damn. He also said he'd be there for me as a friend, if I needed him there or as a cat sitter. Yeah, right. Since he'd proven himself to be such a great friend recently.

He left and again I felt alone. So alone. What an awful, miserable feeling to be in "our" house alone, especially at night. To sleep in "our" bed, to see "our" stuff everywhere. It was awful.

JULY 24, 2008

My first radiology oncologist appointment with Dr. D. Ross Dickson. His nurse was very nice and comforting when I told her about the divorce. Yvonne made me feel better; even strangers cared more about me than my husband and in-laws. Sadly, this was a new reality I would have to get used to.

Dr. Dickson told me so much that I hadn't understood before. He said that he and Dr. Lovett worked together and that Dr. Garino (my oncologist) would work with me with the chemo. Dickson and Lovett worked on my tumor and lymph nodes, and Garino did the *systemic* treatment, the chemo and hormone therapy. After my second surgery, they expected my re-excision (pre-cancer removal) to be negative, but if it was positive again,

I'd need more surgery. After my second surgery, with no treatment at all, my chance of recurrence would be thirty-five to forty percent. With radiation, it would be ten percent. With a mastectomy, it would be five to ten percent. They had me at a grade-three aggression level, which I assume to be highly aggressive. (After research online later, I found out that I was right. A *grade* means how the tumor looks, how abnormal the cancer cells look under a microscope, and how quickly the tumor will grow and spread. Grades are different for every kind of cancer; the higher the level, the more aggressive the cancer. Grade four is the highest level of aggression.)

Dickson also told me that there are "four burning questions" I needed answered. One, *what good was he going to do for me?* He answered that one with my statistics above. Two, *what are the side effects?* For radiation, it is like a bad sunburn in the radiated area. Fatigue is also common in week three of treatment. I wouldn't be nauseated, lose my hair, or vomit. (Whew!) Three, *what are the complications?* There are three long-term effects: 1—scarring of the lungs. Nowadays, the radiation barely affects the lungs, so that chance of occurrence was one to two percent. 2—breaking ribs. Again, the radiation doesn't hit the ribs area much, so that occurrence was less than one percent. 3—heart disease. Since the radiation is no longer treated through the heart, there is a very slim chance of this happening. Four, *what are my options?* He covered those too, above. True, radiation can also cause more cancer, but he promised that result also was rare.

My plan of action would start with my second surgery, my second lumpectomy. Next would come a visit to Garino to see if I needed chemo, based on my surgery results. Chemo would start four weeks after surgery. If I didn't need chemo (please, please, please!) I would instead start radiation soon after surgery. If I needed chemo, radiation would start three to six months after I was done. Finally, my treatment would include Herceptin (hormone therapy), if needed.

However, Dickson threw in one more wrench: genetic testing and counseling. Dr. Noel Laudi and his genetic counselor, Jessica Greenberg, would counsel me on whether or not I needed to undergo genetic testing to see if I carried the cancer gene. For my family, it would be essential to know if it runs in the family and to be on the alert themselves. For me, it meant I would decrease my risk of recurrence through a single or double mastectomy...if I had the gene.

Geez, as if all this wasn't hard enough—hair loss and time off from work to take the chemo treatments—but now losing both breasts?! Seriously, when would it all end?

The radiation itself would amount to once-a-day-for-seven-weeks, Monday through Friday, treatments—approximately thirty-three treatments total. Possibly more or less. Fortunately, the sessions would be only fifteen minutes long. It would start on August 29 with a simulation, giving me four tattoo dots for the radiation machine placement on my chest. I would also get a CAT scan. Dickson would then plan my radiation course. Driving my car while on treatment would be okay too, and I should "tolerate the treatment well."

I learned there are two ways I could get out of radiation. One, refuse the treatment. Fat chance...and go through this again?!

Two, a complete mastectomy. Well, Dickson is very cute and wasn't wearing a wedding band, so maybe that's another reason not to refuse.

I left with one final thought from him: all my medical decisions would be up to four people: Lovett, Garino, Dickson, and me. I decided to leave most of this up to them. I was just along for the ride…and to write my bestseller.

When I got home, I met with my Realtors, Doug and Sheila, to discuss the house. When we all sat down in the living room, they were shocked to hear about everything that had happened in the past few weeks, but they were immensely sympathetic and offered two pairs of shoulders to cry on. They advised me to stay in the house, to keep it myself. They said I needed my "home," something comfortable for me right now. I would also lose at least $10k trying to sell the house right now. I really didn't need to lose even more money on top of everything else. So I needed to try to get him out.

I went to visit Che and Jessica for dinner that night. They again gave me the name of the family law attorney-friend of theirs. Che called her that night and asked her to give me a call right away in the morning; what a great friend, that Che. I was so tired from the day that I went home at 8:30.

My sister Tam called me on the way home. She offered her tough spots for me to think about from her life. It felt good to be there for her too, though at first I felt angry that for once I wanted things to be about me and my problems. Even when I think my life is so tough, there are so many people out there who have worse times to deal with. I needed talks like this one to put my life into perspective. Things could be much, much worse. Maybe my life wasn't so bad. Tam was stuck in a relationship that was hazardous for her, stuck in a few mortgages they couldn't afford, and making money in long hours at odd jobs. Could I handle all of my mess as well as she had?

JULY 25, 2008

I had one hard time getting up today. Not even TaeBo interested me, and I love getting up and working out. I smoked about five cigarettes before 10:00 A.M. When I finally got to working out, Mom called. She said she had a weird feeling about Andy and asked if I could change the locks and jam the garage door. She thought he would come to take stuff from the house.

At that moment, I lost it. I became hysterical to the point of emotional collapse. My chest was closing, my heart so empty it physically hurt. I had nothing left to fight back. Slowly, after talking some more, I started to get some wind back. Mom had a magic way of making me feel better, even when my chest felt empty. I was regaining my will to go on.

I worked that day removing Andy's name from my AAA and T-Mobile accounts. I posted an ad on Roommates.com and started to look for someone to split the costs at home. I also went to my dermatology appointment to get some questionable moles checked out (no use getting cancer #2, right?) When I asked her about Andy's mole on his back, she told me that he should definitely get that checked out.

Sorry, I thought; he's on his own now. I wasn't fighting that fight anymore; he's a big boy who needed his own time to take care of himself.

At 4:00 P.M., I arrived in Uptown for a Girls' Night Out with my Costa Rica friends: Jenni, Randi, and Holly. I had taken extra care that day to make sure I looked smoking hot; I needed to feel better about myself. The looks I noticed from guys were very gratifying, even if no one spoke to me. It was so nice to feel good about myself, even if it was entirely superficial. It hurt to share my story with them, but they were incredibly supportive. Randi offered me a room at her house in Robbinsdale, definitely something to think about. Jenni offered me a place to stay in New Ulm when I came to visit, enticing me with the thought of all the single guys in town.

After two beers, the emotions came out again. I started crying, ruining my fun with the friends I so rarely get to see. I got paranoid about Andy coming over as Mom feared, and I ended up cutting my evening short.

When I got home, I slept on the couch, dreading sleeping in "our" bed. I was so depressed. I was so grateful for my cat Suerte, who spent the night sleeping next to me.

JULY 26, 2008

Camping at the Roshas'! I packed up my car and drove up to St. Cloud to spend the night with my family. On the way, I called Cindy to talk. Again, she left me with a sense of purpose, a sense of strength. She said I'd love being single again and that she'd keep an eye out for single men for me. It was fortifying to see her, a strong and beautiful woman, so happy after her own divorce. She advised me to take time for myself, to do the things that made me happy. She helped me consider that even if it felt impossible now, it would feel good again someday.

When I arrived at home, I needed to keep moving. I started to clean the house while Mom and I again talked about all the crap. I ended up crawling next to her on the living room floor, and she just held me. I cried about not understanding *Why?* How could Andy be so mean? How could he claim to love me and then hurt me so much? Why was he doing this to us? I didn't understand it. Why was *Shawn* being so unsupportive of me? Then I remembered to inquire about what he had asked her that night they were all at my house. He asked her what kind of loan we had, and she answered that she had no idea.

Then she asked him, "What's going on here?" He said that we grew apart, that we had different goals.

Umm, *what?* Sure, if our goals included one of us growing up and one of us living out our single, jackass days. What a hurtful thing to hear from the man I loved and respected.

Then my anger set in. What kind of parent supports his immature son's poor choices? Where was the support, the push to make things work between us? Why were they so quick to see everything end? I began to think there was stuff Andy wasn't telling his parents.

I was glad my brother-in-law Randy was home that day to talk to *me*. He could be ruthless and he could argue anyone into the ground. He said I should keep the house and get Andy to pay his losses. If he didn't want to pay, I should keep more of the savings account and possessions from the house. Otherwise,

Andy should take over the house himself. He also said that he was sorry he had to talk to me about this, that he'd rather spar with me over politics.

That's my Randy!

He also asked if Andy was seeing anyone else. From the details he'd heard from Vic, he'd doubted that Andy was being truthful about that. Yeah, I'd felt that too.

After my conversation with Randy, I called Shawn to see if there was something they were missing from what was going on. He said Andy wasn't saying much to anyone, that he couldn't explain it when someone asked him about it. (That made two of us.) The most hurtful part was when he said that it was good we found this out now rather than in ten years; we still had the chance to have a happy life. To be dismissed from his family so easily made me feel that I was never truly a part of their family in the first place.

I was so grateful to go to church with Mom, Vic, Aeron, and Brit. I got down on my knees and prayed, just as if I hadn't skipped a service in my ten-year hiatus. I asked God for help, strength, and guidance, while I thanked Him for all of my blessings, namely my family. I felt so good and calm, and again I cried. Aeron held my hand the whole time.

Father Albert's homily was about making choices. Our choices show everyone who we really are and what we're made of. Well, I chose me. I chose my family. I chose to be happy.

Our night "camping" was cooking hot dogs on the grill and roasting marshmallows on the fire pit Dad dragged out for us. The mosquitoes reminded us why outdoor camping sometimes stinks. We went inside to watch *Definitely, Maybe*. Yes, a romantic comedy about a divorce, but it gave me some hope that there was someone out there who would be the Right One for me. Even if there's not, through all this mess, I got myself back. Aeron blew up the air mattress for us, on the living room floor, and we slept with our fingers crossed that it wouldn't deflate.

JULY 27, 2008

Gram, Gramp, Vic, Randy, Manda, and Kurt came for lunch today. Seeing Gram and Gramp was so wonderful. She asked me how Andy was doing; apparently, Mom hadn't mentioned to her what was going on. I told her that he'd left me, and I was moving on. She seemed happy for me, which at first made me sad, but I realized that she was happy I got out of the situation. Manda also gave me an incredible massage, and I melted into Mom and Dad's bed. While she worked, we discussed the cancer. She said it didn't feel real to talk about it with me, and I understood what she felt. It still didn't feel real to me either.

I bet it will when the treatments start.

I drove home to go biking with Carrie. On the way back, I called Rachel. We talked about possible anti-depressants that might work for me. Mom recommended them on Friday, and since I discovered Saturday that I fit all the signs of clinical depression, I agreed to try them. She listened patiently to all my new crap, and offered great help and support. Again, I realized that my family was a blessing.

Carrie and I biked around Rice Lake then came back to my house to continue talking. I asked her what her husband KC thought of all of my mess, and he said that he wanted to stay out of it. Not surprising, since he'd always been partial to Andy. Carrie told me a story about someone her aunt knew. The woman had felt sick one day and went to the doctor to find out that she had a rare terminal disease. She died two weeks later, leaving behind four children. Sadly, it made me feel better about myself again, seeing how it could be so much worse.

Andy and I made plans to go to a restaurant to talk at 7:30 that night. I got all dolled up, hoping to make him feel bad, and it worked. One of the first things he said was that I looked pretty. Odd adjective, since I would have preferred *beautiful, gorgeous, incredible,* but it still felt great. The look on his face told me that he meant it. We small-talked for a while, mostly me just listening to him, before we started to talk about the house. I told him he could rent it and keep it, that I would move out as soon as possible. He wasn't interested in keeping the house, so I pushed harder with Holly's idea of renting it out through a company.

He also told me that if I could get a doctor's note, we could get all of our Ireland trip money back. He'd called Orbitz and told them that I had cancer and couldn't travel. So *now* my illness meant something to him? I agreed, but he'll be paying me for it if he can't get the money back as promised. Darn it, because of my struggles with cancer and divorce, I was already missing out on my travel reward.

We went outside to smoke, and he looked weird. I asked him what was up, and he said he felt bad and worried about me. He said he felt like he was ruining my life. Wow, he wasn't giving me much credit, but it felt good to see him feel bad...for once. I asked him if he wanted to keep talking at home, and I convinced him to do it. On the way home, I called Tracy and gloated about how awful he felt and that he missed many things (including my cooking). I was finally freeing myself from the pain of him leaving me, and it felt amazing. I knew it was wrong to feel good about him feeling bad, but it was a selfish gloat I enjoyed, knowing he was realizing how hard this was for him.

Talking was going nowhere, so I did something dangerous— I started flirting. I stupidly started to kiss him, letting things get carried away. I started taking off all of his clothes, and things were quickly moving in the sexual direction. I first wanted to convince him that this was a reason to stay with me, but when he said he was still leaving me, something snapped in my head. I pulled myself together and turned off the kisses. To refuse him then gave me a new sense of worth. Knowing to him it would have been using me for sex but for me it would have been an emotional hole for me to fall into. I stood my ground, said he wasn't giving me enough credit. He got dressed, and our conversation was over.

After he left, I felt liberated! I passed the sadness off onto him—worrying about the house while having to taste me on his lips. I called Sheila to share in my happiness and thanked her for being so amazing and strong with me. Sheila was and is truly a gift in my life.

I went to bed alone and happy, blissfully happy. I thanked God for every member of my family and for Tracy and Carrie. A gentle smile blessed my lips as I drifted off to sleep.

JULY 28, 2009

The last week of summer school. Garnet had been incredible with all her long talks and analyses of my situation. I didn't know what I'd do without her. She was forty and single, and she loved it. She could also personally relate to both my cancer situation and a nasty break-up. She had been such a source of strength.

When I called Andy later on, I realized that I was close to getting him to take the house. It would be so good to move on, just as he was doing, and have a fresh start. I needed that right now.

JULY 29, 2008

So Andy's new "deal" with the house was to refinance together first before he took the house. What? Wow, the apron strings never get cut, do they? Not a chance on his life would I agree to that. Please, just take the damn thing! Just finally let me go and let me move on with my life, just the way he gets to.

JULY 30, 2008

I called my mortgage consultant at Wells Fargo to see what my refinancing options were, and he told me that I'd qualify for a $210,000 loan all by myself. Even better news: if I could get out of this house, I could free myself of seller hassles and be a straight-up buyer again. What a relief! I could also afford this place if I stayed here, but I'd have to sell eventually and find a roommate in the meantime. Great, more hassles I didn't need.

Andy came over in the afternoon to run numbers and ideas.

Of course, I had to look adorable when he came, and he said, "Do you purposely look this good when you know I'm coming over? Because it's not fair." Fair?! He's talking to me about *fair?* Seriously! When he left the house that day, he seemed ready to take the place. I felt that was a good sign.

But did I really want to move? I loved this place, but it was pricey and I might not be able to afford it. I called Vic, Tracy, Che, and Jenni A. to get some advice, but no one could really give me a definitive answer on what I should do.

I went down to Bloomington that afternoon to visit Jenni A. After being diagnosed with multiple sclerosis in 2001, she had been doing so great medically. She'd also been single and enjoying life, also showing me that life after relationships and sickness *does* go on. I loved how she'd traveled to Australia and Fiji all on her own, and I wanted to do that myself soon.

We enjoyed a night of Chinese food and *Dancing with the Stars* while reliving memories of old movies we'd seen. She told me that she'd rather be in my position—divorced—than be single at her age. I disagreed. People could see my marriage as a failure, while she had lived her own life and been more selective about whom she dated. With an illness, I could see how important it was to be very choosy about who you spent your time with, trying to weed out the losers that couldn't handle difficult times. I obviously didn't weed out the bad ones well enough, but at least now I had a chance to find a *good* one.

God, please show me how to take care of *myself.* Please show me first how to love myself so I can learn to love someone else someday. Please don't let me lose myself again in a life of incomplete happiness. Please help me be strong, to overcome all the adversity I was given. Most importantly, please help me to be as loving and supportive to my family and friends as they've been to me. I want to be able to truly show them how important they are to me and to support them in many ways. Thank you, with all of my heart, for all of my blessings.

JULY 31, 2008

The final day of summer school. After work, I jumped into getting the divorce papers rolling. I consulted a mediator, who was of no help, so I contacted a family law attorney. I found Judy Johnson in Edina, and she'd give me a free consultation if I would make a donation to Caring Hands. Andy had already hired his own lawyer, his friend's girlfriend's father, so now the guns were a-blazing.

Please let Andy be reasonable and settle soon, I prayed. I wanted to move out, to free myself of all the mortgage mess, keep $27k from savings, and move on. Please let him settle.

At least he was considering it.

Sheila and Alison came to spend the night. We shared *The Orphanage* horror movie, leftover Chinese food, and "Rock Ya Body" by Justin Timberlake. They also shared in my frustration with my recent e-mail from Andy, telling me he was now leaning toward keeping the house. I was proud of myself that it didn't sway me; I was still set on moving out. Even if Randi's house would be a temporary situation, after talking to her today, I felt content and even excited to have a new roommate, place to live, and control of my own life.

Alison slept with me that night, and I remembered how nice it was not to sleep alone. Someday, if I was lucky, I wouldn't have to, but for now I didn't have to worry about anyone else's sleeping habits but my own.

JULY 31, 2008

I went biking instead of doing TaeBo today. Feeling the cool, fresh breeze on my cheeks and coasting down big hills made me feel free and happy that it was still summer. Rarely did I take the time to enjoy even just the smallest part of happiness in life, the simple things. I needed to do more of that, starting today. I checked with Dr. Moghaddam about getting antidepressants, and she said I'd need to go to my primary care physician for a prescription (damn if I don't have one) and I also realized all the new doctors I'd have to see weren't in my insurance network. Panicking, I called Medica and I was able to add all of them to my network. Who hoo, and thank goodness!

AUGUST 1, 2008

I met Carrie in downtown Minneapolis for happy hour before going to the MN Twins game, the tickets that I "won" in the settlement. How exhilarating to walk amongst the skyscrapers in the hustle of the downtown Minneapolis streets. Walking to happy hour, I realized that I would prefer that bustle to the suburban life of teaching. I felt young again, starting a new life, if even for an hour. I loved the metro life; wished I could afford to *live* there.

When we got to the Metrodome, the blisters on my poor feet

felt awful. Of course, I *had* to dress cute with my hot heels that destroyed my toes. No regrets—they were still just the thing I needed to make me feel beautiful. Upon arriving in the concourse area, I felt immediate pangs of loneliness, abandonment, regret, remorse. I hadn't felt this unwanted in at least a week, hoping these negative feelings were gone. Seeing all the couples reminded me of all the miserable games we went to and, oddly, I missed them. How could I miss feeling miserable? Because I wasn't alone then.

By the end of the first inning, I realized that I wasn't alone now. Happily, I got over my self-pity and we enjoyed the rest of the game until 9:30. So much for meeting my baseball player and running off with him; must have to save that for another game.

Upon arriving back in Maple Grove, I went immediately to Tracy's to meet her and Lindsey for the *Breaking Dawn* release party. After we received our numbers 249, 250, and 251, we realized that we were the only adults other than parents among the hundreds of *Twilight* fans. We were also the few members of Team Jacob (the werewolf in the book who's in love with the protagonist, Bella). Up until Andy left, I was on Team Edward (the gorgeous, educated, polite, strong, well-built, and perfect vampire that is in love with Bella).

In the second book of the series, he leaves Bella. For months, she was trying to pick up the pieces of her shattered life, trying to remember again what made her happy. During her "mourning," she became best friends with Jacob. He never left her side, and he became her sunshine. Edward came back (after

Bella went to get him) and she went right back to him.

In the third book, she realizes she loves both of them, if even in different ways. With Jacob, she doesn't have to give up her life, her future, her family, her chance to have a normal life. With Edward, there's the chance he'd leave her again, though he swears he will not.

Which team would I choose? Now, because of everything assaulting me in my life, I would choose Jacob.

AUGUST 2, 2008

Today I truly realized the importance of reconnecting with "lost" family members. I went with my mom, her sister Sandy, and her sister-in-law Julie to my cousin Marie's bridal shower. It was held at my Grandma's (my mom's mom) apartment. I was nervous to see her again, since she'd spent most of my life ignoring me. I felt abandoned by her through the years, through unanswered Christmas cards and birthday letters, and through her never caring to know what I was up to. Sure, she cared about her grandkids, just not the ones from my immediate family. Before I went, I decided to end the dislike I held for her and to bury the silence.

Throughout cancer, I realized that when you hold hate in your heart, you never feel better in the end. I gave her a big hug when I got there, and I noted the surprise in her eyes upon seeing me. I was still just as surprised as she was, though I was ready to mend the past. She took out a small photo album she had with the pictures of all her grandkids' weddings, and she asked me for a picture of my wedding. I sadly told her that it wouldn't be necessary anymore; I guess that Mom hadn't told her either. I smiled and told her that I'd send her one with me and my cat. She soon put the album away and didn't mention it again.

The wedding talk made me pretty quiet for the rest of the afternoon. I still happily talked to my cousins that I hadn't spoken to in years. Reconnecting with them gave me even more support and love to feel. What kept me from such loving people for so long? My own apprehension and fear. I resolved that I wouldn't let that happen again. The only thing I feared was losing my family again. My aunt Linda gave me a big hug and told me that there would be something better (*someone* better, actually) out there for me. Man, that would be nice, and it will be nice…when I'm ready.

Going home, I received a text from Andy (I thought it would be in response to my earlier text telling him he had a lawyer's letter at my house), but instead he asked me if I had bought *Breaking Dawn* yet, and if I hadn't would I please tell him when I did. I stared in disbelief at the phone, and all I could think of was, *Why?* Why would he care? Why was he making small talk with me? Why was he curious?

I left the text unanswered.

AUGUST 3, 2008

My friends Heather and Tracy came over the next morning to go to church with me. It was Heather's first time at my house, and she loved it, renewing my happiness in staying there. When we walked in the front doors of the church known as the Open Door (conveniently located two blocks from my house) I felt welcomed, and I was impressed by all the members out in the lobby talking. People seemed so happy to take time beforehand to connect with one another, very unlike my Catholic experiences. We picked up some coffee and donuts (also unlike my Catholicism) then headed into the service area. We perused the monthly circular and were excited to see all the extra activities the church offered—for singles, newly marrieds, youth, support groups—that met regularly. I hated to admit that finding someone new was tempting, but thinking I could meet someone with religious values I saw as a bonus.

Reconnecting with God brought me a strength that I had never felt. He was helping me find peace amongst all the mayhem, helping me reach for the person inside that was still there, fighting to live. His love and support brought me the power to make it through the worst days of my life, and keeping my new connection to Him I knew would bring me even closer to complete happiness again. Praying every night as I hopped into bed helped me feel less and less alone.

The hardest prayer I *needed* to say was for Andy. The service leader today reminded me that I need to treat others as I like to be treated, even though it was difficult. I did hope that Andy would find what he was looking for, and that he might end up happy, but the soon-to-be-divorced part of me screamed and burned for him to be as miserable as I'd felt. However, I wanted to be the bigger person, to let go of the hate in my heart and just move along with my life.

Hey, I may not have wanted to wish him perfection just yet, but I thought it was okay just to focus on me, my family, and my friends. My *indifference* replaced the hate within me; I understood that indifference was the opposite of love, and that understanding was helping me recover for now. My body needed it, as I was heading into surgery again the next week.

AUGUST 4, 2008

My first genetic counseling appointment with Jessica Greenberg and Dr. Noel Laudi at Mercy. I really wished that I'd brought a tape recorder with me—or Mom; it was all very emotionally overwhelming, not to mention scary, to think of what my possibilities were.

Jessica began by explaining what genetic defects are. Based on my parents' DNA, they could have the cancer gene or be a carrier of the gene defect. If one was a carrier, I started with a normal gene and a defect gene. The normal gene could become a defect, leaving me with two defect genes and giving me cancer. This cancer could develop sooner and lead to more varieties of breast cancer. If the cancer was sporadic (not genetic) I started with two good genes right away, and one became defective.

After mapping out my entire family tree—immediate family through aunts, uncles, cousins and grandparents—she said she found a fifteen percent chance I was a genetic defect. With such a clean family history, she doubted that I was genetically linked.

My immediate thought: *yeah, and I had a seven percent chance of getting cancer in the first place!* So much for favorable odds. I decided I'd avoid casinos just now.

I asked Jessica about skipping my upcoming surgery, whether

I should wait to find out if I was genetically positive and get a complete mastectomy. She said no because we didn't know how destructive my cancer was. I was weakly estrogen-receptor positive and progesterone-receptor negative, so no more Nuvaring—the estrogen in this contraceptive was too destructive. My new birth control options became an IUD or condoms. Riiiiight. Like I would need either anytime soon.

More random thoughts from the appointment:

~ If I'm genetically positive, a mastectomy isn't necessarily the next step. Who hoo!

~ It's rare that my lifestyle would have caused the cancer.

~ With my mom's mom being so much older than I am when she was diagnosed (58), it's most likely I'm not genetically positive.

~ My breast cancer concern is my age—could there be a gene? It could be a weak gene influenced by the environment.

~ The genetic test, if positive, would also show if I have a greater risk of developing another form of breast cancer or ovarian cancer.

~ With breast cancer, sixty percent of cases are sporadic, thirty percent are familial, and ten percent are hereditary. Within the ten percent of hereditary cases, fifty-two percent have the BRCA 1 (breast cancer gene), thirty-two percent have BRCA 2, and sixteen percent have "other."

  • All of us have a gene from each parent, and it's the genes' job to prevent cancer and regulate cells.

  • In the "other" category, I would need further testing, for other genes my family doesn't have.

~ If I am genetically positive, all of my sisters have a fifty-fifty percent chance of the same. They can choose to be tested as well. Once one of us is positive, testing becomes easier.

~ A test is a simple blood test. The sample is Fed-Exed to the one lab in the country that has the gene patented, the one in Utah. I will get the results in three to four weeks. If my results are positive, results are clear. If negative, results are unclear and doctors need to test my family.

~ After all my chemo treatments, Dr. Garino can give me a survival rate (chance of recurrence). She may also "upgrade" me from annual mammograms to annual MRIs (which can see more than a mammogram).

~ If I am BRCA 1 or 2 positive, my chance of recurrence is sixty percent.

- If positive, I will get an ovarian cancer screening through ultrasound. However, there is a high error rate. Très reassuring, no? It's also difficult to detect early. Also, my interim care still includes chemo, family screenings, annual checkups, to clarify cancer risks, and change my screenings.
- If negative, there's more testing. It may be the P53 (li fraumeni) gene, which would mean only I am affected.

~ My testing starts with BRCA 1 and 2 screening, which detects ninety percent of genetic patients. Step 2, the BART screening, detects more forms, but most insurance doesn't cover it. Step 3 is the P53 test in another lab. The lab in all cases calls my insurance provider to make sure it's covered beforehand. Amazing...finally *less* work for me to do!

INFORMATION FROM DR. LAUDI:

Chemo will stop ovulation, causing temporary menopause (Good Lord!) This shouldn't affect having children in the future. He also said that Garino will talk to me about Herceptin, since I'm her-2-neu positive (umm…what?!) and this drug will suppress the growth factor. The best thing he told me? That it was a Godsend that my cancer was detected early. Great time to have good luck, eh?

Even now, I am blessed, and I mean that.

Andy came over that night at 9:00. He officially wanted nothing to do with the house, the schmuck. Sure, it was easier to walk away from everything; just leave me to deal with it all, right? Wouldn't be the first time he'd done that. He did offer me $30k and splitting the furniture, which was a better offer than before, but he was pissing me off. How come he was the only one who got to walk away from the past? Why did my life have to be more difficult for his to be easier? Did he *ever* think of me?

Tracy and Jason helped me afterwards with the idea of keeping the house as an investment. Honestly, I thought I'd feel more comfortable with more money then. Frustration building…

AUGUST 5, 2008

I called my school district's benefits department today to get information on leaves, just in case I needed one. Depending on how severe my treatment and reaction will be, I learned that I had two options: one, use up my twelve sick days and apply for fifteen more from the sick leave pool if I need intermittent days off; or two, if I'd need over ninety days, I could apply for long-term disability to receive two-thirds of my salary. Just another reason to pray for no chemo.

I went to see the collaborative law attorney in Edina, Judy Johnson. She was wonderfully helpful (and counseled me for free for the first session). After I explained the situation, she said Andy seemed like a big kid (yup) and if he was going to stick me with the house and medical bills, I deserved *everything:* the money, the house, and everything in it. We could quitclaim the house to me when we were divorced, and out of the kindness of my heart, I could release him from the mortgages. The only thing that keeping his name on the mortgage would do was to boost his credit rating, since I would be paying the bills. She said that a "simple assumption" that would cost $1000 would release his name from both mortgages; this would be preferable to having to refinance. The best part came when she told me that splitting the savings fifty-fifty in our case wasn't fair, with my liabilities. She was certain that if he took me to court, I would get *everything.*

Damn, that felt so good! I left her office with air in my step, genuinely smiling at the optimism of the divorce proceedings.

As I shared dinner that night with my pal Jenni, Andy called. I told him that I talked to Judy, didn't hire her, but she gave me an idea of what would happen in court. He was *livid,* yelling at me so loud that I had to pull the phone away from my ear. He screamed that all I wanted was more money, that everything he offered wasn't good enough. I said that I still wanted to settle out of court, so I offered him $5000 to walk away from everything.

Again, he freaked out. So I mentioned that the alternative would be for *him* to take the house and $18k, more than enough money to cover renting the house out and having money to spend. Then he got even more upset, telling me that I shouldn't be telling him what his options were.

Hey, even if he didn't like it, it was still an option. I felt that I had finally showed him what I was made of and that I wouldn't let him tell me what *my* crappy options were. I was afraid I had made things with him worse. But still, now I knew I could legally get everything, minus the $3000 maximum in legal fees.

I had a new ace up my sleeve.

AUGUST 6, 2008

Talk about being a little distracted this morning. While I was on the phone with Orbitz trying to take care of the Ireland trip, I rear-ended a Mercedes. Sure, couldn't have been a jalopy. Swiping the cancer card for the first time, I told the other driver that I was on the phone with my oncologist. She checked out her fender, said there was no damage to her car, and said there was no need to call in a police report.

Wow! Did that cancer card swipe just work?!

As Garnet and I were on the way back from a training in St. Paul, Garnet saw an injured pigeon on the side of the road, nearly getting squashed by oncoming traffic. She plucked a sweatshirt (no pun intended) from her back seat, wrapped up the little guy, and placed it in her lap. As a passer-by heckled her for picking up the diseased bird, she retorted with, "Yeah, it has diseases, and you have no brain."

She told me later on that humans are in the center of their universe, and we think that all animals are less than we are. All animals just try to live with us, and all humans do is build obstructions and kill them off.

It really stopped me in my tracks, making me realize that I was just like that passer-by. I thought that pigeons were just rats with wings, dirty little intrusions in my world. It was a perfect time for me to again be grateful for what I had and to appreciate every living being.

There was always more to daily life than my own little existence.

Later on, I attended my first appointment with Ardith, my counselor. Reliving all of the past month's experiences ripped the wounds wide open. A lot of good came from it, though. She said that, with his drinking, she saw signs of chemical dependency in Andy, and that his behavior was "twenty-five going on twelve." His parents had raised a co-dependent child.

All of this wasn't news to me, but the part that did hurt was when she said he had probably cheated on me for a while, most likely with someone from work. I kept thinking, who was there of *any* substance at that place? The only people there were drunken twerps with no real purpose in their lives. Skinny, big-chested bitches who threw themselves at him night after night. How could I compete with that? I was older, more mature, sensible, and enjoyed a good job. Yep, nothing he seemed to want.

I'd love to know who it was, just so I could pity her and hate her guts at the same time. Who would honestly want to date a guy with a drinking problem, little sense of responsibility, who left his wife days after her breast cancer surgery? No one with any moral code, anyhow. They deserved each other and the misery, to be alone to become adults.

Ardith told me to also keep up on my healthy habits—eating well and exercise—while cutting out the diet soda and smoking. Damn.

Well, I'd now met another person who had my well-being on her mind. Why was I complaining again?

I removed the SteriStrips from my excision today. It's not a horrible sight, just a two-inch reminder that will be there for the rest of my life. I immediately fast forwarded to having someone else see it someday. I couldn't imagine trusting or loving someone enough to show them. Where did that level of trust and intimacy get me before? That will be a big step; for now, just the idea of it still made me nauseous. I was going to focus on *me* for a while. Why complicate life with trying to date? I had too much to deal with besides the dating drama.

The Myriad lab (genetic testing company in Salt Lake City, Utah) called to tell me that my genetic test for the BRCA 1/2 genes was approved by Medica at 100%! Thank goodness! That's $4000 I didn't have to pay. I couldn't imagine *not* having insurance right now. I was more determined than ever to make sure I didn't lose my job in the next two years. That became my new life goal (other than beating cancer, I guess.) The BART test wasn't covered, though, which was fine for now. Anyhow, BRCA 1/2 would come first.

I met a potential new roommate today (with Tracy's presence

and guidance)—Jared. He seemed chill, like he'd be a good roommate or at least someone to help cover the monthly bills for now. How nice would it be to have someone help pay the mortgage without having to deal with his emotional needs? What a great change!

Andy texted tonight to say he was still thinking about the $5000 offer. I prayed for a resolution, and soon. I was being torn apart worrying about his childish ass, when it should have been me worrying about my own ass.

AUGUST 7, 2008

I started off my day with more trainings, where I ran into another ESL teacher from a high school in the district. She's married to the father of her son, not necessarily enjoying the wife part of her life. When I told her a little about what was going on with me, she told me about how she craves her freedom and he craves an obedient wife who cooks and cleans without complaint. She said how she'd love to be single again, like me.

Imagine trying to make that work with a child in the middle. Whew! All I could think was how I'd gladly trade her my "freedom" for having someone at home that loves me.

Right after our lunch break, I got a text from Andy, saying he'd e-mailed me. Instant nausea. I couldn't think of concentrating on work anymore, so I told my colleague that I felt sick (not a far cry from the actual truth) and I drove home. I prayed for a reasonable resolution. His new request: $7000 and the TV, and he would pay me for half of August's mortgage.

I responded with a counter offer.

I waited so impatiently for his response. In the wait time, I furiously cleaned the house, trying to get my mind off of my non-ringing cell phone. When Mom came over later on, we had Mexican Noodle Bowls for dinner as I gave us both pedicures (I love pampering Mom! She needs more things to take care of her like that.) We indulged in Dove ice cream treats, as I prayed to also crack open the celebratory champagne.

Finally, at nine P.M., he called back. He gave his final counter offer, hoping I'd go for $6000, and I stayed firm with *I'd rather not.* He finally agreed. He also added that we could talk about the smaller stuff later on. However, I didn't mention that I wasn't willing to discuss the small stuff. He was getting so much more than I was already willing to give up. He would find that out soon enough. He thanked me for being civil through everything, and I shouldn't have replied with, "Ditto," since I sure didn't mean that. He told me that he'd call Orbitz again to see if we could get a refund on our Ireland trip and that he'd let me know what they said.

I hung up the phone, yelled a big *Who hoo!* and danced around the living room. FINALLY, an agreement!

Mom and I popped the cork on the champagne and celebrated the beginning of the end of my old—married—life and the beginning of a new life. I happily sent Judy Johnson an e-mail saying he'd agreed to the terms and he'd agreed to working exclusively with her; he'd appreciated how little she would bill to file the papers for us, and I liked the work she'd do for me. I could finally ask her to draw up the papers.

I couldn't have asked for a better evening. I had my incredible mother, a good meal, heavenly desserts, a pedicure, a couple of glasses of champagne, and more love and support from everyone around me than ever before. Sure, parts of my life seemed grim. I still had moments of desperation and sadness, moments of feeling that I'll always be romantically alone, but I had *me* back. I could be happier doing things I wanted to do, no longer doubting what a good person I was, no longer sitting at home thinking and waiting for life to begin *someday*.

I reminded myself: Even though it may be difficult at times, with my family and friends my time is now. My someday is today.

AUGUST 8, 2008

In hindsight, it's funny that I remember this day more for the 2008 Summer Olympics beginning rather than my second lumpectomy…

An easy morning this time. I knew what surgery was all about, and I wasn't going into it nervous. Mom and I had a relaxing morning with coffee and breakfast. She then tortured me with making her homemade chicken soup for after we got back. It felt like torture because I was now cut off from eating before surgery. Tracy came over at 1:30, and I shared with her a letter I found from Andy on the computer. It was written while I was in D.C., saying how sorry he was for screwing up but that he needed to find what he was looking for. Already then, he was leaving, but he said nothing to my face.

I thought this would have hurt when he wrote it to me, but now I was disgusted by his lack of ambition when it came to us.

I was over his childlike behavior; I didn't have time to be his mom anymore.

Tracy and I did have a good laugh at a date offer that I got from Roommates.com. Another member saw my profile, thought I was beautiful and asked me out. I thought I'd be nice, though I wasn't interested or attracted to him in the slightest, so I e-mailed him a thank you and asked him more about himself. He replied back with calling me "Cutie," spelling a lot of the message wrong, and signing it OXOXOXO. Ugh. I lost what little interest I had. He asked me nothing about myself either, so I knew I was not losing much by not talking to him. It was awfully nice to hear that I'm still attractive, even if it came from weirdos on the Internet.

We checked into Mercy at 2:30 then sat around until 4:00. We three watched the clock in the waiting room, and this time there were no tears heading into the surgery prep. I could laugh, smile, and joke about it. No tears for my husband or my mother-in-law, just happiness for my mom and great friend. What great changes in a few short weeks! I was a new person.

I made sure to ask my anesthesiologist for good anti-nausea meds for after surgery. He (the cute German guy again, Dr. Doberton) looked guilty about my nausea, and he promised he'd take care of me this time. No worries here. Anything would be better than the nausea of last time!

I woke up in recovery later on; Mom showed up soon after. I remember them putting the ACE bandage around my chest, getting some pain meds, no big deal this time. We got me dressed in my street clothes, and we were on our way home. I felt so good that we even stopped into Blockbuster to trade our movie for another. It felt surreal, to be right out of surgery and walking around Maple Grove. My chest felt a little tight, but I chalked it up to the ACE bandage being wrapped so tight. We went home, ate the soup, and I relished that my second surgery was over.

AUGUST 9, 2008

I woke up and Mom was already downstairs, reading on the couch. It was still so weird to feel so great after a surgery. I ate a normal breakfast, washed it down with a Vicodin, and we started making chair cushions for Aunt Lisa. My chest kept bugging me all morning, so to prevent more complaining, I took off the bandage to ease up the pressure on my chest. Still, the pain continued.

When my heart would beat, I felt a clicking in my chest. Breathing was getting even more difficult—no deep breaths allowed now. I held Mom's hand to my xyphoid so she could feel the clicking too, and we decided to call Dr. Lovett's on-call doctor.

I called, and was told they'd return my call within fifteen minutes. After twenty minutes, I called again. Finally, they paged him, and he said I should go into the E.R. Dammit! I *just* got home, and I didn't want to go back again. And anyhow, doctors will always tell you to come in if they don't know what is wrong. Couldn't he just tell me that I'd be fine, to just wait it out?

We drove back to Mercy at noon. In the E.R., they hooked me up to an EKG machine to check my heart, and then took an x-ray of my chest. All of a sudden, Dr. Ito ran in, followed by Dr. Baker and two nurses. Dr. Ito told me that I had a pneumothorax. Dr. Lovett, while giving me my chest Novocain, had pierced my lung with the needle, causing my lung to collapse. They had to immediately put a tube in to re-inflate it, but they promised to put me out while they did it.

I was immediately readmitted to the hospital, issued another patient I.D. bracelet, and I cried myself to anesthesia-sleep again. I woke up not more than fifteen minutes later in intense pain, comparable to that of breaking my collarbone in 2002. Then the drugs started, but they couldn't come fast enough for me to be *out* of pain. I was checked into room 203, my new home for a while.

Mom went home to get some things for me, instantly making me feel worse because she had to do so much to take care of me. I knew she was my mom, and took care of me because she wanted to, but I still felt so awful that she had to spend so much time with me. Damn Andy should have been there instead, but I'd rather be *completely* alone than stuck with him. I knew she was here because she cared, and I hoped/*would* repay her for everything she'd done for me.

I couldn't have been given a better supporter if I had to dream one up. The love of a mother for her daughter never diminishes with time or age, and never will I stop needing her with me. Even if I felt like a twenty-eight-year-old baby, to be near her made every tear bearable. She slept on a recliner in room 203 that night, waking up with me every time another nurse came in for meds. She never stopped watching over me all night.

AUGUST 10, 2008

Oh, pain and more pain. In the morning, right away, Mom found a nearby church to attend while I went off for an x-ray and bathroom break. I was so proud of myself for going in by myself. Getting back into bed, now that was a different story. The nurse Tania and a PCA had to slide me back into bed, and that's when the pain hit a ten, the highest on the hospital's pain scale. I just sat there and cried through the pain, and Mom cried through it with me. I imagined that it could never be easy to watch your children go through so much pain. Morphine was no longer enough to sedate me, so they added a longer-lasting drug to my pain cocktail. It took a few hours to get my pain down to tolerable.

Making the time more tolerable were all of the visitors— Mom, Kathryn, Sheila, Alison, Brit, Rachel, and Dan. They spent the afternoon with me, enjoying the Olympics now on TV. All I could do while they sat around me and chatted was to lie there with my eyes closed and just listen to them. I couldn't even open my eyes, trying not to be conscious enough to feel the pain again. Later on, Tracy and Lindsey stopped by with flowers, and Garnet stopped by with video games. Mom went home to get a good night's sleep and more of her own medication, but I hoped she would take more time than that at home. She needed to rest more, much more, than I did, and I prayed she would. This upcoming weekend, I wanted to take care of *her*.

I called Andy to reschedule our paperwork plans, and he called me "Sweetie" and said that it wasn't a problem. Of course, he had no interest in *why* I needed to reschedule.

I was *so* much better off.

AUGUST 11, 2008

Another morning at Mercy. It's nice having someone just bring breakfast right to your door and to eat it in bed, even with the pain and crumbs. I could get used to this, just without the painful tube in my side. Dr. Lovett and his nurse Linda came early to remove the tape and bandages, saying if my x-ray was okay, the tube could be removed and I could go home later today. However, just the tape removal was excruciating, feeling as if my skin was ripping right off with it. Oh, the awful pain! I cried and yelped in pain, but nothing eased it or could take my mind off of it.

Mercifully, it finally stopped, but the pain eased all too slowly. Linda was kind, trying to ease my agony after Lovett left, but only time truly helped me.

Vic came by with Syd, Aeron, and Luke. We played Boggle and watched more Olympic fun. Ah, to feel "normal" for a little while. I loved having family around during the hardest times. They left shortly before lunch, before my chest x-ray. Even Che stopped in to say hello, keeping my mind further away from the thoughts of pain.

I got the great news from Linda at about 2:00 P.M.—I was getting the tube out and I was going home today! The tube removal was not as bad as the tape removal, but it was still nearly the worst pain I've ever felt. She cut the sutures holding the tube in, I took a few deep breaths, and she pulled it out. Honestly, I thought part of my lung was coming with it. The tube was about one inch in diameter, and it was at least six inches into my chest. No little tubes here at Mercy. Ironically, most of the stabbing pain left my body as the tube did. I was still sore and moving ever so slowly, but I instantly felt better.

My two Julies from work visited me as I waited for Mom to come. I sat carefully on the bed and explained my life while they sat patiently and quietly listened. I felt relieved to have people from work really caring about what was going on in my life. They seemed very supportive.

Mom came at 4:30 to bring me back to Maple Grove. Like an angel, she washed all of my dirty laundry and rugs while I was in the hospital, bringing fresh-air cleanliness into my home. We grilled up our dinner, enjoyed *Pay It Forward*, and all was perfect.

AUGUST 12, 2008

Oncology D-Day, though I was nervous more for Lovett's follow-up on Wednesday. When I was being discharged from Mercy, Lovett personally called me and asked if I'd bring my mom with me to the appointment, so he could give both of us the results. Fearing the worst, I thought he had bad news from my pathology report and wanted me to have support there. Mom and Garnet thought he was just covering his behind legally and didn't want me to sue for the pneumothorax. Darn it, I wouldn't sue as long as he would just cover the extra bills that I accrued from it. The next day, we'd see what he was up to.

Mom and I went to my oncologist's office (Dr. Garino) at one P.M., and half an hour later, she finally showed up. So many new details from this appointment:

~ Because I'm weakly estrogen-receptor positive and her-2-neu receptor positive, there's a great chance chemo will work for me. Chemo is inevitably my next step. Damn.

~ If I am BRCA 1 or 2 positive, I can choose a bilateral mastectomy to prevent my cancer recurrence or a second primary breast cancer from developing. I could also remove my ovaries to prevent breast or ovarian cancer. However, the bilateral mastectomy will not help me avoid chemo with my aggressive-grade cancer. It will, however, prevent me from going through radiation. She suspects, with my age factor, that I am genetically positive. Double damn.

~ Provided that I have clear margins from the second lumpectomy, I have three treatment choices with chemo:

• 1: Adriamycin + Cytoxan come first, given every other week for four treatments, with injections of Neulasta each day following a treatment to keep up my white blood cell count. Then Cycle Two of Taxol and Herceptin, Taxol every other week for four treatments, Herceptin weekly for a year. TAC are all chemo drugs; Herceptin is a hormone blocker. This "dose-dense AC/Taxol" is the most common treatment, and (I believe) what Garino favors for me.

• 2: TCH: Though Adriamycin is seen as most common/important for my treatment, this

Taxotere/Carboplatin/Herceptin treatment will be every three weeks for six treatments, Herceptin still weekly for a year. This option is usually for older patients.

- 3: Aggressive hormone therapy. This will kill off the estrogen in my body to prevent a new breast cancer and block my ovaries for two years (or even remove my ovaries). She didn't recommend any of this treatment for me, because I'm only weakly estrogen-receptor positive and ovary removal is too radical for me at this point.

So I'm going with option 1; bring on the big guns and kill it off *right*.

MY PLAN, AS OF TODAY, IS:

1. heal up for two more weeks from surgery
2. tell Garino my treatment choice
3. get a MUGA scan on my heart and a port inserted (a port is a catheter inserted into my chest so I'm not injected with needles constantly during chemo. It is implanted into my chest by a surgeon and attached to my jugular or supraclavicular vein. It can, though, become infected or clot.)
4. take the Chemo 101 class at the Cancer Resource Center
5. do chemo
6. determine cost of treatment, to prepare data for divorce proceedings
7a. wait for genetic results, possibly get a bilateral mastectomy and avoid radiation, or

7b. get radiation

8. get fabulous breast reconstruction (damn it, I deserve a nice rack out of this whole mess!)

9. take a long-awaited trip with Mom

10. Live. Enjoy all my blessings, be grateful for every day.

I went to the Cancer Resource Center and spoke to Marcia, a social worker, who was able to offer me some great tips. She urged me to be open and honest about my condition with the people at work, to go into a discussion with them about what my treatment is, what my plans are, and an outcome that I'd like to see at work. She also gave me three grant applications for money to help pay my bills. What a relief to know that financial help was out there! I would use it if I needed it.

I spent a leisurely evening with Mom making more reusable grocery bags for her sisters. These nights with Mom made all the crap worth it. Her presence was a blessing to me and my sanity.

AUGUST 13, 2008

I loved having breakfast with Mom in the morning; I wished I could do this with her every day. It was a long day for me though, being only a few days out of surgery.

I had a leadership meeting that morning at work, and afterwards, I asked my assistant principal Julie if she had time to talk. I told her about my prognosis, what my treatment plan would look like. I was ungodly nervous to open my mouth, to tell her that I wouldn't be working at full strength. I was two years away from getting a continuing contract (tenure). I'd been performing well, so I *shouldn't* worry. But I did. She seemed so wonderfully supportive, offering any help I needed, such as switching classes I teach, giving up my new department-leader position until treatment was over, moving my schedule around, etc. I felt extreme relief once she knew about all of this and that I wanted to proceed as normally as possible. I refused to let cancer and divorce ruin my professional life. I prayed that her openness and willingness to help weren't feigned, that she meant it.

Mom and I met at Dr. Lovett's office at 4:00 P.M. Worst-case scenario arose again. Lovett couldn't get all the pre-cancer; he recommended a full mastectomy. Damn.

Well, now I wanted to wait to see what the genetic results were; I could do a bilateral right away if I was positive. Lovett said that cosmetically, immediate reconstruction with a tissue expander was best, but I would first need to make sure the pre-cancer hadn't spread to nearby tissue. I'd need radiation to get rid of the rest. Immediate reconstruction would also mean I would be out of work for at least four weeks, not ten days like the mastectomy without reconstruction would be. With school starting soon, I didn't have time for that.

Lovett also painfully shared with us his own personal cancer story, how his son died from lung cancer at 28. He reminded us both how cancer can be harder on the parents. When Mom looks at me, I could see—through all the love and support—that she'd do anything to prevent me from going through this, even take it on herself. Because of her support, I had the strength to take it on myself.

We left the office and walked to our cars, and I cried again and gave her a big hug. I hated to leave her, if even for a day. I was becoming her little shadow again, always wanting her around. When she was around, I was peaceful and happy. I could face anything. I was strong. The second she left, I ached in my heart. I was aware of being alone. Life seemed bleak and scary. Mom gave my life a reason to keep moving on, showed me that I have people who love me, no matter what.

I met Andy at 5:30 at Caribou in Maple Grove to fill out the divorce paperwork: a financial/asset questionnaire and a retainer agreement. Of course, he was late, which made me fear that he'd gone to the house. Nope, just ran late. I immediately got out the papers and showed him where to fill in information, and then I stared off to the right side of him, refusing to even look at him. I was now disgusted at the sight of him, this person who left so quickly and easily (easily only for him).

I didn't hate him, but I stayed indifferent. *Indifference is the opposite of love,* I kept reminding myself. I just wanted nothing more than to be done with him. I was relieved when he didn't bring up hashing over my retirement plans. He did bring up dividing the rest of the household items, kitchen items specifically. Point blank, I informed him that I wanted it all.

He smiled at me, probably thought I was kidding, and jokingly asked me if "this was how it was going to be." I said yes. I argued that it was for my health, not being able to lift more than fifteen pounds and having to replace all the heavy things in the house. (And, of course, he didn't ask *why* I couldn't lift more than fifteen pounds.) Even though he mentioned that I had people that could help me if I needed it, I stayed firm on what I said.

It placated him when I said he could have the plates, mugs, and bowls, and he agreed. I'd always hated those big, clunky things anyhow, but I didn't say that aloud. His mother picked them out for us. Whew! The rest of the house stuff would be mine. He asked if we needed to fill out all of our other property items on the questionnaire, like my wedding ring and the TV, and I answered, "Only if you're going to be a dick."

How mature was his answer: "I won't if you won't."

He signed the agreement questionnaire, and *then* I told him about my other plans. From his $5000 settlement, I would be keeping $625 for his part of the lawyer fees. I was keeping $500 to take his name off the mortgage. I'd also be keeping $1600 for my half of the Ireland trip, and that when the "refund" from Orbitz came, I'd sign the whole thing over to him. He sat with a surprised look on his face, but he agreed to it. He questioned if I'd heard anything from the travel company, and I informed him that they'd told me they'd take two to three weeks to respond. We shared a smile about them being slow to refund money, but I wasn't being friendly, with my fake smile. He wasn't getting any of my real happiness.

I held out my hand and requested his house keys and garage door opener, which he handed over. As he got my blanket out of his car, he stood waiting by my car, giving me that cute, seductive smile and seemed to wait for a hug or more from me. I simply said, "Well, I'll call if there's anything else," got in my car, and drove off without looking back.

What was he thinking? I had nothing left for him, whether he realized that or not.

I celebrated with Tracy and Jason over MexiBowls, a bottle of wine, and a membership to AmericanSingles.com. Wow, was I *not* ready to date right then. Besides, who would honestly want to deal with a bilateral mastectomy and chemo? Sure, my profile pictures looked cute now, but reality would soon hit…and hard. I couldn't trust any man to stick by me right now, except for the blood-related ones. I didn't need the frustration of dating. Yech. Sure, there were two guys on there that I'd go out with, but still, back to my chemo point. Best for now to think of this new membership as entertaining material.

When I talked to Judy Johnson about getting the signatures in order, I filled her in on my pneumothorax fun.

She was irate, saying I had a malpractice lawsuit on my hands. She quickly added she'd tell some of her colleagues about my situation and would get back to me with advice. Originally, I'd just wanted them to cover my additional medical costs from it, but now, a little award for my "pain and suffering" might be nice. I could use that money to pay off my second mortgage and be able to give a ton to Mom and Dad to help them out. It would feel so great to pay it forward to them.

AUGUST 14, 2008

Class was rough today. My heart kept racing, pounding so hard it rattled my whole chest like a tympani. It was impossible to concentrate on ESL lessons when I couldn't concentrate on anything but the beating of my heart. Okay, that, and finding a new surgeon, lawsuits, wigs, breast prostheses, new doctor referrals, insurance coverage, running errands, getting a roommate to help cover bills. And that was all just during the morning. No wonder I had an anxiety attack after all that. I spent my hour lunch on the phone setting an appointment with a new surgeon, Dr. Dana Carlson.

Tracy gave her my name and they added an extra opening for me Tuesday at 10:30. She'd been rated as one of the top surgeons in the Twin Cities, and I hoped she might be able to refer me to a better oncology team, if needed. After the surgeon, I called Medica with two important requests: will they cover my wigs/breast prostheses, and are my new doctors covered under my insurance plan? Well, the bad news was that they wouldn't cover wigs, but good news that they would cover breast prostheses up to eighty percent with a network provider, and all of my doctors were now in my plan coverage. However, I had only three visits approved for Dr. Garino and Dr. Dickson but none for Laudi.

How fun that I'd have to keep calling again and again for more approvals.

I couldn't get my other errands done fast enough that afternoon. I furiously ran all over Maple Grove, picking up this and that. I packed up myself and Suerte and we went *home*.

There was no better emotion than to pull into my parents' driveway and see my loved ones sitting outside, smiling because I was now there. Why did I miss out on this for three years of my life? The two neighbor kids, Madison and Kaden, gave me big hugs hello and goodbye as they went home. Then I got to hug my beautiful Mom, Dad, and Vic, who were also sitting outside. My heart was full of happiness again. It felt like a Sunday dinner with my sisters Vic, Sheila, Alison, and Amanda, along with their families, stopping by. All those happy faces and supporters. I felt so loved.

How could life get any better than it was at that moment, with so many great people around me?

Sadly, though, we always had cancer talk. My Aunt Sharon called to tell me to contact the Piper Institute in Minneapolis, the best cancer treatment center in Minnesota (and all I could think was, *really? More work?!*) Rachel also called later on, and I briefed her on my chemo cocktail. She liked the Adriamycin route, considering it a common treatment and a good "bang for your buck" drug. What a fabulous pharmaceutical supporter! She also told me that morphine could cause your heart to race, especially after taking a large amount for an extended period of time. Whew, at least I knew I was not dying, and hopefully this feeling of death would go away soon. Rachel and I sat on the phone for an hour and a half that night, until almost midnight. I snuck into the living room when Dad came out for his midnight snack, and instantly I felt like I was a teenager again, busted for being on the phone so late. Some feelings, engrained so deeply, are hard to shake off even after twelve years.

AUGUST 15, 2008

What a way to start off the day: the realization that I was supposed to be on a plane to Ireland this morning and not waking up on my parents' couch....

Finally, I could remove my second pair of TED socks. The post-surgical, circulation-cutting, knee-high, anti-embolism (blood clot-preventing) socks. They're horribly unattractive, but I rocked in them for a week, even in shorts.

While waiting for Amanda, I spent the morning writing thank-you cards to all the people who came to see me or sent flowers while I was in the hospital. I agonized for hours about sending my father-in-law Shawn a birthday card, and in the end I gave in to the temptation. I signed it simply, "Thinking of you, Gwen." I knew that I wanted to send that card as more of a jab-in-the-gut-reminder-that-I'm-still-here card, but when you're angry with someone, the only person you hurt is yourself. I knew I just needed to let go of my anger toward them. What good for me would ever come of it?

Amanda picked me up and we were off for pedicures. Her first ever, my second. We were like little girls admiring something pretty, watching our beautified nails glisten in the sunlight. During our pedis, I asked Amanda if she wanted to know if I'm genetically positive (the conversation I'd been dreading to have with all of my sisters). She replied without hesitation: "Uh, yeah!"

I knew how hard and deep that information was to deal with, so I never wanted to pressure anyone with that knowledge if they didn't want it. All that could come from knowing was the added stress of realizing that you could develop the cancer someday too, or worse, pass it along to your daughters.

Not even *I* wanted to know my results! Why would I want to

burden any of them with knowing too?

While Amanda and Kurt were packing up their truck for the weekend at the cabin with Kurt's family, I got to play a little with Alec. We played with his train, read some nursery rhymes, and jumped on his trampoline. I loved getting that time with him. I hated that he didn't know who I was when I visited, that I was not around enough for him to know me. My heart swelled when he asked Manda if I was going to the cabin with them.

After packing up their cooler, I got a call from "X" (Andy's new name in my cell phone). He asked if I had looked for his auto-opener for his car. Not having the time, I apologized (not that I needed to). He told me he'd locked his keys in his car. I told him I was in St. Cloud, and he responded that he didn't have keys to the house anymore. Pause. He waited and then said, "Well, I guess I'll have to call someone." I happily said, "Good luck!" and hung up.

What did he expect I'd do or say, help him? Oh please, can *I* help *you* in your time of need? Sheesh. I also realized that the car opener was for his car, and he had his brother's car (switching cars after his had his plates removed because of the DUI). What good would having that opener do anyway?

Why couldn't I just wave my magic wand and open his car?

Sure enough, fifteen minutes later, he texted me and said the opener wouldn't work for the same reason I already knew. It killed me to see how much he still relied on my help, even after leaving me.

I found out today that my friend Jill's father passed away after falling off a ladder. He'd been in a coma for a week before passing away today. I texted her with my condolences, hoping that she'd get it even with my crappy cell reception. I sure didn't want to call her with all that she was dealing with. Death is much, much harder to deal with than cancer or divorce. I feel for Jill. I could not fathom losing anyone right now—or even within decades.

Part Three:

SERIOUSLY, DATING AGAIN ALREADY??

AUGUST 16, 2008

Dad woke me up at 6:00 A.M. to go to the Swapper's Meet with him and Gram Rosha. We walked around checking out the produce, scouring for deals. Sharing those moments with both of them was so precious to me. Reminded of my own mortality, I understood this may have been the only time I would ever have to do this with either of them, especially Gram, and the time became that much more important and special to me. Even when I felt as if I was yelling at Gram so she could hear me, having her conversation and smiles made me feel loved and immensely important to her. Even my ride home with Dad, after dropping her off, was a new experience—sitting as an adult with my dad, talking about how my grandparents were changing with age, getting more and more advanced with sickness.

It was surreal, being an adult talking to my dad now, and at the same time, remembering back to when I was little, sitting by my dad and knowing little about the world around me. I always thought my dad hated me when I was growing up, as teenagers tend to think about their parents. But looking back, he was only trying to protect me from bad decisions, from bad things happening to me. I couldn't explain how good it felt to be able to talk to him now, to feel the love he had for me, to know he cared and still only wanted to protect me, no matter what.

As Brit and I were making strawberry sauce with the strawberries Dad bought for me, she said she was confused about my "ex-husband Andy." When I tried explaining how he didn't want to be with me anymore, she just grunted in disgust.

My thoughts exactly.

I slipped into a low point while talking to Mom later on that day. I asked her, "When does it stop hurting?" She thought I meant surgery, but I meant with Andy. I cried for my envy of him, of his just walking away and starting his life over. New apartment, no house responsibility, no cancer. Just him, work, and his social life. What I wouldn't give to have less to deal with, to just lead a normal life with everyday worries. Was what I had now *normal?*

That night, Syd gave me a breast cancer awareness bracelet of hers. Since my diagnosis, she'd been obsessed with collecting them in support of me. What a great niece! Vic also became very interested in my American Singles profile, really into seeing my options and perusing their profiles. I was just turned off by the thought of dating altogether, completely freaked out by the very thought of it. Why even try to deal with this *now?*

I freaked out the one normal person I found on there by

comparing myself to Steve Carrell's character on *Little Miss Sunshine*. Nice one, Gwen. Now you're suicidal. I just meant that we all had bad days. Oh well. I didn't want to date anyway.

AUGUST 17, 2008

Church of St. Luke with Mom, Haley, and Hunter this morning. In his homily, the Very Reverend Jacob Yali spoke of powerlessness. It felt that the church recently had been speaking right to me, applying directly to my life. Powerlessness? Where did I begin? Everything lately had stripped me of decision-making, but I refused to let it kill me. Sure, life handed me dilemmas, but I was serving up that "dillemonade" (thanks for that cheesy line, Danny Tanner). Divorce? Cancer? Neither was going to break my spirit.

Another recurring theme in the Catholic Church was forgiving those who have wronged us. Man, was *that* a constant struggle for me. But you know? I always felt better inside when I let go of that anger, that frustration. When I chose to be happy and focus on what's pure and healthy in my life, my body felt lighter. I didn't have that negativity to hold me down.

May I please hold on to that.

After church, we went to get our "reward" for going: cappuccinos. While we were there, Hunter and Haley made a blunt comment about me getting divorced and Hunter said, "Andy drinks too much." I was not sure why that hurt so much—maybe getting it thrown in my face unexpectedly? Made me wonder what Kathryn and Jeff say to them, not that any of what Haley and Hunter said wasn't true.

I looked forward to the day when hearing his name didn't make my skin crawl or make me sick to my stomach.

Before Luke's birthday party, Mom and I snuck off for a quick walk. We didn't go very far, but we had a great conversation. We somehow got on the topic of the ultimatum Mom gave Dad so long ago—the alcohol or her and the girls. Dad was strong enough to choose Mom. He hadn't drunk for over thirty years. When I asked her what she would have done if Dad had chosen differently, she said, "I don't know."

Thank God she never had to find out. I wouldn't be here today, nor any of my little sisters. I hoped I'd inherited Dad's strength, if even just a little bit.

The first part of the party became "Talking with Randy's Mom" time. She talked to me about the cancer, and she needed to tell me something: one of the best things I could do was to keep a positive attitude. She told me, "Let go, and let God." I agreed.

The second part of the party became "Let's Check Out Gwen's AmericanSingles.com Profile." Kath and Vic started screening guys with me. Disheartening! That's what it felt like. Where were all the normal single guys? Not that I needed many, just one. Kath and Vic were excited to see all the guys and check them out, but it just made me sick, partly from the fear of dating again but also from fear that I might never find someone to love me.

I was just happy to fall asleep on Mom's couch again.

AUGUST 18, 2008

I woke up early, wanting to absorb all the family time I could before heading back to the cities. Jessica Greenberg wasn't answering her calls or pages, so I had to head out, regardless. I held so tightly to Mom, refusing to let go, and she didn't make me—or let me—let go of her. It was hard to leave the center of my support circle. The only thing making it easier was knowing I would see her soon.

Jessica did have the results of my genetic test, but of course, nothing much was easy in my life. I discovered I was neither positive nor negative for the BRCA 1 or 2, but they did find a variant (mutation) on my BRCA 1 gene. Best-case scenario, it was nothing. Worst case, it was a rare cancer gene (P53), li fraumeni syndrome. However, my family didn't fit the picture of it—we have no random cancers at young ages. I opted at this time NOT to have the P53 test for an out-of-pocket $1500 and to wait to see if Medica will cover it and if I would need radiation. If radiation would be necessary, then I had no worries on getting the test anytime soon. Radiation treatments could also cause problems, if not cancer again, so I'd have to do it soon.

Jessica said that the only step forward at this point would be to test some family members, Mom first and possibly her mother as well, to see if this variant was genetic. Their testing would be free, just so the company could study the variant and compare it to different occurrences in other families.

My variant had been seen on seventy-four other tested people, in fourteen other families. In five of those families, it tracked with cancer. In nine, there was no rhyme or reason, so it wasn't informative for cancer risk. Jessica said that at the end of the day, I was not likely to be a carrier. Even with P53, there was only a less-than-two-percent chance I was positive.

Not that statistics meant much to me anymore.

I checked my e-mail eagerly that afternoon, hoping to hear from the one seemingly-normal guy I found on American Singles: Jeff. His messages interested me, and he asked great questions. I couldn't help but be interested in him. However, I still was not interested in taking it further. I couldn't imagine dropping the cancer bomb on someone and having them actually stick around.

Thank goodness for online dating—no face-to-face pressure.

I spent the night with Rachel and Dan. Rach was great, reviewing my chemo options with me. She e-mailed her oncology pharmacist connections to see what option would be best for me. Being able to sleep on another couch was just what I needed. Anything to prevent feeling lonely at home.

It made me sad to think that I could have been doing this with my family for years, but I was so absorbed in making my marriage work that I now realized I'd missed out on three years with them. I refused to ever let that happen again. Never will I lose the closeness to the people who mean everything to me and who will always stick by me.

FROM CARINGBRIDGE.ORG, TUESDAY, AUGUST 19, 2008 2:07 PM, CDT:

I just met today with a new surgeon. I'm not as comfortable with the last one after the pneumothorax, but I appreciate everything he did to help me. The new surgeon, Dr. Dana Carlson, has an office here in Maple Grove, and made an opening to see me, thanks to my amazing friend Tracy, who referred me to her. (Thanks a million, Tracy!)

Dr. Carlson was incredible. She concurred with Dr. Lovett, and recommended a mastectomy for me. I decided to opt for the bilateral mastectomy for genetic and future-cancer-risk options, and she said it would be easier for reconstruction as well. She also recommended getting a second opinion on my chemo options, especially since I don't feel comfortable with my nil knowledge of how the drugs would work for me. She also recommended oncotyping, genetically testing my tumor and cancer to see which drugs would help me the best. I've already called two doctors to see what I can do. So many doctors, so little time before school starts!

From her referral, I have an appointment with a plastic surgeon that would do a gradual reconstruction, starting directly after my mastectomy. This appointment is on Friday this week. I'm lucky that they can squeeze me in so soon. I'll need to take time off of work now, something I was desperately trying to avoid, but Dr. Carlson reminded me that I need to take care of myself first. It's a good reminder once in a while.

Have a fantastic Tuesday! I'm off to see Mamma Mia tonight with Tracy and Lindsey.

AUGUST 19, 2008

After Pilates at Rachel and Dan's (and a cup of coffee that Rachel had waiting for me, what a sweetheart), I drove back to Maple Grove for my first appointment with Dr. Dana Carlson, my new surgeon. I will sum it up in one word—WOW!

She came from a woman's perspective, knew and related well to my situation, and made me feel so comfortable. She concurred with Dr. Lovett, that I'd need a mastectomy, and she agreed that the bilateral would be a good idea for reconstructive purposes. She said that otherwise, it would be nearly impossible to be symmetrical again. She referred me to a plastic surgeon in Edina, Dr. Jennifer Harrington, who "gives you great cleavage." SOLD!

She also gave me names of some new oncologists that could give me a second opinion about chemo options and also do oncotyping, genetically testing my tumor to determine which chemo type would be best. Dr. Harrington would also start immediate reconstruction following the mastectomy.

Great news: I won't have to get prostheses or be flat-chested for a year!

I got my second opinion from Dr. Laudi via his nurse—either chemo option would be good for me. Wow, thanks for the clarification. So much for a true second opinion. Now what? I still had no idea which one to pick.

Finally, a night that I could go out and feel "normal" again—dinner and *Mamma Mia!* with Tracy and Lindsey. To sing along at the top of my lungs with Tracy, as Lindsey looked at us in embarrassment, was just the elixir I needed to feel good about life again. After the movie, I went over to Tracy's and checked my e-mail. Jeff had asked me to meet him. Whoa! Nervous, but a little excited. I haven't been on a date for over three years. What if he's different in person? What if he doesn't like me?

Tracy was excited for me and encouraged me to just have fun and enjoy the distraction from regular life.

AUGUST 20, 2008

A quiet morning at home. I spent the day sleeping on the couch, completely absorbed in my self-pity and depression. How I hated being that way. Why should I let everything going on in life wreck my chance to be in a good mood? Darn, I wish the Celexa would work harder!

When I finally snapped out of it, I snuck in a quick energy-reviving workout before meeting my friend Jenni for a night at the casino. It felt so great to talk to someone who really gets what I'm going through medically, how the process of illness and work will play out.

AUGUST 21, 2008

When I got home that morning, I had no energy or desire to do anything. To try to get myself back on track, I decided to take a bike ride with no destination in mind. For once, I was going to fly by the seat of my pants, quite rare for the planner in me. For an hour, I just rode my bike aimlessly, around Maple Grove and Rice Lake, enjoying the cool, overcast afternoon. It was actually difficult for me to be left that long, alone with my thoughts.

I felt happy and stronger when I got home, so I started to tackle cleaning the garage and storage closet downstairs. Ah, to purge the rest of the remnants of Andy. Gone now were our wedding pictures, with the exception of the ones with my family. Gone were the ticket stubs, restaurant placemats, and other trinket souvenirs of our relationship. Gone were all the pictures of us in frames. Gone was my wedding dress, the one that never quite fit right no matter how many times it was taken in. (I saw that now as an unrecognized omen.) Gone was the teddy bear he gave me that I kissed on nights I fell asleep alone. The place was slowly but surely starting to feel more like *mine*.

I made a CaringBridge.org update about my cancer journey on Tuesday, and I had fun reading the guestbook entries daily. Already there were over 200 visitors to my page! I forwarded it to darn-near everyone I knew, excluding any of Andy's family. Even if they eventually got the link forwarded to them, would they *honestly* care about what was going on, or would they read it like a tabloid magazine? All they cared about was keeping up with appearances, not people. However, the site had connected me with friends all over the place: grad school friends, high school pals, and former coworkers. It uplifted me to know so many people cared about me even through the hard times.

So many good, honest people out there.

I got an e-mail from Shawn today, thanking me for the birthday card I sent. I was surprised he even replied, even more by his message. He asked how I was doing and feeling, saying he says a prayer or two for me every day (like what, *Please, Lord, let her give Andy more stuff?*) and that I'll always be a part of their family.

WHAT?! This coming from the man who hadn't contacted me, not even to check in, for over a month, who had been painfully indifferent towards me? Honestly. If I even wrote a reply, it wouldn't be as nice as the one he dutifully sent to me.

Another e-mail I received today was from Andy, asking me when I'd stop by his workplace. I'd told him I'd be in Dinkytown and that I'd stop by in exchange for drinks for Carrie and me. I had a change of heart, not wanting to be nice to him anymore, so I told him that I didn't think I'd make it. He also asked me for the sheets from the bed, since they were a gift from his friend, and for the Pottery Barn shelf on the fireplace mantel. Was he *mad* when I told him no! He wondered why the "keeping gifts from friends" rule didn't apply to him too. To placate him, I told him I'd think about it.

In the end, he said it would be nice to see me. He hoped that I was feeling well, that I would get all I can from life, and that he still thinks of me. Of course he did, but now he was just trying to weasel more stuff from me. Sure he wanted to see me.

Wished I could say the same.

Foolishly curious to see him, and Carrie's presence giving me more courage, I decided to bring his mail to him at work. He smiled and waved when I walked in, while the other female bartender and wait staff glared at me. What was *that?* So much for being friendly with those little skeezes. He deliberately shook my hand in agreement for getting us drinks, seeming eager to touch my hand. Even the feel of his hand disgusted me.

We intentionally sat on the opposite side of the bar, out of his view, though he made it a point to come over and tell me that he was moving the rest of his things out on September 3rd. Why did he have to come over to our table just to tell me that?

We left after our four free drinks and appetizers without saying goodbye.

We traveled down the road for our actual destination in Minneapolis: the Hope Lodge, for my first meeting of the Young Survivors Group. Some women there were more obviously going through cancer treatments; the short hair was usually my signal. So many young women, so many bilateral mastectomies, so much chemo and radiation were apparent in that room. It was utterly depressing, but it did feel good to know that I wasn't alone on Cancer Island. These women were all going through it, but they were doing it with their partners and husbands; some women were lucky enough to have someone who stuck with them through sickness and in health.

That was the hardest part of the meeting, being reminded that *my* husband left. When we were going around the circle to share our personal cancer stories, it finally came around to me. When I started to speak, all I could say was my name before I started to cry uncontrollably. I cried because I realized how scared I was of everything, and I finally felt comfortable enough to let all of my hidden emotions out from underneath my façade of strength.

Not once did anyone make me feel embarrassed for crying, but just the opposite—they all understood. This was a new feeling for me. Yes, my family had been wonderful, but these were all people who could relate first-hand to my frustration. They knew how it felt to have no control over your life. They knew what it felt like to lose all of your hair, even the eyelashes. They knew what it felt like to be thrust into the world of oncology and make important medical decisions. One woman, Mary, said that people would ask her how she stayed so positive about her life, and she'd reply, "It was the only choice I could make about my life today." Well said.

One woman at the meeting, Kathy, came all the way from Fergus Falls to attend. She had just celebrated her ten-year anniversary of being cancer-free. She had been diagnosed at 26, and with the limited oncology knowledge that was out there ten years ago, she had undergone an intense clinical trial. Through the trials, they lost six of her fellow trial patients. Kathy and the others showed me that, yep, the process stinks, but life happily goes on afterwards.

It was an emotionally-draining meeting, but in a month from now when they meet again, I'll be ready.

Emotionally spent after dropping Carrie off, and desperately needing to feel "normal" again, I got all cute and called Jeff to see if he'd like to meet up for a beer. He agreed. Yikes! When he walked in, I was pleasantly surprised that he was even better-looking in person—gorgeous brown eyes, happy smile, great body (from what I could see through his black button-up shirt and jeans). However, after being with him for a few hours, I did a lot more listening and nodding than talking, and the conversation wasn't much I could comment on: his family and his computers. He seemed very jittery, almost like he was taking drugs. Maybe it was just nerves. Who knows? He hugged me before we left (sweet that he didn't try to kiss me) and I mentioned that maybe we could get together when I got back from my parents' house over the weekend.

I decided I'll try hanging out one more time, but I was still *not* looking for anything relationship-wise. I needed to enjoy this "me" time!

AUGUST 22, 2008

More purging of possessions in the morning. I started by cleaning out the guest bedroom closet and moving all of my things into my closet, anticipating a roommate sometime soon. Again, the place was feeling more like *mine*. I wished I could carry Andy's dresser and mattresses out to the garage myself. My room would look so much more "Gwen" when I had my reading corner and bookshelf in there. Aah, the thought alone was comforting.

Ten A.M. brought me to an appointment with Ardith. She was proud of how assertive I'd been with Andy, how I hadn't given him power by giving in. I'd need to work on changing my thoughts of what others think of me, from "What are they saying about me?" to "Who cares what they think?"

I've been going crazy thinking about Shawn and Diane's opinions of me, wondering what Andy's told them about me. Also, I needed to see "success" as getting out of a one-person marriage and moving on. I couldn't see myself as a failure in marriage, but as a strong person that doesn't have to raise her husband anymore.

Not surprisingly, I've also been officially diagnosed with separation anxiety from Mom, bursting into tears every time I leave home. Ardith told me to remind myself that Mom isn't leaving me, but she is living her life. My other official diagnosis was adjustment disorder, not clinical depression, thank goodness. She said that I just needed to talk things out for now and eventually I'd be just fine. She comforted me by telling me that Andy would continue to coast through life, never achieving success in life if he kept running from responsibility. However, I was using my anger in a good way—to detach myself from him emotionally and start my new life.

Yea me!

Two-fifteen P.M. brought me to an appointment with Dr. Harrington, my plastic surgeon in Edina. What another amazing doctor; she even hugged me! She told me that Andy was without character for leaving me right now, that there would be something better out there for me. She shared with me that she was also divorced, so she knew how the separation feels.

Surgery-wise, I'll have the gradual reconstruction. After my mastectomy, she will lift up my pectoral muscles and put the skin stretchers in. She will also place a piece of Alloderm—cadaver skin (eek!)—between my muscle and where it meets the rib cage, so my breasts will have "nice drop" later on. She made me really look forward to the "reward" later on, but I was not looking forward to the two-to-three weeks off from work for the recovery from the surgery.

Happily, I drove home to St. Cloud for the night and the weekend. Back to my happy support circle. Back to the one place I was happy.

AUGUST 24, 2008

"Back to School Soup" Day at the Rosha House. We were a

factory in the kitchen, chopping up the vegetables and meats for our annual soup that meant fall days were upon us again. I adored the chaos of all the people, the yelling, the crying, and the laughter that lit up the house. Every day spent at home with all of my beautiful sisters, parents, brothers-in-law, nieces, and nephews formed a beautiful gift. It was humbling to ask my little sister Al for the TV that I gave her, but she happily brought it for me now that I wouldn't have one anymore. Hey, not a bad trade—a plasma TV for freedom from my husband.

I was glad that Al was able to bring my old TV back to me; it was definitely hard to ask for the return of the gift I gave to her. Fortunately, she was wonderful and had no issue with it. One less expense took a load off of my mind.

On the way home, I called Jeff back to see if he still wanted to get together later on, and he agreed to meet me at my house so I could get help from Rachel and Dan with unloading the TV from my car. While sitting in my living room, we small-talked about religion, not wanting to scare him off with the news of The Big C, but it was all I could think about. Finally I caved, asking him how much he could handle to hear about me. He had already, on his own, guessed the first part about cancer, seeing my breast cancer support books underneath the coffee table, and he remembered my talking about my recent return to church. I even tried to freak him out by telling him about my upcoming hair loss, weight loss, vomiting and nausea, but he asked me why I was trying to scare him off.

So I went to Plan B with Bombs 2 and 3 to drop: being married already and still being married. He just looked at me calmly and said that he liked hanging out with me, that none of this would stop him from wanting to hang out with me more and getting to know me better. If things would work out, they would.

I sat in complete disbelief, staring at him. Was he *serious?* Even after hearing all of that, he still wanted to spend time with me? Umm, what?! So he dropped his bomb on me—he was being deployed to Iraq or Afghanistan soon.

Okay, so we both had our issues.

He asked me what I was doing tomorrow night, if he could cook dinner with me. Honestly, how could this guy who only officially met me three days ago want to stick around, knowing full well of my cancer and pending divorce? How was it that this stranger cared more about me than my soon-to-be-ex-husband? Was it actually true that mature and responsible men still existed? He quickly kissed me, and I knew he meant it.

What a whole new world was now opening up to me.

AUGUST 25, 2008

Day One of Back to School workshops at Northdale Middle School. Relief washed over me, grateful for the distractions from life. It was still extremely difficult to keep focused on work though, but I tried to bury it with more work and kept going through the motions. Getting ready for a new school year, knowing that I wouldn't be there for a few weeks, felt almost pointless. If even for a few weeks, I'd happily welcome the distraction from Cancer College and return to being in my comfortable, old, normal life for a while.

I met Jeff later on at his house in Brooklyn Park; together we ran quickly to the grocery store for supplies. He seemed so abstract-random to my concrete-sequential as we wandered around the grocery store. He had no real dinner plans, just came up with ideas as we walked up and down the aisles. It was weird to relinquish control to someone I hardly knew, but for once I just went with it.

While we were making dinner, I asked him where he'd like to be in five years. He said simply, "Happy, and maybe with kids." His casual approach and outlook, lack of professional goals or ambition took me off guard. Could I even handle this lack of motivation? Or was it just that his goals were so different from mine? Instantly, I was put on the defensive, ready to protect my future from this, but trying not to judge.

Sure, being around someone affectionate was nice when I felt lonely, but I felt like I was trying to convince myself that "settling" for now would be okay.

I'll see how Tracy feels when she meets him.

AUGUST 26, 2008

Jeff's been messaging me all day. Cute, but a little much when I'm supposed to be working. I talked to another ESL teacher in the district about her husband leaving her. He had been cheating on her for a year, got the other woman pregnant right after my friend miscarried, then cheated on his new girlfriend/mother of his kids with a one night stand and got *her* pregnant with twins. Damn. My colleague said it had been four years and she'd found it tough to get over seeing happy marriages, but she realized he was a loser, that she was better off without him.

It made my mess seem easier to deal with, seeing how my divorce negotiations could have been so much worse for me than they were.

How do you make life with cancer even more frustrating and scary? Attend your mandatory "Chemo 101" class at the Cancer Resource Center. It started off all fun and cute, borrowing a hot little blond wig from the CRC. Trying on all the sassy little wigs was like a miniature fashion show for the women working there that day. I felt sassy too, like a new woman with every wig I tried on. Still, it was hard to see what I'd look like in a few months, to feel the heat and scratchiness of the synthetic hair. I figured wearing a wig would be better than being bald or "scarfed," looking more like a cancer patient.

Then the actual chemo instruction started. It was an extremely informative event. Of course, I was the youngest person there again. ("But you shouldn't be here! You're so young!" Geez. Again, I was very tired of hearing that.) Marcia, the CRC nurse, explained the basics, such as ways to treat cancer, how chemo works, and the goals of treatment. Since chemo kills all the fast-growing cells in the body, that's why my hair will fall out, why I'll need Neulasta injections to bring up my white blood cell counts, and that I'll get diarrhea and constipation. Oh, the joys of cancer!

Chemo is meant to help cure cancer, keep the cancer from spreading, slow its growth, kill metastasized cells (cells that have spread to other parts of the body), and relieve cancer symptoms.

JUST SOME OF THE FUN SIDE EFFECTS OF CHEMOTHERAPY:

- ~ Nausea, vomiting, diarrhea (that will subside within a week of the full rounds of chemo)
- ~ Lowered red- and white-blood cell counts
- ~ Fatigue (and it will take months to return to pre-chemo energy levels)
- ~ Hair loss (*all* the hair on my body)
- ~ Anxiety and depression
- ~ Physical pain
- ~ Peripheral neuropathy—numbness in the fingers and feet
- ~ Mouth sores and sensitivity, alleviated with salt water
- ~ Metallic taste in my mouth
- ~ Heightened senses of smell and taste

WAYS TO ALLEVIATE SIDE EFFECTS OF CHEMO:

- ~ Call the doctor for anti-nausea meds
- ~ Avoid red meat if it tastes metallic
- ~ Eat a high-calorie diet to maintain a healthy weight and a high-protein diet to rebuild blood cells
- ~ Drink a lot of water to maintain hydration
- ~ Avoid spicy and high-fat foods
- ~ Eat small meals frequently or exercise before eating to increase hunger
- ~ Brush with an infants' toothbrush to avoid excessive bleeding in the mouth and skip shaving my legs to prevent excessive bleeding when my counts are down
- ~ Wash hands and face with a gentle soap and constantly

wear sunscreen SPF 30

~ Skip wigs and wear scarves and hats that will be gentle on the sensitive skin of my hairless scalp

~ If I have pain of any kind, call my oncologist for anti-pain meds

THE FEARS OF CHEMO SIDE EFFECTS:

~ I can often go from diarrhea to constipation without notice

~ If I can't keep up my red/white blood cell or platelet counts, I can get anemia, neutropenia, or bleed easily

~ I have to limit exercise if my white counts are low, due to increased risk of injury, which can cause internal bleeding

~ I'm at high risk for infections, so I need to avoid crowds (like a middle school, perhaps?)

~ If I have shaking/chills, flu-like symptoms, fever over 100 degrees, or a sore throat/coughing, it may be a medical emergency and I'll need to go to the emergency room immediately

~ An ER visit may require a five-day hospitalization to bring counts back up and bring me back to a healthy level

~ If I get a rash, it is a conduit for bacteria and more serious infections, so I'll need to call the doctor

~ The funniest part (not funny-ha-ha, but funny-depressing) of this section is that there are many side effects of chemo on sexual activity too, but since that's far from an issue for me right now, I happily get to skip listening to this part of the class.

The chemo infusions themselves are a whole other ballgame. If I have the Cytoxan/Adriamycin, the duration of infusions (the "drip-drip" of the IV drugs) is two hours. First, I'll get an anti-nausea injection to combat the nausea that will come after the chemo is finished for the day, plus Benadryl just in case I am allergic to the chemo drugs. The Adriamycin takes twenty minutes to infuse. The Cytoxan takes thirty minutes. The Taxol/Herceptin weekly treatments will take four hours of infusions. For the first Taxol/Carboplatin treatment, I'll need to make sure I have a driver to bring me home in case I have a bad reaction or I'm too tired to drive. The Herceptin (the hormone therapy targeted at my her-2-neu positive status) won't be nearly as bad as the other three drugs, but they will be on the same day as the Taxol/Carboplatin and every week until I'm done with full treatment. This one takes an hour and a half of infusion time all by itself. *(Note to reader: Are you confused yet? Yeah, don't get me started. I already know how confusing it all is. I'm living in it.)*

What an information-heavy class, all in two hours. In solidarity, I shared in the fears and questions with three other chemo patients in attendance with me. This whole process is still tough, even with knowing what to expect.

Jeff said he wanted to see me as much as he could before I went home for the weekend (and before surgery made me more fragile), and since I wanted Tracy to meet/evaluate him, we went over to visit with Tracy and Jason. He seemed very polite, but I was still nervous to hear Tracy's evaluation. After a few glasses of wine, a little Guitar Hero, and many military conversations between Jason and Jeff, we went back to my place. It must have been the wine; I got a little "into" kissing him, but it felt good to feel normal, beautiful, and sexual again. Good isn't quite accurate; I felt like a woman again.

FROM CARINGBRIDGE.ORG, WEDNESDAY, AUGUST 27, 2008 6:21 AM, CDT:

It's a rainy day in Maple Grove, and I love it! What a fun thing to wake up to, the gentle sound of the rain, the strong thunderclaps. Great way to start the morning.

I've been waiting to update the site until I had my next surgery date. I'm going in at noon on September 11. At first, I was disappointed to hear I was scheduled on such a black day in US history, but I got over it and decided that it was going to be a good day in Gwen history, The Day the Cancer Was Gone.

I also decided to take some extended time off from work, at least three months. I will be starting reconstruction at the same time, thus the extended time off needed. With the surgery and follow-ups, not to mention starting the first round of chemo, I finally listened to the wise people around me, and I'll be out until mid-December. Scares me to think that this will be the first amount of time I've taken off of school since I started in kindergarten! It will be good for a little R&R, considering how the summer played out, and I really look forward to finally tackling my ever-growing reading list.

Have a fantastic day, raining or not! I will be thinking of all of you, grateful that you are in my life, while at Open House tonight :)

FROM CARINGBRIDGE.ORG,
MONDAY, SEPTEMBER 1, 2008 6:14 PM, CDT:

Aah, Minnesota...the last day of "summer" for me, and I'm enjoying the warm sunshine before heading back to work tomorrow. I enjoyed the afternoon at Weaver Lake, getting in as much sunshine as I can!

I will start my leave from work on September 11. If you'd like to contact me after, I will only have my personal e-mail accounts and cell phone number. For the three days following surgery, I will be at North Memorial recuperating, then up to my parents' house in St. Cloud for two weeks. A few weeks after recovering from surgery, I'll be starting Round One of chemo: Adriamycin and Cytoxan every other week for four treatments. I'm not sure how I'll be feeling after surgery or during treatments, but please continue to e-mail or call me. If I feel "cute" enough for visitors, I'll be sure to let everyone know ASAP!

I've been asked many times what people can do to help. First, THANK YOU for all the offers! I couldn't ask for better friends and family. Right now, I feel good, so it's hard for me to think of ways people can help me out. I can tell you that all of the cards, calls, hanging out, and e-mails have been wonderful for my daily inner strength, so please keep them coming. When the time comes for help in other ways, I'll be sure to ask (tough for an independent woman, but I know it helps!)

Have a great beginning to the new school year and September!

FROM CARINGBRIDGE.ORG,
WEDNESDAY, SEPTEMBER 3, 2008 8:05 PM, CDT:

Wow, is being back to work full-time a big change! I love the chaos of the beginning of the school year, sixth graders with their deer-in-the-headlights looks while trying to find their lockers or the gym, seeing my students from last year and how they've grown taller over the summer, and having former students stop by to visit. However, for a while, I'm right back to nap time after work!

I had my pre-surgical check-up this afternoon with Dr. McIntyre in MG. I'm happy to report that I have a healthy heart and lungs, no signs of other illness or infections—I'm cleared for surgery next week! He advised me to take care of myself and be careful not to get sick in the next week, or I'll have to reschedule surgery. Not going to let that happen, even if I have to drink orange juice/take more vitamins nonstop until then.

I can't tell you how great it is to be back at work, focusing on the positive (and having my student, Afra, list me on her math questionnaire as the person she admires most). I will relish these few days I have at work, but I will try to sneak a Teacher's Edition home so I can work on plans for when I get back. Have a great evening, and enjoy the fall weather!

SEPTEMBER 4, 2008

Forget trying to go back day by day and try to remember what was happening! I'm just going to try to update my thoughts here when I have the chance to catch up on all of the chaos.

First, the medical updates. I had a pre-surgery check-up with Dr. McIntyre, my primary care physician (as I had to now call him…all the darn doctors keep asking me who my PCP is, and I had to start naming someone so they'd get off my back) at Allina Medical Group, Maple Grove. My heart and lungs are a-okay, ready for surgery. He made sure to tell me to be careful in the next week and to not get sick, otherwise I would have to reschedule my surgery. No way was I doing that! I'll scare the damn germs out of my body before I reschedule. Now I was just waiting for the big surgery day…

Next, Jeff was freaking me out. Here, I didn't want to date in the first place, and he now wanted to see me constantly! I finally realized that we were just too different in what we like to do, and I was afraid to just tell him that, fearing he would hate me. I knew the longer I waited, the harder and uglier it would be. I've avoided him, trying to give him the hint, but I just didn't know if it was working. He's nice, just not The One for me.

However, Tracy went backpacking this weekend with Jason and Jason's coworker, Mark. He's the single hockey referee/accountant that she wants to set me up with. She not-so-casually talked to him all weekend about me, even showing him my Facebook page and pictures. To be honest with him, she told him pretty much everything there was to know about my life drama. After hearing all of that, he *still* wanted to meet me.

What's wrong with men? Are they all gluttons for my punishment?

After we talked about the weekend, she told me to add him as a friend on Facebook, and *damn*, he is cute! He found my number on my Facebook page and even gave me the first call.

We've already spent nearly five hours on the phone getting

to know each other. He is fascinating, with all the ambition he has for his life and how great he is with people. He regrets not putting enough into his last relationship and he vows not to do that again. He's going for his CPA license, enjoying skiing and scuba diving, and reading educational books. He co-owns his own house in Minneapolis, and he's a great conversationalist. He invited me to go with him to church this coming Sunday and even to a wedding with him on September 27th.

Before accepting his wedding invitation, I decided that it would be a great idea just to *meet* first before committing to more plans. I looked forward to meeting him.

Finally, Andy drama. He came on Labor Day along with Diane and Shawn to move the rest of his things out of my garage, as I conveniently sat vacuuming out my car as they worked. His brother Devin had to bring over Andy's notarized divorce papers, which he forgot in Minneapolis (surprise…forgot the papers and *still* had his family helping him with everything. Some people never grow up.)

He was irate when I told him I gave away the wine cooler he didn't want. Seriously, man?! He even had the gall to ask when I'd be in Minneapolis next, if I could bring his mail to him the next time I came. I rarely go to Minneapolis, so he asked me why I was in town the last time I came. I intentionally kept the conversation vague and said, "A meeting."

He wondered aloud why I told him some things but I wouldn't tell him others. I said I kept him strictly on a need-to-know basis, letting him know only what I need to tell him about medical issues so he understands why I need my settlement. I tried to play up the sympathy card and told him that Medica wasn't cooperating (though it was true), and he actually apologized. I reminded him that I am a spitfire, that I get things done. It sickened me when he smiled at me and said, "Yeah, you do." I turned away. However, the drama continued when he was upset that I was keeping the DVD player—as we'd already agreed.

After Devin dropped off the divorce papers (and was nice to me as we briefly talked), they had everything packed and were ready to leave. Andy took me aside and asked if he could see me sometime. I stopped cold. The only response I could choke out of my repulsed mind was, "Why?"

He started to cry. I was agape with blind shock, but I asked if he needed to talk for a minute inside. Sniffling, he asked me for two minutes. We stepped no further into my house than the entryway when he proceeded to tell me that even if he legally didn't have to anymore, he wanted to take care of me.

When he asked me for one last hug, I brushed him off. I looked him straight in the eye and I firmly said, "I don't need you. I am strong and I already have a great support system. You have *no idea* what I've been through. You will miss out on everything, including a fantastic set of boobs."

Pause for reaction: yes, I actually *said* that to him. Hey, it was all true. He still told me that I could call him for anything, and I said I wouldn't. Part of me thought he said supportive crap like that just to tell his family and friends that he said it to me, but most of me thought he finally realized it was over and realized he missed me.

It felt great to close the door on him, hopefully, for good.

Of course, the next day he e-mailed me, looking to find the receiver instructions and a receiver-computer cord. What part of telling him to leave me alone didn't he understand?

I felt so happy again. Getting back to me had been an incredible journey thus far. I missed being happy just being me, not who I thought I was: a wife. Being alone for these weeks had been wonderful for me, even though it was hard to get through them. Thank God for giving me my life back. I'm a better person now, and I love it.

FROM CARINGBRIDGE.ORG, TUESDAY, SEPTEMBER 9, 2008 5:46 PM, CDT:

I have the most amazing sisters and mother. This past Saturday, I was upset that my family was getting together without inviting me; they thought it was the weekend I was staying in MG, but I wanted to go visit anyway. I was delightfully surprised and humbled to see what the real plans were: they were having a "beading" party in my honor, making BC Awareness bracelets for each of us! We all now have unique and beautiful bracelets for each of us, and we shared a great afternoon of spilling beads all over the kitchen floor, eating my sister Victoria's caramel apple pie, and taking pictures of all the fun. I have an incredible family, and I know how lucky I am.

After talking to my family this weekend, I've decided that I will roll the dice and take only a two-week leave instead of the three months. I know that keeping busy and working through treatment will be better for me, for my students, and for my colleagues. Besides, how many books can a person read before she loses her sanity? I look forward to maintaining normality as much as I can, and I'm already happier just from making the decision to stay here. My plastic surgeon's nurse is worried, but I'm not going to overdo it. I will take it day by day, and when I can finally return to work, I know that I'll handle it well. I have a mountain of people to help and support me; there isn't much that I cannot do!

The sun shines in on me through the windows of the media center, reminding me that the days are getting shorter. I look forward to enjoying the evening later with my college friend and roommate Jenni, as we take on the Chanhassen Dinner Theater. I made sure to dress up a little more today, just for the occasion!

FROM CARINGBRIDGE.ORG, THURSDAY, SEPTEMBER 11, 2008 9:59 AM, CDT:

D-Day! I'm soon heading in with Mom. I'm not nervous, more looking forward to getting the recovery ball rolling. While I'm out of Internet service, my sister Victoria agreed to keep some updates on here for me (thanks a million, Vic!) as to how I'm doing and visitors at the hospital.

The sea of pink yesterday at work, the wave of e-mails and text messages, and the hugs will be with me as I continue on today. Thank you so much to everyone for all that you do for me. Again, I am grateful for having such wonderful people in my life. Hugs to everyone!

THURSDAY, SEPTEMBER 11, 2008 5:05 PM, CDT:

I have only the briefest of brief updates: Gwen is out of surgery, which went well, is in recovery but not awake.

It was also relayed to me that she was in good spirits, which is inspiring and amazing.

More to follow as I get more information.

~Victoria

FRIDAY, SEPTEMBER 12, 2008 12:36 PM, CDT:

The updated information, as I've received it:

From Mom: All of the doctors are so nice, as are Tracy and Lindsey for keeping vigil with Mom at the hospital during surgery. The doctors were amazed at Gwen's poise, at her wonderful spirits. She (Gwen) got a little of "the riot act" for being too thin, but surgery went well and the port is also in for upcoming treatments.

From Gwen: Surgery went fast since she was through surgery and recovery by 6pm. She has two sets of drains coming out for drainage of unsightly stuff. Said tubes are making her look all frumpy and bulging. She is on a muscle relaxer, which is making her sleepy, as well as something to manage the pain (which she says isn't bad—the pain, that is). Today's assignment is walking around her ward (is that what it's called?) four times in what she refers to as "Mr. Burns' posture" (from the Simpsons, hunched over and very stiff). She said any movement at all hurts but also said she could go home today. Using her better judgment not to rush herself, she's staying until probably tomorrow.

From me: Thanks for all the prayers. It seems God is answering them. Any other prayers you care to send her way are always welcome!

~Victoria

FRIDAY, SEPTEMBER 12, 2008 2:48 PM, CDT:

I neglected to mention that Gwen's plastic surgeon said that her new breasts look fabulous already. :)

(I hope it's okay that I shared this. I have a feeling that Gwen might be too modest to do so herself. I guess we'll find out!)

~Victoria

SATURDAY, SEPTEMBER 13, 2008 7:06 AM, CDT:

I hope today is the worst Gwen feels during this whole ordeal. She, understandably, is in a good deal of pain and looks terrible. How it's possible that she's still in a good mood and is chipper I'm not sure. Our mom is now her nurse, helping her manage pain medicines and trying to make her comfortable. Not much else to add except that she looks the part of a patient: propped on pillows, eyes closed and cringing in pain, a side table with books and medicines, tubes, bandaging and those funny compression sock-things that prevent clotting (she says they're so annoying).

Hopefully, good news and improvements tomorrow...

MONDAY, SEPTEMBER 15, 2008 6:52 AM, CDT:

There is a chance that Gwen will get to post an update herself today, but for now I'll briefly share her news.

Unfortunately, yesterday wasn't better. She said "the pain is the same, it's just easier to handle."): She can eat, sleep and sit propped up. Talking seems to be a challenge. We are blessed to have Kathryn, a nursing student and PCA, to help with Gwen's care: she was able to help her shower on Sunday. The worst part of the pain seems to be from the drainage tubes (there are four). If these tubes are moved the wrong way, Gwen says she gets the dark tunnel feeling that accompanies nearly fainting.

~Victoria

MONDAY, SEPTEMBER 15, 2008 1:34 PM, CDT:

The freedom of Internet access! I scuffled over to Victoria's house to check e-mail, and I was shocked to see how many new visits my Caring Bridge site had. It feels so wonderful to know that the support continues to roll in, and I use that strength every morning. Vic tried to get me to post a picture of what a "patient" I look like, but I wasn't excited about sharing that. No need for everyone to see me without makeup, with my glasses on, hair in every direction, and dressed in ACE bandages, a sweatshirt, and pj pants. Yep, can't see why I wouldn't want to share that :)

Today is MUCH better than yesterday. Mom and I realized that we were scrimping on the pain medication, so we increased it this morning ever so slightly. I was almost giddy with the excitement of feeling relatively normal, being able to even reach up to put my hair in a ponytail. I'm already having a hard time focusing on recovering and not feeling bored, but I just need to keep grabbing Hatchet and reading a little more.

Hope you are all enjoying the fall weather as much as I am. It's fun to wrap up in a blanket and enjoy the breeze, just like high school football games.

SEPTEMBER 16, 2008

So many changes! I finally met Mark and we went on our first date on September 4 to Valleyfair and to church. Since then, we've been on the phone nonstop, seeing each other whenever we can, and I really like him. However, on our first date, he talked about his ex-girlfriend nonstop, leading me to end the night in tears. We talked through things, and it's been good. Before our first date, he sent me three books on alternative therapies to chemotherapy for cancer, and I've been trying to get to reading them ever since I received them. It's been tough thinking of a path other than chemo, but it does sound like a good alternative if it works.

My surgery went very well on the 11th. Lindsey and Tracy accompanied Mom and me to North Memorial for the bilateral mastectomy/immediate reconstruction at noon. I was in and out before I even knew it. Mom stayed with me for most of the night in my hospital room before she headed home to St. Cloud. *Any* pain I had was nothing in comparison to what I felt with the pneumothorax. I was on morphine just that first night, then moved to Percocet and a muscle relaxer the next morning. I happily greeted Julie, Julie, and Joanna from work. It felt good to hear that I didn't look like I'd just had surgery. Kath stopped by wearing her "I ❤ Gwen" t-shirt, and Rachel and Dan stopped by as well.

Mark also braved meeting my family Friday night and stayed there with me past midnight, walking my "laps" around the hallway as prescribed by the surgeon. I felt so embarrassed that he saw me as such a patient, but not once did he make me feel awkward. With the way he looked at me, I felt beautiful despite being on an IV, lack of shower for the day, and walking like Mr. Burns from *The Simpsons*. I was glad he came over for dinner the night before surgery and I could show him my non-patient side, that I was normally up for anything. Thinking about how he wanted a relationship that others would look at and be jealous, that he wanted a wonderful wife and kids, made me regain hope for my future.

Is he human? No one is this nice. Who still bakes homemade bread from scratch too?

FROM CARINGBRIDGE.ORG, WEDNESDAY, SEPTEMBER 17, 2008 1:20 PM, CDT:

A great big hug and thank you to all of my supporters! The prayers, positive thoughts, good karma, and extra brownie points have paid off in spades. I got a call yesterday from my surgeon, Dr. Carlson, and she was proud to tell me that I am now cancer-free! The third time was the charm. Great to hear, with all of the painful recovery I've been through; makes it worth every moment.

Mom and I are hoping that with the great news I can skip chemo (nothing wrong with hoping). I will hear from my oncologist tomorrow with the plans of upcoming treatments.

Dr. Harrington, my plastic surgeon, also said that I am recovering very well. She removed my first set of drains yesterday afternoon. In a week when I go back to see her again, though she isn't promising anything, I hope to get the second set removed and the ACE bandage around my chest removed as well. The bandage makes for labored breathing, and I'd love that freedom back. She said that since I'm doing so well, and if I'm not rushing myself, I can go back to work as soon as I'm ready. I'm planning on going back on Wednesday, the 24th, if the follow-up with her goes well. I'm not pushing myself harder than I can go, and I'm really enjoying the downtime, but getting back to "real life" as soon as I can will be so nice. Can't say that I'm not enjoying the sleeping later, leisurely reading, sipping fresh coffee with Mom, playing "trains" with my godson, and all the extra visits from family!

I'm also proudly to the recovery stage when I can get up with a dull, aching pain rather than a bone-crushing stabbing pain. I'm now a step down again with the Percocet, and I will start a simple acetaminophen tomorrow. I can wash my own hair (I felt like a little girl with my mom and sister Kathryn washing my hair!), strip my drains, sit/stand up without help, take slow walks, and for the most part dress myself. It sounds funny when I look at all of these things and remind myself that I still needed help with these things even yesterday. Every day gets so much better in so many ways.

My family is the greatest...again. Starting with Mom's pink ribbon shirt, all of my sisters have made "I ❤ Gwen" t-shirts and have sported all of them throughout the weekend. Even my brother-in-law Kurt had his "I ❤ Beer" shirt made in honor of me. I hope to get them all together this weekend and get a picture of all of them with me in my "I am loved" shirt.

Please enjoy the late summer days with me by going for a walk, ride a bike, or another fun activity. These, and the great people around me, make each day worthwhile!

FRIDAY, SEPTEMBER 19, 2008 8:15 PM, CDT:

I got another appointment rather than a definitive answer from my oncologist regarding my chemo. I'll be talking to her about my options on October 2. The fun of cancer treatments...all the waiting.

Good thing I'm keeping busy with spending quality time with my "peeps!"

WEDNESDAY, SEPTEMBER 24, 2008 10:51 AM, CDT:

Good news: I was allowed to get my teeth cleaned after getting clearance from my plastic surgeon to do so (the bacteria produced in a teeth cleaning can get directly into your blood stream, causing heart problems with patients that have had implant surgeries). Who knew that would ever be an issue? However, my gums are wonderfully better than they were in January. Flossing pays off, folks.

More good news: Dr. Carlson's appointment went well yesterday too. She reviewed my stellar pathology report results, concluding that I won't need to see her again until I need my port removed after chemo ends. She is very optimistic that I will have little to no reoccurrence of the invasive cells. Yea!

However, there is not-so-great news too. Doctors seem to know their stuff once in a while. I was advised by my plastic surgeon NOT to do anything for two weeks, no driving, reaching up to high shelves, vacuuming. Well, two out of three were enough to push my recovery back at least another week. (Vacuuming was the one that I wasn't in a rush to try again.) My drains aren't slowing with the amount that they produce. I am at about 65 cc's of liquid a day, and I need to be lower than 30 cc's for at least two consecutive days before I can get the drains removed and resume getting back to normal activities. I'm shooting to finally be done with the drains by this coming Tuesday, September 30th. I learned the hard way to just listen, and I'm focusing on being done by Tuesday.

More not-so-great news: Dr. Garino, my oncologist, finally gave me a little insight to what my upcoming treatment will include. I've been pushing to get some information before deciding how much time I'll really need off from work. She said that she is planning on chemo for me, and she'll discuss why she made that decision when I go in on October 2nd.

Therefore, I've been faced with another difficult decision. I need to take the original time off that was planned for me, staying away from crowds to prevent serious infections and keeping my blood counts up, as well as focusing on getting over treatments before forcing myself to go back to work. If I can get a definitive answer from the district office and the LTD contact as to whether I can be approved for LTD after the 90 days, I'll be out until December 15. Sure, I can plan all I want and make my own recovery schedule, but I've finally learned to just listen. My body is clearly asking for more time to get over all of this, and I need to pay attention to it and to my medical team.

Even with the mixed news, I am positive that things are going to work out for the best. I have so many reasons to be thankful for all that I have and the strength that I get from the amazing people in my life. Thank you again for continuing all the phone calls, cards, e-mails, and offers of food. With the weight and lifting restrictions, I can't cook, so it will come in handy!

FROM CARINGBRIDGE,
FRIDAY, SEPTEMBER 26, 2008 9:58 AM, CDT:

Day 15 post-surgery. My drains are slowing a little, but they still have a long way to go before I can get them out. Come on, Tuesday!! I dream of how great it will feel to get my "tentacles" out.

I shouldn't complain about having some time to enjoy myself and relax for the first time since I was fourteen, but darn it, I wish I could go to work! I miss being around all of the people, the students, the keeping busy, the enjoyment of my work. And my computer will shut down on me if I spend any more time on iTunes. I don't have a good personality for sitting around, especially when it's not my decision to do so. I cheated a little and made cookies for the folks at work, but I took it easy—no heavy lifting, I used my step ladder to reach the high cabinet shelves, and enjoyed a lot of the raw dough. Walnuts have omega-3s, so it was more of a health necessity!

I do enjoy my daily walks too, since it's the only exercise I'm allowed. Target, Wal-Mart, and Rainbow Foods are going to be sick of seeing me around, but they're so darn close to home. I love finding any excuse to walk somewhere, even to doctor/dentist appointments. The 3.6 miles to and from Tracy's house last night were great. Ahh, the freedom, the breeze in my hair, the open highw—well, sidewalk.

Thanks, Julie G for stopping over yesterday! She cheered me up with her infectious energy and brought me some food to last through the next week. I have some great people around.

SEPTEMBER 28, 2008

This past weekend, Mark brought me to his hometown for his friend's wedding. He rarely left my side all weekend, and I felt so adored and appreciated. His friends, our hosts, and everyone I met were very nice to me. I was even introduced as his girlfriend by our host's mother, and I didn't know how to respond to that. No, I'm not his gf, but I did feel like it. We spent hours on the phone, especially the week after surgery when I was at Mom and Dad's. He seemed to really listen to me and care about what I have to say. He told Tracy that he wanted to take the relationship slow, build the foundations of a relationship, and not to rush anything (especially the physical activity). Fine with me! I wasn't even planning on dating until mid-2009. For someone so close to perfect for me, and a man not scared off by my baggage in life, I'll happily make an exception to my no-dating rule.

FROM CARINGBRIDGE.ORG, MONDAY, SEPTEMBER 29, 2008 11:15 AM, CDT:

What a fun weekend! I went to Cook, MN for a wedding, and seeing all the fall colors turning in northern MN was such a gift. I haven't been able to go camping this year, and to be out with all the blazing colors on the trees, cool and fresh fall air, and dense blanket of stars at night, I no longer minded the missing tent.

I had a rough weekend with the drains, however. Even though I was able to hide them (and the port...yea!) under my dress and appear "normal" at the wedding, they weren't kind to me in the draining department. I was at 87 cc's on Saturday, but I dropped back down to 40 yesterday. Fingers crossed for today; if I can get them to 30, I am going to push to get them out tomorrow afternoon.

With the guidance of friends, I've been looking into alternative treatments. Since the cancer is gone, and I have some other small but important reasons not to go through chemo right now, I'm hoping to find a path that isn't as invasive or as hard on my body. So far, I've looked into the Gerson Institute in southern CA, which focuses on a complete overhaul of the diet and ways of preparing food. I'm not

*ruling out the western medicine, but if I can find a plan that would
be good if even just for now, I'm willing to look into it. I still have
my oncologist appointment this Thursday, where Dr. Garino will
explain why she believes chemo is still my next choice and what my
future treatment would look like.*

*Enjoy this beautiful fall day! How lucky we are that the sun is
shining and we can enjoy the weather for as long as it will hold out.
I have a bag of apples from this weekend that are calling me to make
Double Crumble Apple Dessert...*

WEDNESDAY, OCTOBER 1, 2008 6:31 PM, CDT:

Ah, the joy of drains! I was at 33 cc's yesterday, so I'm honestly
thinking that Friday is the big day now. Someday, "Tentacle"
and "Ganglion" (the names I gave my drains after my sister
Kathryn said I should name them) will be a distant memory.
Tomorrow is the big oncology day, so I'm looking forward to
the news...

WEDNESDAY, OCTOBER 1, 2008

More medical updates. Recovery from surgery was going
well. I got the first set of drains out after only five days, but
"Ganglion" and "Tentacle" are comfortably still nestled
underneath all my shirts. Well, comfortable for them, still
uncomfortable and painful for me. Yesterday I was finally down
to thirty-three cc's of fluid; if I can get down to thirty-ish today,
I can get my drains taken out! Freedom from the drains and
the ACE bandage around my chest was on the horizon. It was
amazing how three weeks with painful drains could make you

appreciate being able to move about freely, to cuddle with someone without worrying about pulling on a tube or resting on the tube-incision site, to be able to go shopping without desperately trying to hide the drainage system underneath your shirts.

It took me a little over a week to wean myself off the Percocet and muscle relaxers. Mom and I learned the hard way to go easy on myself by not cutting them out so quickly. Sunday after surgery was awful: so little movement, so much pain. Monday morning came with two Percocets and a giddy relaxation that normally only comes from a few glasses of wine. I could see how people easily become addicted. It was the drinking without the hangover.

I've been "drug-free" for two weeks now. I thought I'd be able to get back to work if I could just get off the meds. WRONG. I was still in way too much pain and draining so much that there was no way to meet my "deadline" of September 25 for returning to work. So decision-lacking Gwen went from taking a three-month leave to taking two weeks, then going back to taking three months off.

Good news on the leave front, however. With the ninety-day leave, I'll have to burn up all of my sick leave days. I can then apply for long-term disability leave. Granted that I am approved for LTD, since I am a member of the Sick Leave Bank at work, I can apply to the SLB to pay for the rest of my ninety days that my sick days don't cover. (Sick days = eleven days, SLB = forty-nine days of full salary). LTD will pay for the few days that I would be out on LTD; then I'll be back to work, all benefits and salary restored. The SLB will also cover fifteen more days of chemo visits if I still continue to burn my newly-accrued sick days when I return. Seriously hope that I'm done with chemo by then.

Mark continued to educate me on alternative therapies. He sent four books plus one DVD to my house about these alternatives. One book was on the Miracle Medical Supplement, a solution of chlorine dioxide. It's been used to cure malaria in Africa, but now it claims to be a cure for other diseases, including cancer. Still reading that book. Another alternative Mark has offered was to send me to the Gerson Institute in Mexico. It promotes an organic vegetarian diet consisting mainly of vegetable and fruit juices, not to mention foods prepared in glass pans and without microwaves. Max Gerson believed that the human body could cure itself if the toxins were removed and it got the vitamins and nutrients it needs.

It sounded like a fantastic alternative—better to feed my body vitamins rather than poison, right? Well, too bad. The two-week Gerson stay cost $11,000. I couldn't spend my money—*that* much—on the hopes that within two years it would "cure" me of cancer. My family all pushed for the chemo; Mark and Tracy wanted me to try the "detox" method. The way I saw it was that all of this was a crapshoot. There were no guarantees with either chemo or alternatives that the cancer wouldn't come back someday.

To me, either decision sucked.

Everyone tried to be helpful and supportive. I kept hearing

comments like, "Your hair will grow back!" "It will be over in a few months!" "You'll have perky boobs forever!" or "You can always adopt!" It seemed so easy for everyone to say such things; they will hopefully never have to make those decisions.

"Wow. Tough one. I don't know what I'd do."

Yeah, neither did I, and here the decision was, nagging me every day, whispering in my ear, controlling all of my thoughts. How would you feel, knowing that poison would be ripping through your veins? How would you feel being exhausted and nauseated for four months? How would you feel to have people staring at your port that awkwardly sticks out from the thin skin on your chest? How would you feel looking down at the long, diagonal scars that hold together what you have left from both of your breasts being taken away? How would you feel to be in constant awareness of the small cotton prostheses you've stuffed in your tank top and fearing that they'll stick out again or pop out in front of others? How would you feel knowing that the children you finally realized you desperately want someday may only be a blind hope or stab in the dark?

Please, I hoped that people might remember this when they talk to someone who faces all of these fears at once. It's impossible to imagine how that feels. I just prayed that people can offer support to the ones that painfully know how that feels.

The American Cancer Society has been wonderfully helpful as well. I had no idea how many services they offer, like getting people rides to chemo, free wigs to patients, connecting people to other survivors for support, not to mention the incredible source of so much cancer information. I was able to call them and get a $50 voucher for a wig, plus shipping costs. The wig I chose was so close to my real hair color, though very short. Now I had three wig options—the short blond one I just ordered; the short black one from Rachel; and the shoulder-length blonde one from the CRC. They were all fun and so much cuter than being bald. However, they got *so* warm and itchy. Scarves would be so much more comfortable on my sore scalp; they were just not as cute, and they really made me feel more like a cancer patient.

I also made another relationship revelation this week. My separation anxiety continued to work me over. Just like Ardith told me over a month ago, I needed to realize that those closest to me were *not* going to leave me (i.e., Mom). I was on constant high alert when it came to disagreements with Mark. If he seemed upset, whether he was or not, I'd pick it apart so much that I jumped to the decision to leave, that it was over between us, that he'd be done with me.

I was deliberately finding reasons for ending our relationship before I could get hurt or be left again. I'd walk away from an incredible person rather than see that not everyone is a coward like Andy. I couldn't imagine letting myself get so close to someone again and opening up my life and heart to love again, only to be left just when I needed someone. How could I begin to honestly trust someone if I couldn't be sure if he'd be there? Not even my husband would stay with me. Why would someone I'm dating?

To make the dating conversation even more interesting, Mark and I had a long talk that lasted two days. The evening started off well, after I made dinner and dessert for him and his roommates. He later made a joke about me stuffing my bra, which completely crushed me. He tried to apologize, but then things took a turn for the worst. When I packed up my things to go home, he got mad at me for wanting to leave.

I went home to try to figure out what was going on. He e-mailed the next day trying to figure out what I wanted. I wrote him a letter that night and read it to him over the phone, saying that I wanted to be happy, but I was afraid of again losing someone close to me. I felt vulnerable and exposed after revealing so many personal and secret feelings to someone else.

That's when it all hit the fan. He compared me to his ex, someone who was "near perfect, then God sent [him] someone on the opposite end of the spectrum." *W.O.W.* She hadn't been divorced, was still a virgin, and didn't have cancer, all of which he pointed out to me.

That hit me right in the gut, especially when there was nothing I could have done to prevent any of these things. How should I have felt about being compared to her perfection? He said that God had to teach him unconditional love and how he needed that before he met me. Great, now I felt like a test project of his, seeing if he could successfully "put up" with me and test the lesson he learned.

I remembered something that Mark said to me in his e-mail earlier that day: that he put his faith in God. I started to do the same. I had two choices—to be angry with Mark, or put my faith in someone else…God. I knew that through anything, He would be there for me. I put my faith in God and back in myself. I knew that I was a good person. I'd made good choices in my life. I'd surrounded myself with good people. I attended church and I prayed for peace and good things to come. I didn't take Mark's perfection comparison to heart, but I took my inner faith and clung to my inner strength. Peace came to me after that.

However, I was still at 38 cc's today…stuck with Tentacle and Ganglion for another week…

OCTOBER 2, 2008

Chemo D-Day. It killed me how the office told me to be at my appointment twenty minutes early, then Dr. Garino proceeded to make me wait for forty-three minutes for her to come into the exam room. I couldn't trust my oncologist to be on time; how could I trust her with my body and putting poison in it?

Straight off, I wanted her to explain *why* I needed chemo. In my case, she said, it was preventative. Cancer is one cell, which grows locally and spreads to the lymph nodes first and then invades blood vessels. She said that I had no high risk of recurrence, that I had an eighty-five percent chance of being cancer-free after the mastectomy. However, I still had a fifteen percent chance that the cancer cells bypassed the lymph nodes. Normally, people with less-than-a-one-centimeter-in-size tumor with no involved lymph nodes could bypass chemo. I, on the other hand, landed in the gray category since I had a grade-three (very aggressive), estrogen-receptor-weakly-positive, and her-2-neu positive cancer. Therefore, Garino still recommended chemo for me.

Chemo works best, she explained, on patients with a low tumor load (me).

She also removed Adriamycin from my treatment plan (Whew! Adriamycin is a vesicant—a drug that could eat away at my veins and internal organs if it would escape from my vein during treatment, and it could have also caused leukemia later on in my life). My new plan focused on TCH—Taxotere, Carboplatin, and Herceptin—every three weeks for six treatments. Herceptin would also be administered weekly for a total of fifty-two weekly treatments. With this TCH plan, there would be energy/hair loss and lower blood counts. The Herceptin would be huge in helping my chemo plan since I was her-2-neu positive. The final part of the treatment plan involved being on a hormone suppressant for five years— Tamoxifen. My chemo would also stop my periods for the year that I was in treatment; if it didn't, I'd need shots to stop menstruation. My period should come back within two or three months of the Herceptin ending. Ninety-five to ninety-eight percent of women resumed their periods within a few months.

My favorite part of this plan was that this course would bring my rate of recurrence from fifteen percent down to five percent. I liked those odds!

Plan B: if I didn't want to do the chemo, I could do an aggressive hormone therapy. To block my periods and put me into temporary menopause, I would get shots of Zoladex for two years. This would also protect my ovaries and long-term fertility, but it would also affect my bone density. I would still get the Tamoxifen for five years, and this would not block my periods.

This plan would bring my rate of recurrence from fifteen percent down to ten percent. Still not bad odds, but not as good as those associated with the chemo.

What finally freaked me out about all the treatment plans was my mortality rate if my kind of cancer returned—on average, I would have two years to live. Damn. This was the first time in two months that anyone mentioned the possibility of death from this.

I was scared into action. I wanted a second opinion, a third, to try any alternatives, to harvest my eggs, to pray for the eighty-five percent chance of being cancer-free, to scream, to pray for help. How scary to all of a sudden see how quickly your life can end before your eyes, especially when you haven't had enough time to truly live it. What did I have to look forward to if I had so little time left?

Later that day, I tried to tell Mark about my options. I had no reservations about telling my family and friends; I knew they'd support my decision, no matter what. I tried to go over my notes and explain to him what it all meant. What I really got from telling him was something I really didn't expect. I expected from him opposition, anger, frustration, annoyance. What I got was frustration and annoyance *with myself.*

He asked me great clarification questions, for which I had no answers. I had no idea how to explain what her-2-neu was or what estrogen receptors were. What I got from telling him was a call to action, to get the answers I knew I needed to answer before starting chemo.

I didn't sleep at all that night, with all I had on my mind.

FRIDAY, OCTOBER 3, 2008

I went right to work that morning on the computer, researching all of the unknowns I had from the night before. I started on estrogen receptors and her-2-neu then moved on to my drug cocktail info—what they were meant to do and their side effects.

1. What is her-2-neu? (For more information, use Herceptin.com)

HER2-positive breast cancer is a breast cancer that tests positive for a protein called human epidermal growth factor receptor-2 (HER2), which promotes the growth of cancer cells. In about one of every three breast cancers, the cancer cells make an excess of HER2 due to a gene mutation. This gene mutation can occur in many types of cancer—not only breast cancer.

HER2-positive breast cancers tend to be more aggressive than other types of breast cancer. They're also less responsive to hormone treatment. However, new treatments that specifically target HER2 are proving to be very effective: Trastuzumab (Herceptin). Herceptin, which specifically targets HER2, kills these cancer cells and decreases the risk of recurrence.

2. What is the significance of estrogen receptors?

From BreastCancer.Org: Your doctor will order a hormone receptors assay, a test to see if the cancer is sensitive to estrogen and progesterone. If a tumor is estrogen-receptor positive (ER-positive), it is more likely to grow in a high-estrogen environment. ER-negative tumors are usually not affected by the levels of estrogen and progesterone in your body. This is one time when hearing the word "positive" may really mean something good (so often, a "positive" test result really means that something not so good was found). ER-positive cancers are more likely to respond to anti-estrogen therapies. If you have an ER-positive cancer, you may respond well to Tamoxifen, a drug that works by blocking the estrogen receptors on the breast tissue cells and slowing their estrogen-fuelled growth. A study suggests that Herceptin may be beneficial regardless of your ER/PR status.

3. *(Side note: For more drug information on Taxotere, go to taxotere.com. On Carboplatin, AmericanCancerSociety.org. For Herceptin, use the site Herceptin.com. They are fabulous!)*

Finally, I felt comfortable with all the mess I had made with the decision to start chemo. Kath and Rach came at 10:00 to accompany me to Dr. Harrington's to hopefully get the drains removed. Well, technically I'd fudged on their true fluid output for the last few days, but I was so close (and so tired of them!) So I convinced Kim the nurse to talk to Dr. Harrington about it. (Kim had said my "magical output" number for two days was 25 cc's, not the 30 I was originally told.) Finally, Kim came back with the great news. I would be freeing myself of Ganglion and Tentacle. I would still have to take it easy for one more week, no heavy activity, and continue to wear the ACE bandage. If I did, in a week I could start getting the tissue expanders pumped full of saline.

Kath held my hand during the removal; it was so comforting

and comfortable to have her right there. I took a deep breath in, then exhaled deeply and felt the snake-like tubes being pulled from my chest. Happily, the extraction didn't hurt at all, just odd to feel the plastic running so far within my body.

After I got redressed, I couldn't help but admire my "new" flat stomach for the rest of the day, both in mirrors and running my hands over my abs. However, it did make me conscious of how my waistline had expanded in four weeks. I couldn't help wanting to jump right back into working out again. I'd now put on ten pounds since surgery. Normally, I'd freak out about it, but I was oddly proud to be back to 115. I'd been on a fun diet—eating anything and everything in sight, no longer worrying about the fat or calorie content. All three of us celebrated the weight gain and drain removal with snacks, candy, and a good female-friendly movie of *Made of Honor*, a movie that normally, with their husbands, they'd have to skip.

OCTOBER 5, 2008

I was so eager to attend church with Tracy at the Open Door this morning. She picked me up and we headed straight for the donut area. I started to free my stresses with singing of praise and worship when a stabbing pain in my heart sidelined me. Honestly, it felt as if someone was putting a knife in my heart. Instantly freaking out ensued. Did I remove my drains too soon? Was I doing too much? Was this the heart trouble Rachel warned me about? Was this just drain-removal pain?

It was such an intense pain that I just sat there for the rest of the service, on the edge of my seat. Even walking out of the church afterwards was uncomfortable. The second I got home, I just reclined on the couch. I was so glad that I had my roommate Jared there, just in case I needed to go to the emergency room.

I felt good enough later on to carve some pumpkins with Tracy and Lindsey before heading to church (yes, again) with Mark in the evening. On the way there, Alison called to find out what was going on with my chemo plans. I was very hesitant to talk about it in front of Mark, since he'd been so against it in the first place, so I told her to talk to Mom, Kath, or Rachel. He knew something was up, so I was forced to tell him that I started chemo on Tuesday. He was very upset, even saying he'd thought I was smart and would want all the information on alternatives before I made a decision *(ouch)*. He said that he'd also bet that I hadn't made one phone call to any of the people he'd given me names for about the Gerson Institute. *(Double ouch)*.

As one might expect, our time at church was very quiet. So I again did what Mark had already told me to do—put my faith somewhere else. I prayed to God that He would help me be strong in my decision making, that I knew everything would be okay when He was with me.

I wrote out that prayer and placed it in my car, to remind myself of my desire for strength and who I needed to ask for it. (Note: even today, I still have that note in my car.)

On the way back to my house, Mark finally spoke to me again. I reminded him that I needed only two things: support and respect for my decisions. I couldn't be around him if he couldn't give that.

He did get me to call one of the Gerson references, though. (So much for support, eh?) The woman, Paula from California, said she'd been a vegetarian since she was eighteen, meditated since she was twenty, but was still diagnosed with breast cancer in her mid-forties. Since she'd never considered chemo as an option, she fell in love with the Gerson plan, as labor-intensive as it was. I still wasn't convinced, especially with her "seventy percent cure rate" statistic. Heck, even chemo was ninety-five percent!

I was now set on chemo more than ever. Even Mark seemed more supportive of the chemo plan, but I considered this whole discussion as a "probation" of sorts. Did he really have what it took to stick with me through anything? Only time would tell.

FROM CARINGBRIDGE.ORG, MONDAY, OCTOBER 6, 2008 9:42 AM, CDT:

Day 25 with the drains...no wait! I'm still drain-free! I love enjoying the freedom of not having my little pals following me around everywhere. It does remind me that I need to keep working on the abs now. I'm taking it easy, though. Dr. Harrington plans to start filling up the skin stretchers on Friday. I'm looking forward to getting that process started. The sooner I can start, the sooner I can be done!

Getting an oncology appointment is usually torturous, but not when it comes to getting your chemo started. I called on Friday after I got the clearance from Dr. Harrington, and Dr. Garino got me in for this Tuesday at 9:00 A.M. Her nurse told me to bring a book because my chemo would take all day. I'm not scared but more interested to see how the process works. I'm bringing a camera to document the process, and I'm hoping to also get a video in there to see how it works. I'm starting on a steroid today to prevent the nausea that will come from the drugs tomorrow, and I'll take them three times tomorrow and Wednesday as well.

The Cancer Resource Center at Mercy well prepped me to deal with the possible side effects, so I know that if I have any of them I need to contact the on-call oncologist immediately. The only one that really bothers me is the higher temp one; if my temp is over 100 degrees, it becomes a medical emergency that warrants a five-day hospital stay to bring my blood counts back up. It's more important now than ever that I safeguard myself from infection and germs, because I'll be darned if I'm going back to the hospital for anything other than visiting a newborn.

I'm not scared about starting it, but I'm hopeful and praying for a safe treatment. I have so many helpful people around me that it's been wonderful for my optimism. Thanks to Julie S. for bringing over Sophia and to Michelle for bringing over Chinese food and Penelope on Friday. Thanks to Kathryn and Rachel for hanging with me through the appointment on Friday and for sharing in quesadillas and spinach dip. Thanks to Tracy and Lindsey too for carving some amazing pumpkins with me yesterday. I have an incredible tribute to Twilight on my deck now. Support from family and friends means everything to me.

Part Four
LET THE CHEMO BEGIN

OCTOBER 7, 2008

Chemo Day 1. Mom came to my house at 7:30 in the morning to drive me to Mercy. She'd read in *Reader's Digest* about a Swedish study that ice packs on your head during the chemo infusions would help to retain your hair, so she came armed with two large ice packs. What a sweetheart. That woman really loves me.

We started the whole process with consent forms and getting information on a clinical trial I'd agreed to participate in— Coenzyme-Q-10 ("Co-Q-10"), an enzyme being studied to find its effects on energy levels in breast cancer patients on chemo. Rach said it should be harmless enough, since Co-Q-10 is produced normally in your body and is also sold over-the-counter. In this trial, I will be taking either a Co-Q-10/vitamin B supplement or a placebo/ vitamin B supplement three times a day for twenty-eight weeks. Sheesh, *more* pills? I was already taking ten milligrams of dexamethasone, an anti-nausea steroid, three times a day the day before/of/after chemo.

The dexamethasone burned like the malaria pills I'd taken in Costa Rica, like a lit cigarette has been dropped in my stomach. Oh, the pain and the burning in my stomach. Amy, the RN coordinating the clinical trial, said I'd receive the pills free of charge in a few days and to start taking them as soon as I received them. Now, off to chemo…

Cynda, my chemo nurse, started at 9:00 A.M. drawing five vials of blood through my port. One vial was for the clinical trial, one was to check my blood counts, one was a pregnancy test (yeah, no worries there, though), two more for unknown reasons. I was so nervous to use my port for the first time. It turned out to be really no big deal. It popped in there easily, stayed put with tape, and did its little job well. I didn't have any more vesicant worries, since that was part of the port's job—to prevent tissue-eating. After the blood draws, she flushed my port with saline to clean out the tubes.

At 9:18, my blood counts came back all good. Although "normal" for white blood cells is four to ten, I was at sixteen. Another *hmm*. Was that bad?

At 9:28, I was given decadron aloxy for the nausea to come later on and Benadryl for allergic reactions I might have. Both of these were given via IV as well. These took half an hour to infuse (drip through the IV and make their way through my veins). A machine actually monitored and pumped in everything, not a person, as I'd thought. I suppose it *was* much smarter to leave a machine and port to do all the work rather than to suffer the possibility of human error. [Side note here: one wonderful part of all the screenings/surgeries/hospital visits/chemo treatments was the hot blankets you cover yourself with during everything. It's so cuddly and warm, making all the hell you're going through almost something to look forward to. I needed a blanket warmer at home.]

At 9:55, Taxotere started infusing. Unlike what my pal Laure and I feared (thus, me listening to the *Scooby Doo* theme song on my iPod) the actual drug wasn't a bubbling green ooze. It was clear, mixed into a 250 cc bag of saline. The Taxotere took one hour to infuse, and during the whole time, I never felt anything. No skin bubbling off, no violent bleeding from all orifices, not even vomiting or nausea. Whew.

Beginning at 10:55, Carboplatin infused for half an hour. Sadly, another clear liquid and nothing fun to watch.

At 11:37, Herceptin. The last clear liquid infused for an hour and a half.

When I finished, Garino's nurse Gail ordered my Neulasta shot from Walgreens Specialty Pharmacy. She told me that with Medica, WSP had been delaying the shipments to beyond the required twenty-four to forty-eight hour window needed to inject the medicine. I prayed that I could get it before the forty-eight hours were up, but with my white counts so high right now, I figured I might have a small window of opportunity to work with.

These specialty shots also cost $5000 each through WSP and would cost $10,000 in a hospital.

For the love of Mike! Please come through for me, Medica!

While we were on the way home, the fatigue officially set in. When Mom and I got back to my place, all I could do was lie down. My entire body felt heavy, as if I'd been hit by a truck or was carrying an additional 200 pounds. Mom just sat with me, rubbing my knee, comforting me. Seriously though, if *this* was all chemo was, I could handle it!

I reclined on the couch for a few hours before feeling up to moving again.

To try to make it up to Mark for the "evil chemo" I had taken against his will, I went to his house later that night to make him dinner. Maybe that would help him ease up on me...?

FROM CARINGBRIDGE.ORG, WEDNESDAY, OCTOBER 8, 2008 11:07 AM, CDT:

The Day After Chemo 1. Not a bad morning! I feel fine, still tired, but that is the only side effect I'm feeling so far. I think the steroids, even when taken with food, are making my stomach burn, but I'm not nauseated—a good trade. It's still surreal to think that yesterday I was getting injected with all kinds of toxic liquids and that today I am resting up at home.

I'm getting the Neulasta shots (three of them) delivered tomorrow so I can keep up the blood counts. Good to hear that things are moving right along so far. Patience is indeed a virtue when it comes to cancer and its treatment.

OCTOBER 8, 2008

Walgreens Specialty Pharmacy finally set up a delivery of the Neulasta for me for tomorrow. My co-pay was $50, a far cry from the $5000, but still a lot of money for me. Thank goodness medical expenses are tax-deductible.

Later on, I still felt fine. It was hard to believe how easy chemo seemed. However, around evening-time, it started to come down on me. What I thought was heartburn turned into a stabbing and burning that kept me awake all day long and throughout the night. I felt like I had diarrhea, but I didn't, just gas and painful bowel movements. (WOW! Are side effects oh so fun, or what?) My scalp started to hurt when washing my hair or brushing it, but I was retaining it all. Whew, no hair loss. My tongue felt "furry," like it was constantly burned or coated in plaque. My skin hurt. My pinkie and pointer fingers felt numb and tingly, but not all the time. *That* scared me the most…that this numbness might lead to peripheral neuropathy. Good grief, what's next?

FROM CARINGBRIDGE.ORG, THURSDAY, OCTOBER 9, 2008 3:48 PM, CDT:

Okay, so chemo does take a little while to settle in. I still can't complain about my symptoms, as they have been easy enough to deal with, but I can sure feel them now. The stomach burning continues even without the steroids, but my great friend Heather (who has also gone through chemo recently) told me to get some Prilosec to prevent that. Last night and this morning, I felt I was getting a fever, but the thermometer showed only 97 degrees. I also had a hard time eating last night and at lunch today, with a little nausea. Still, even with all of this, I am just taking it easy and it isn't as bad as I'd feared. It's just a lot to take in at once. I keep reminding myself, it could be worse! Keeping a stiff upper lip helps through the rough moments.

The Neulasta came early this morning, and my friend Angie gave me the shot in the tricep before we headed out for pedicures and lunch. The shot was a little painful, but it was quick, and now I don't need one for another three weeks. My toes are ready for spring weather, so I'll need to show off the flip flops for a few more weeks.

OCTOBER 9, 2008

My friend Angie came over to meet me for lunch and pedicures, and I greeted her with a *Hey, want to give me a shot in the arm?* Now there was a way to get someone's attention. Or even to make them never want to visit you again. Not a bad job, she did; no pain from that one. I was grateful that I didn't have to figure that one out on my own or make yet another trip to the cancer center. Our lunch and pedis were fabulous, but the grease from lunch made me nauseated. Not only was I struggling to find something on the menu that sounded appealing, I made myself sick with the one choice I made. I guessed I needed to avoid Applebee's for a while.

Still more side effects today too. I made a marinated salmon fillet for dinner, and its spices tore my stomach apart. In pain, I put my head in Mark's lap for an hour. I hadn't felt this special or beautiful from a relationship in so long. He made me feel blissful, so incredibly happy and loved. Even when he was busy at work or studying, he never forgot about me sitting there. I was showered with attention, kisses, hugs, backside pats, smiles, laughter, kisses on the forehead, notes left for me everywhere, and e-mails throughout the day. He was truly good for me. I loved when I would catch him just looking at me and when I asked him what's up, he would smile and say, "I hope you know how beautiful you are." This one seemed like a keeper.

OCTOBER 10, 2008

I didn't know what was wrong with me today. I was in an awful mood, just wanting to sleep all day. I purposely slept through my volunteering meeting at the library at 10:00 A.M., just because I refused to get up. I gave in to the fatigue, thinking we're all allowed these days once in a while. Finally, the thought of getting my skin stretchers filled today perked me up enough to get cute and head to Dr. Harrington's.

Her nurse Kim filled me with 60 ccs on each side. It was such an interesting experience. First, Kim used a magnet to find the valve on the stretcher implant. Then she filled the stretcher with a needle and syringe. I couldn't even feel the needle since my chest was so numb.

Being able to see the beginning of new breasts was a wonderful treat for me. No longer was I completely flat-chested; I even had the beginnings of cleavage! Who hoo! I couldn't help but stare in the mirror afterwards. Finally, it was happening: the beginning of feeling "normal" again.

OCTOBER 11, 2008

Still nauseated, but becoming easier to deal with. I enjoyed a day at an orchard with Rachel and Dan, sitting on the hill in the fall sunshine, soaking up the warmth of normalcy, away from the oncology of my real life. The fresh apples were one of the rare things that didn't make me nauseated. Oh, the joys of chemotherapy.

OCTOBER 12, 2008

I brought the one and only Anjou pear to a Vikings tailgating event. People kept looking at me funny as I carried it around, but after my scrambled eggs that morning, my stomach felt so awful that I didn't give a crap if people stared at my fresh produce. I did get a lot of good stares too; I was gratified to feel attractive.

Church that night was wonderful too. There's nothing like the feeling that comes from being so uplifted in church. How was it that *now* I could feel God's presence in my life, but for seventeen years I couldn't? Was I just ready for it now? In any case, it felt wonderful to be rejuvenated and ready for the week.

I was getting a little nervous about how much time I spent with Mark. I loved his company, but our time together felt so domestic already, as if we were a married couple that lived together (just out of overnight bags). I would stay home, cook and clean, and kiss him goodbye in the morning when he went to work. It was nice, but I was not ready to be "married" again. I was not even ready for girlfriend status. (Heck, I was not even ready to be felt up!)

The daily routine was what I was used to, and he treated me better than I was used to, but then conversations like the one tonight would come up.

We had a long talk about the causes of cancer. He expressed his opinion that he doesn't think God would cause it intentionally, but He did it so I'd learn something from it and grow to be a better person.

It was hard for me to accept that I may have done things to

cause it myself, lifestyle-wise. But I hadn't always lived the healthiest of lifestyles, so it was quite possible. All the drinking in college up until last year, smoking, unhealthy eating, little water consumption, little sleep, little exercise, and a negative attitude about life. Yep, hard pill to swallow, but darn possible.

I was proud of myself for making better choices now. It was great for my recovery and for preventing cancer in the future. Knowing I was on the right health path now made it easier to block out Mark's effort to tell me I caused this cancer on my own.

Another discussion topic we had concerned all the books and movies he gave me to read and watch. I felt that he was trying to change who I am, and it was making me feel imperfect. I finally told him that I felt he was searching for someone not so like me (imperfect in many ways). He became pretty upset and told me I was already darn near perfect. *(Darn near* perfect? Ouch.)

I liked who I was right then! If he did too, I believed, he would ease up on the books and making me read them constantly.

However, I had been reading one of them, *The Purpose Driven Life.* The book was actually helping me find out what my reason for being was. I came to believe that my purpose (through God's presence in my life) was to help others. I reviewed the facts of my present life: I teach. I am there for my family. I am a good friend. There are many ways that I help others already.

How good it felt to know I have a purpose in life! Now I realized what it was. Knowing and understanding my purpose would motivate me to do more with my life and daily activities, rather than just sit around accomplishing nothing.

OCTOBER 13, 2008

I continued on my quest to help others today by making dessert for Tracy and Jason and making Mark dinner again. I was also hard at work concocting a birthday present for Julie at work. Funny how I could spend a whole day just cooking and baking.

OCTOBER 14, 2008

Chemo #2 of Herceptin today. Not all bad this time. It was reassuring because I had an idea of what to expect. However, my side effects changed again today. Now, I developed a measles-esque rash all over my face and chin. It looked awful to me, so I overkilled with the application of the foundation and cover-up. It didn't itch or break into a pus-filled peak like acne. My chemo nurse Cynda said the steroids I took last week could have caused the break-out. It all seemed to get worse after the Herceptin today, so maybe that was the culprit?

Another fun new side effect: my nose hurt. It felt as if someone punched me in the nose; it was that tender and sore. (It also became difficult to kiss now, having to avoid getting my nose in on the action.) Along with the sore nose came a horrible nosebleed. It started this morning before chemo. It took about five tissues and half an hour of pinching my nose to make it stop. I'd never had so much blood pouring out of my nose. I didn't think it would ever stop. I was beyond relieved when it finally did cease flowing, fearing that I'd have to go to the hospital for a transfusion.

Side effect #3: I believe my menopause has started. Rather than freeze at night as I was used to, I sweated all night long and preferred to sleep atop the covers. I'd also been avoiding being close to Mark, as he seemed like a portable heater and increased my discomfort. My face constantly felt feverish too, yet I never had an elevated temp.

Side effect #4: the "furry" feeling in my mouth persisted, and I finally detected the metallic taste they'd warned me about. Thank goodness I haven't lost my sense of taste, though.

Blood counts today: WBC: 32.14 (normal is 4.3 to 10.8), RBC: 3.85 (normal is 4.2 to 5.4), hemoglobin: 11.7 (normal is 12.0 to 16.0), platelets 153 (normal is 150 to 400). At least the Neulasta worked! However, yikes, 32.14? Now bring on the protein to increase the others.

In my boredom at chemo, I took a handwriting analysis test in a magazine. I learned that my super-connected cursive means I hold on tight emotionally, and intellectually I'm logical but inflexible. My straight slant that leans to the right says my gut reaction is well-balanced; it's suppressed, but I cry easily. The tiny letters of *o, a,* and *m* indicate that my ego is focused and less social. Feeling the "Braille-like" impressions I leave on the back of the page is heavy pressure—I'm asserting myself in the world. The smaller-than-an-*m*-space between words says that I keep my distance with social boundaries. The tops of my connected-but-mostly-closed *o's* and *a's* is how much I reveal—I'm balanced, sharing just enough information. My signature being stylish and similar to my normal handwriting means, "What you see is what you get."

I thought that all of these taken together produced an accurate description of me.

Gail said to try Benadryl (25 mg) for the rash. Hoped that would help. I also found out from Cynda that my Herceptin level was only 5 mL mixed into a bag of 250 mL of saline. SO reassuring to know that not *all* of the IV bag was drugs!

OCTOBER 15, 2008

No new symptoms, thank goodness. I still had: an achy scalp, a sore nose, the rash on my face, and the metallic taste in my mouth. No news was now the best news.

My godson Alec (Petey) and I hung out all day. What a treat he was! That smile was infectious. He wanted to put on my makeup for me. He did well with the powder and eye shadow, not so well with the lipstick and mascara. I loved the pictures I took of his work.

I called Kathryn last night to ask if I could relax at her house the next day rather than at home, and she happily agreed. She knew as much as I did that staying at Mom and Dad's could be taxing on the psyche. My true motive, however, was different, but she had no idea what I was up to. Mom confided in me that Kath had been stressed out lately with work, school, and being a wife and mother. I knew that I wanted to help her out somehow. Mom and I snuck over to her house after she'd gone to work, Mom collecting the laundry while I stayed behind to clean the house. It took a good two hours to finish, but when I left and listened to Christian music on the radio on the way home, I felt uplifted and happy, knowing I had made a difference.

Kath came over to Mom and Dad's later on that night and thanked me, saying it was better than winning the lottery. Then she burst into tears. I knew that feeling all too well: feeling so helpless with everything you have going on that it's burying you deep into depression, like no light is visible at the end. I just hugged her, also knowing how a simple hand of help and support could make the light shine so brightly around you. I hadn't felt so good about myself in such a long time. Simple things—like laundry and cleaning—could make such a lasting impact.

Heading over to Mark's that night, I drove into Nosebleed City in the middle of I-494 and Highway 62. I bled down the front of my shirts and jeans, completely soaking the four napkins I could scrounge up in the car before getting to his house. I felt like a horror movie victim when he answered the door, seeing me covered in blood and clutching a handful of blood-soaked napkins. I soaked a few tissues when I got into the bathroom, and then the blood clot came out of my right nostril, the size of an oblong quarter. I iced my nose with a bag of frozen pineapple and held the bridge of my nose for over an hour, when the bleeding finally stopped.

Yuck! And wow, that was fun.

Just to make my nosebleed evening even better, I got an e-mail from Andy too. Paragraph one told me that house arrest for his DUI would be for the month of December, and how he hoped it wouldn't interfere with our divorce proceedings. (Why would it? We will be officially divorced any day now…?) Paragraph two asked if I'd received a refund from the Ireland trip yet (a big fat *nope*). Paragraph three related how he always thought of me, how I do well in "adverse situations," and that he'd make time for me if I needed him.

Adverse situations? How coldly-worded of a compliment. Vic said it best—complete with emoticon—when she said about him making time for me ("Not in December, obviously." :D)

The whole e-mail just felt like one big excuse to ask where his money was. It felt good to respond devoid of emotion, saying merely that his house arrest shouldn't affect anything with us, and I'd seen no refund yet. Again, I refused to be *his* crying shoulder through anything.

I could not be the bigger person and just support him, not then or ever. Where the heck was he when I needed someone? Starts with a "w-" and ends in "-ork." Fortunately, I recognized that the end was close at hand, although no divorce papers were waiting for me at home today.

I slept (well, sat awake for hours) sitting almost completely upright and as far away from steaming-hot Mark as I could get in his bed, fearing I'd start bleeding again. Nope, and whew.

FROM CARINGBRIDGE.ORG, THURSDAY, OCTOBER 16, 2008 10:00 PM, CDT:

What a joy to visit school again! Before chemo on Tuesday afternoon, I went into Northdale Middle School armed with an apple crisp. It felt so good to get the hugs and smiles from so many coworkers. My students were flabbergasted to see me: "Are you our teacher again? Can we have a party today? I thought you were sick! Why do you still have your hair?" It felt good to be missed. It made me even more ready to come back when I can. I just loved walking through the busy hallways during passing time. It's amazing how much I missed that.

The Herceptin-only chemo treatment wasn't so bad on Tuesday. It only took an hour, not even enough time to get a day done in my journal. I eagerly took off to go back to Mom and Dad's that night. The only side effect that is bugging me now (now that I'd learned that the burning stomach was caused by me not taking the Co-Q-10 with food as directed) is daily nosebleeds. It's an outpour of blood, usually taking many tissues being soaked to stop it. Yesterday, I was on Highway 62 going 60 mph when it started out of the blue; tough to drive and not bleed on myself in the meantime! Figured I had a good reason if I got pulled over, which made the drive that much more exhilarating.

I got a blood test to see how I was doing before chemo on Tuesday, and my red/hemoglobin/platelet counts were just barely in the low end of normal range, which was still good enough for receiving treatment. The Neulasta did its job—and then some—in keeping up my white blood cell count. Again, normal for an adult is 4000-10,000 cells. Mine was over 32,000 this time, double what it was last week.

Next up: Plastic surgeon tomorrow, heart scan on Monday, and chemo (Herceptin #3) on Tuesday...

OCTOBER 16, 2008

I went to Buffalo Wild Wings for dinner with Tracy, Jason, and Carrie. After eating way too many wings (and the former bulimic in me kicking in), I ended up vomiting in the bathroom, fearing I'd get fatter if I kept eating that way. Sure enough, nosebleed #3. Sadly, this one was self-inflicted.

I was a little upset with Mark for making other plans for the evening, even after I'd invited him to come and meet my friends and me for dinner BEFORE he'd made other plans. Then I had to come quickly to my senses—we weren't even officially dating, so why should I care? I should have been excited for all the friend-time I had!

Still, it bugged me that he'd blown me off, so I tried calling him again when I got home. No answer. No response for another hour and a half, after I'd gone to bed.

I sat in bed freezing that night, but woke up drenched in sweat hours later. Darn heated mattress pad did a good job!

FROM CARINGBRIDGE.ORG,
FRIDAY, OCTOBER 17, 2008 3:59 PM, CDT:

Another fun and successful trip to the plastic surgeon! They said I am doing very well, that my skin is fantastic for this sort of thing (Why, thank you!) They also asked me to be a model for the Breast Cancer Conference's fashion show next October 3. They said they want a greater number of younger women to model, to show people that BC does affect many younger women too, and they thought of me and my "cute little body." How fun to be able to add modeling to my resume! Kidding. I was very flattered that they asked.

Mom convinced me to call Gail at Dr. Garino's office to tell them about my nosebleeds and measles-esque-looking allergic reaction. They snuck me in to see the nurse practitioner this afternoon. The allergic reaction was to the Herceptin, so I was put on meds for that. If it didn't get better, they might need to adjust the timing of the Herceptin treatments, making them farther apart. Not good news for me as I'd like to get them done ASAP. I was willing to go daily if they'd let me. The nosebleeds, it turned out, were caused by bleeding ulcers (oh, I know...yikes and yuck!) trailing all along the top of my inner nose. The chemo caused the nose lining to shed, and this was the result. Now on meds for that too. Blood counts were still all good.

Bring on Dave and Buster's tonight and church rummage sales tomorrow. I will enjoy the weekend and all the time with my fun-lovin' sisters and friends.

OCTOBER 17, 2008

Thirty exhilarating minutes of Tae Bo in the morning. What a relief to get back into exercise, but no relief in the burpees—too much pressure on the pecs.

The "girls" continued to look great to me, especially considering they were now bigger than what I'd lost in the mastectomy (100 cc's on the left breast, 130 cc's on the right.) I was proud to put on my first bra (sans underwire, of course) since September 10. I didn't even need the teddy-bear-stuffing bra stuffers anymore! My bra and I looked fabulous alone. No more worries if/when the stuffers shift or move. Kim told me that they'd aim for late December for my implants; they like to wait for at least four months of pectoral stretching after the mastectomy for the real implants.

In that case, I'd have to extend my leave for a week or two. Since I had no sick days to use when I come back, I would need to stay out on leave until all major surgeries were completed. Darn…a few more days off sounded like torture!

All the pleasure was worth all the pain. It sure was, especially with the implants.

Side-effect check: sore nose, face rash, sore scalp, but no more tingly fingers. No worries about those now until I started dropping things, if that comes back. Another fun side effect kicked in today as I sat killing time at Rosedale Mall; perfume now kills my nose. I was enjoying my Caribou coffee when the perfume wafted on by, stinging my nose with severe pain. Note to self: avoid indoor malls for a while. The nosebleeds scared Mom enough to make me call Garino's nurse, Gail. So much for lunch with Julie and Jenni from union work; now I'd be at the doctor—again—this afternoon.

Nurse practitioner appointment with Carmen went great. Carmen said my nose sure looked painful (reassuring that I hadn't made it up in my head). It was funny how no one even bothered to look inside my nose when I'd told the nurses that my nose hurt at chemo on Thursday. Carmen also said that my allergies were probably hurting me more now since my body's energies were being used to fight the chemo, thus adding the pressure to my nose and sinuses.

Also got some good news, though: my resting heart rate was running much faster than normal (89 today, when 50 is normal for me), my metabolism was running faster as well, and my face felt warmer trying to fight the chemo, so I was glad to hear that I was not going through menopause yet.

I left with two more prescriptions: Claritin for the allergies and numbing cream to place atop my port skin before chemo, so I could avoid the "sour face" when they stick me with the needle. All of my blood counts were also good today, even with the WBCs down to 16.0.

My ex-boyfriend, Justin, came to visit me tonight. I hadn't seen him in three years, but it was so great to see him again and his familiar, comfortable smile. I'd invited him up to have a night of wallowing, since he'd broken up with his recent ex. He'd brought the two journals I'd written to him when we were together all those years ago, and it was funny yet surreal to relive some of those moments from our relationship. So much of it I'd completely forgotten, while some I still vividly remembered. We had a fun night of SkeeBall and trivia. I guess he proved the point that you *can* be friends with an ex. He'd always said that, but I'd never believed it.

OCTOBER 18, 2008

Mark and I had our second official date tonight. All dressed up, I went to his house with roses for him. He was adorable, asking me to wait in the house for him to pick *me* up. He ran outside, and when I opened his front door when he rang the bell, he had a single red rose for me. He drove us to my restaurant of choice, a pasta bar in his neighborhood that came highly recommended by Carrie. We started to debate politics over dinner, tough when he was a strong conservative and I was very liberal, so I tried to keep the conversation lighter and avoid all controversial talk. After finding out our bowling alley was full later on, we picked up a movie and went back to his house. While setting up the movie, he stepped out of sight and came back with the other eleven red roses he'd hidden away in his roommate's room. I was pleasantly surprised!

I finally felt comfortable enough to at least remove my shirt, but nothing else. I'd prefaced it with letting him feel the skin stretcher above my tank top line earlier that night. I was starting to feel a little more comfortable with letting go a bit with him, letting down my wall of staunch resistance. I admitted to feeling a little mixed up in my reactions to the activities, though. On one hand, I was young and hormonal and enjoying feeling sexual again. On the other hand, I was committed now more than ever to share myself with my partner—boyfriend, husband, or otherwise, but preferably a husband—and be committed to just one person before sharing the most intimate parts of myself: my heart and my body. Where should I draw the line? How would I know what I'd be comfortable with, and when? Thank goodness he was patient about sexual activity.

I'd now realized that I no longer knew how to date. All I knew about being single was being-in-college single, not grown-up-post-divorce single. No long nights of drinking, waking up next to someone. No roller-coaster emotions and fights, running away from the person. I wanted stability, loyalty, friendship, kindness, consideration, help/partnership, laughter, quality time, and love. Long cry from starting out my "qualifications list" with "someone who's nice to me." I think I was just not ready to date yet, to be exclusive with just one person.

OCTOBER 20, 2008

My first MUGA scan was this afternoon at Mercy. No side effects!

FROM CARINGBRIDGE.ORG,
TUESDAY, OCTOBER 21, 2008 11:22 PM, CDT:

Yesterday, I had my first MUGA (MUltiple Gated Acquisition) scan to see how the left ventricle of my heart is doing from the chemo. They injected me with pyrophosphate (PYP), a radioactive liquid that will highlight my heart during the scan, I waited twenty minutes for another injection on PYP (both injections done through an IV in my arm—the PYP can clog my port), then I was hooked up to the machine by the little white heart scanning pads with cords attached to the machine, like the ones used on TV (for all you fellow Grey's Anatomy fans!) They scanned the left side of my heart for ten minutes, then another scan straight-on for another ten. Nothing to it! I should get the results next week at my next appointment with Dr. Garino.

I wish that the Herceptin treatments were all there was to my chemo. I had H3 (Herceptin treatment #3) today, and it gets easier every time. I was also given an INR (International Normalized Ratio) test to see how my blood is clotting, due to the nosebleeds last week. I will also get those results next Tuesday.

My side effects have been much better too. Still have the metallic taste in my mouth, but that is getting easier to cope with now that it's more "normal" to me. I also have some allergic reaction "measles," but the lotion prescribed last week is really helping those go away. I felt like a hormonal teenager with all the little red bumps on my face. Thank goodness they're disappearing. I'm also tired every day, but naps are wonderful gifts. I'm lucky that my side effects aren't as bad as some reported by other patients.

Even if I don't have a chance to thank everyone for their guest book postings, I can't tell you how much I appreciate and read every single one. You are the bright points of my days. Thank you for all of your support, love, and hugs!

OCTOBER 21, 2008

Herceptin treatment #3 today. The INR test showed that my blood was clotting just as it should be. WBC: 6.3, RBC: 4.0, HGB: 12.3, PLT: 139.

Still not divorced yet. @*&^#@!! Andy sent me yet another e-mail asking if he had any important mail at "the Maple Grove house." (Umm…no, *my* house!)

I replied, "None that I've seen."

He quickly sent back, "Thanks. I appreciate it."

I said nothing.

The clindamycin topical lotion for the Herceptin allergic reaction "measles" helped, thank goodness. I hated being so embarrassed for people to see me, even with a ton of makeup on. Not that anyone *couldn't* see the bumps through it all. No more nosebleeds either. I was still horribly congested, though, making it so difficult to breathe at night (or when trying to kiss someone.)

I called Medica today to ask them about two bills I'd received—one from North Memorial for my 9/11 – 9/13 stay there, and the other from Suburban Imaging for the 6/25 and 7/15 mammograms. The North Memorial bill's total came to over $45,000. Thank goodness for insurance. I will have to pay only $1200 for my twenty percent cost of room and board from the reconstruction (my insurance will pay only eighty percent for all reconstruction costs. I guess it was better than them covering nothing. I'd be flat-chested for the rest of my life if they didn't cover that much.)

The mammograms, they discovered, should have been covered, so they will re-file the claim and pay the $536 that I was charged. Who hoo! I had that check all ready to mail today. It really paid—literally—to check on those. I would have been out all that money. It made me want to double-check on all of the bills I'd paid until now.

Feeling lucky in the money department, I decided to call the social worker at the Mercy Cancer Resource Center, Marcia, to check on a grant application I'd submitted a few weeks ago. She found it, buried under a pile of papers. The Mercy Oncology Outreach Program will pay for one month of my two mortgage payments. Another $1100 saved. How *lucky* was I for all this help.

OCTOBER 22, 2008

The love of a godchild. Petey was all smiles, watching me from the living room window as I arrived at my parents' house today. We invented a new game of "Rock-a-Bye-Petey," in which I "rock" him like a crazy woman, as he squealed in delight and asked me to do it again. We feasted on hours of playing with monster trucks, when the neighbor boy Kaden came over to give me relief from all the playing; man, I needed a nap! When Kaden's mom dropped him off, she told me how he was rushing her through the getting-ready process because he "didn't want to miss Gwen!" When I asked him what I should name my own little boy someday, he gave a pensive look before he responded, "Kaden!"

Over the last few months, I'd realized just how much I'd love my own little "Kaden" someday. May I be that lucky.

OCTOBER 23, 2008

I snuck over to Kathryn's house again to clean up before Pete's party, though Mom had beat me to the laundry. I didn't volunteer her to help! That amazing woman.

The party was a riot, complete with a Dee Snyder and black afro wigs, a piñata made out of brown paper bags, a whoopee cushion, root beer barrel shots, a monster truck birthday cake, and all of my favorite people around me.

FROM CARINGBRIDGE.ORG, FRIDAY, OCTOBER 24, 2008 12:02 PM, CDT:

Darn if the inevitable started, just as the nurses predicted, exactly two weeks from the date of my first chemo treatment—I'm starting to lose my hair. For some reason, I envisioned the clumps on the pillow when I'd wake up, or brushing out a lump of it after a shower. The process is much more subtle, starting this past Tuesday with a little more than normal human daily hair loss, going up to double the normal rate on Wednesday, a little more yesterday than the day before. I woke up this morning and a minute bunch came out. Not the massive clump of my nightmares, but enough to admit to myself that I'm not going to be one of the lucky women who gets to keep hers. (Hey, we can all have delusional dreams, can't we?) People keep saying, "It will grow back," and I know that, but it is a reminder of the cancer process. It's sad to see it go, like a part of who I am is leaving. I feared this point: without my hair, looking more like a cancer patient.

HOWEVER! There are so many positive aspects to remind myself of. I have three cute wigs to sport and a pile of beautiful scarves from my sister Kathryn, from my mom, and from my student Afra. I look forward to the rotation of them all, being a new person every day of the week. I'll fit in more at chemo sessions too, since I was one of the only people on Tuesdays left with hair. It will be the chance to start over on my hair regrowth, since I was trying to grow out the highlights since last November. And who won't be jealous of the fact that I'm gaining at least fifteen minutes of morning prep time from skipping the shampooing, conditioning, leave-in conditioning, brushing, shine serum, blow-drying, heat protecting spray, and flat-ironing? Doesn't sound so bad now, does it?

Plastic surgeon appointment also went well this morning. Kim, the nurse, still raves about how great my skin is doing. Again, positives all over the place!

Enjoy your weekends! Even with the clouds and rain, I adore the smell of the damp fall air.

OCTOBER 24, 2008

The morning started with another fill at Dr. Harrington's. I was now up to 240 cc's on each side. According to Kim, I was now a full B or a small C, but I feel *huge!* I cannot stop staring at them all day. Working out when I got home, in a sports bra, I felt so curvy. Kim said I won't even get stretch marks, so now I was not worried about filling them up too fast. Maybe one more set of 90 cc's would be enough? Hmm.

I found a brochure for "Chemo Care" at Garino's office, a co-pay assistance program for chemo treatments. If my annual income was lower than $41,600, I'd qualify for help from them. I may just hit that for 2008, since Andy left and I was not getting paid for months. Each chemo appointment charged a $20 office co-pay, plus the cost of drugs. Maybe I should look into this program, considering the price of Neulasta…?

OCTOBER 25, 2008

Last night, I stayed up late cooking for Shel, Al, and Amanda, enjoying a few beers and a call to Mark as I cooked. Mark called back around midnight to read a chapter in *The Purpose Driven Life,* but I was so tired that I asked him to postpone. I didn't want to be tired and only half-listen. Mark was irate with me that I wouldn't take the five or ten minutes to read with him, that I chose working out as more important than him and God.

Even after time to cool off, I was still upset with him for saying all that. I knew where he was coming from, but I was really trying my best. I felt that any decision I would have made at that point would have been the wrong one. I was glad he eventually apologized, but his anger at my choice drove a deeper wedge between us, keeping me from becoming closer to him.

My heart became more apprehensive.

Carrie also told me a fun story last night about Andy via her husband, KC. KC saw Andy grabbing a female bartender's butt and winked at KC, saying how great it was to be single. At first, I was furious; what a complete jackass to even make that reference about me to someone he knew would pass it on—to eventually get back to me. And how illegal—to grab an employee's butt!

Then I realized the only person I was hurting was me. I should really just be happy that he got what he wanted from life. Really, it gave me more reason to be happy he was gone and all the more reason to move on with my life.

OCTOBER 26, 2008

I went to a movie and dinner with Jenni and Julie from union work this afternoon, and I actually looked forward to going "home" to Mark afterwards, to go to church together. Was that a sign that I was starting to avoid my friends to hang out with him? No. I could clearly see how much my avoidance of my friends and family hurt me before, and now I could clearly go into a new relationship knowing what *not* to do in the future. What good man would want me to give up part of the best part of who I am to be around him more? It was all about finding a good balance of both worlds and in the process not giving up who I am.

There was nothing better than enjoying a good evening at church. I could be free to sing, worship, and enjoy the ambiance without fear of being ridiculed for being "crazy-religious" or weird. Still amazing to me how I could now say that I was a Christian, giving up drinking and swearing, and doing random acts of kindness for others.

As I kept telling others, cancer really changes you.

OCTOBER 27, 2008

A full hour of Tae Bo Advanced today! It felt so difficult, so much more difficult than in the past, with a sore chest, no full range of motion, and the very labored breathing. How great it felt, though, to get back on the working-out path!

Even with a full day of great friends—Julies S. and G. from work and Erin from high school—Mark had to wreck my evening by being unsupportive again. I mentioned to him that I was back on my "roids" and he took that to mean that I wasn't taking my chemo seriously. He said he felt like he was the only one who cared about how this affected me. He asked me if I even knew what steroids can do to me. I started to cry, telling him I was fully aware of what they could do, since my college roommate Jenni had a hip replacement at age twenty-three from excessive steroids that her doctor had prescribed for her. But how was I supposed to live my life in constant fear of possible side effects?

I reminded him of the two things I needed from him—support and respect for my decisions. I went to bed that night, completely unable to trust him. I wanted to be able to know that I could be supported no matter what, because I needed that strength to truly live life. But I couldn't imagine how tough it would be on him either. Knowing how strongly he felt against chemo, it would be so hard to sit back and say nothing to change my mind. But I had made this decision before I met him, and I didn't want to go back on that huge decision upon meeting someone new.

What a hard time to start dating someone.

OCTOBER 28, 2008

Full Chemo #2 today. I got a good hour of Tae Bo in before Mom came to meet me. Washing, blow drying, and flat ironing my hair made a TON fall out. The look on Mom's face confirmed just how much was falling out. It was a look of sadness, not quite pity, but like she was losing it all with me.

I avoided the washing/styling process now to slow down the hair loss. I had the cold packs Mom gave me to prevent my hair loss also in the freezer, but I didn't think they'd really help me keep what I had left.

I told Mom about the conversation that Mark and I had the night before, and she recommended checking out the book for people living with cancer patients, so he'd get a better sense of what I was going through or how to deal with it himself. Not a bad idea. (It also reminded me of how I checked out the book for Andy and how he just returned it right after I gave it to him to read. Of course, I had no idea until weeks later that he hadn't actually kept the book, when I reminded myself that its return date was coming due.)

This was the first morning I used the Lidocaine to numb my port skin, but apparently, I didn't use enough; it still stung. My MUGA scan came back at seventy-three percent, what my "normal" heart performance was. My nurse practitioner Carmen said that anything over fifty percent was considered normal, but if I had any significant drops by my next scan in three months (such as down to sixty percent), then I'd have concerns that the Herceptin might be affecting my heart.

Darn—of course the drug that might affect my heart was the one that I'd be on for a year.

Carmen did assure me that exercise would keep my heart function higher. My blood clotting was also tested, and it came back perfect: 1.0 out of 1.0. My counts: WBC: 16.1, RBC: 3.78, HGB: 11.5, PLT: 320. The chemo process was quicker this time. I did get Decadron for nausea again, but no Benadryl for allergic reactions.

I was getting pretty tired sitting there, and the fatigue became even worse after we left. We tried to sell my wedding rings at a quick stop at Rosedale Mall, but they offered me only $400 for a $5000 set. Guess I'd keep them a while longer. I was not *that* desperate to get rid of the rings.

We stopped at Panera for lunch, but I was even too tired to eat there, so we took it back to my house. Mom left at 7:00 P.M. I didn't know what I'd do without her. If I didn't have her presence and support, I'd feel awfully alone. Wasn't I supposed to have The One who promised "to have and to hold me, in sickness and in health"? How awful to actually have to go through this completely alone, with no family or friends to lean on.

I felt so incredibly blessed to have my vast support system.

When Mark came over later that night, he again asked me to watch the Gerson Institute video with him. Instantly, I fell back on trusting his support of me. I went from being happy to sad in two seconds. Why was he still pushing me, even after our conversation last night? I told him I'd watch it after going grocery shopping and I wasn't budging, even after hearing his pleas to the contrary. I took my time in coming back, especially since he was on the phone with his mom when I left.

I came back more than an hour later, almost expecting that he would have left, but praying that he hadn't. He was writing me a letter at the dining room table. When I asked if he'd want some space, he said he didn't think he was good for me. Whoa. He felt like he was dragging me down, and even though he didn't want to, he thought he wasn't best for me and he should leave.

It was July déjà vu all over again, someone promising to be there for me but later deciding it was too much.

My heart was falling, tears quickly springing to my eyes. I couldn't handle Mark leaving me now too. I knew how much this was for ME to deal with, and I couldn't imagine how hard it was on people around me. But how could I honestly expect someone to live with me through this, someone not related to me? Someone I'd only been dating for two months? How could I be so selfish?

I gave him the opportunity to make his own decision—to support me, even if it was too difficult for him, or he could decide it was too much for him to deal with. He responded by flipping over his letter and writing, "I love you."

He wanted so much for me to be able to share with him what I was going through, to not hold back from sharing my true feelings. So I finally told him this: I was scared shitless about what was happening to my body; I was trying to minimize my effects for everyone around me so no one would have to suffer too; I was freaked out about trying to share my new scars with someone someday; I was afraid of being told that I couldn't have kids.

He looked at me and said that true love wouldn't care about scars but would see past it. Now *he* was beginning to tear up. He said he didn't want to leave me, but he didn't want to drag me down.

I went upstairs to bed and decided to "let go and let God." If it was going to happen for us, I just needed to let it happen. So I did what any normal girl would do—worked the lingerie I was wearing and enjoyed the glow of the soft lights coming in from the window. He reassured me that he was different, that he truly cared about me.

We stayed up until almost five in the morning, just talking and enjoying our time together. However, my hair was really bothering me, as I found clumps throughout my sheets. What a mood killer for me, though I tried to ignore it. I fell asleep peacefully in his arms.

FROM CARINGBRIDGE.ORG, MONDAY, NOVEMBER 3, 2008 4:37 PM, CST:

The joys of insurance. I received a statement from Medica today referencing my reconstruction in September, telling me that I'll be *receiving a massive bill from my plastic surgeon for "services not covered." After a while on hold, I got them to realize they coded the surgery wrong and they were charging me for services indeed covered. Another $8000 bill saved. Pays to keep on top of these!*

I spent my morning volunteering at the World Vision Experience: AIDS in Edina this morning. After the twenty-minute tour, I was ready to sponsor a child in Africa. It's amazing to live my life here, easily feeling sorry for myself about how life is going, and then to experience the life of a young child living with AIDS in Africa. Talk about getting a real perspective about what is truly important. Here's a link to check it out: http://www.wvexperience.org/ I will enjoy the experience as a great reminder of how my life can have a positive impact on so many others.

OCTOBER 29, 2008

Home again, home again! I finally let my hair loss get the best of me, and I asked Kath to cut my hair short. Not shaved, just short. It was now above my chin in the front, almost spiky in the back. It was so much easier for me emotionally than losing the long strands, though now my hair came out with only a simple run-through of the fingers. Wouldn't it just be easier to shave it? Sure, but it was emotionally difficult for me to let that part of me go. I was already struggling with the fact I was back up to 120 pounds. I saw my face "filling out" (as Mom put it) and people were telling me I looked "healthy" (eating-disorder-mind-code for "fat").

I was already going to be bald; I sure as heck didn't want to feel fat too. Kicking up the exercise and cutting out the crap food then. I'd feel better with my face thinning out a little, maybe getting down past 115 (but no lower than 110). My new chest had to weigh at least five pounds, right?? It might not be tough for me to cut out some eating with the heartburn/stomachache that came back today. I wanted to lose weight in a healthy way and be smart about it, taking better care of myself from here on.

Oh, and the best part of the day? I was divorced!! I got a call early in the morning from my attorney, saying she'd received notice that the courts had finally passed the judgment. Now I could wait eight weeks to get the papers from her, or I could go down to the Hennepin Family Court Building in Minneapolis and pay $10 for my own certified copy. Was there even a real choice to make? I immediately jumped into my car, drove down there, and happily requested a copy. Five minutes later, I left with the highest hop in my step and dopiest smile on my face, a joyful look that they'd probably not seen in the courthouse in a long time. I immediately drove to the DMV to get my new driver's license and passport, free and clear of the tattoo of my former last name. I smiled pretty for the camera, fully ready and blissfully happy to be Gwen Rosha again.

Free at last, free at last! Thank God almighty, I'm free at last!

OCTOBER 30, 2008

Couldn't get myself up to going to the Exotic/Erotic Ball with Heather tonight. I felt so foggy and tired; "chemo brain" must be kicking in. I couldn't even write e-mails today. I had to concentrate on the words I was typing, not even able to focus on spelling or forming complete/logical sentences. What an awful feeling—to be so out of it. I felt useless even to myself.

OCTOBER 31, 2008

I was up to 300 cc's at Harrington's. I asked Kim for 330, but she "white-knuckled" my injections up to 300, so no extra 30. But hey, I was looking cute! I loved how I could fill out "real" shirts now. Kim said I was nearing the end of my expansion process—that better mean that I could still get some more saline into these stretchers before "the end."

NOVEMBER 2, 2008

Rachel and I went shopping this afternoon, mostly so I could get fitted properly at Victoria's Secret. So apparently, I was a 32D. Riiiiiight. There ain't no way I was that big. I thought they were vanity-sizing their bras to make women feel bigger than they really were.

Church sermon tonight talked about God offering us doors to go through to build relationships with people. I knew of a person in financial trouble, another battling addiction, yet another facing health issues, but what was keeping me from reaching out to them? Was I too concerned about my own schedule to make time for those who meant the most to me? Why was I not walking through these doors? It was interesting to reflect on how someone who claimed her family meant everything to her was so timid to take the necessary action to spend time with them.

NOVEMBER 3, 2008

I volunteered this morning at the World AIDS Experience, and with every picture I saw or every African-simulated room I walked into, I felt even more grateful for what I had in my life. Seriously, if I could have chosen an illness, I'd much, MUCH rather have breast cancer than AIDS. After my grateful-for-what-I-have morning, I went over to Tracy's to chat. She told me about Jason's new plan of wanting to join the Air Force Reserves. It would mean extra monthly income and a guaranteed position after twelve years of service. She was afraid of him being deployed to Iraq if he joined, leaving her with a baby at home.

Either way, I was glad that I was not the one in that position. How do you support your husband in his dreams while sacrificing the dreams you have together?

NOVEMBER 4, 2008

After changing my name at the district office and at Wells Fargo, voting for Obama, and dropping off cookies at work, I went to Herceptin #5 at 2:30. No wonder I'd needed a nap before driving home to Mom and Dad's.

Kathryn, Sheila, and I enjoyed my homemade limoncello that evening while watching the election results. We danced around the kitchen and ate random chips and snacks like drunken teenagers, though we weren't drunk. The vodka infusion made my haircut-to-come easier to deal with, even a little fun for a while. Kath gave me a Mohawk just for giggles; how often in your life can you even actually have a Mohawk? We laughed at how silly I looked with my new hairdo, complete with my little kid's deer towel/poncho around my shoulders. That limoncello exacerbated the laughter. Then the electric razor came out. Kath first used the shortest razor guard that she could, and the short hair I had left started falling to the floor around me. It was sad to see the little chunks on the floor, but weird to feel the peach fuzz I had left on my head.

Shel took a picture of me looking in the mirror at my shaved head for the first time, and I gave a shocked laugh before instantly bursting into tears. Kath immediately hugged me around the head and shoulders as she violently started crying too. Shel grabbed my hand and held it while all three of us cried together.

I felt Kath's tears falling quickly on my face and arms, mixing in with my own. Through her sobs, she told me, "That was the hardest thing I've ever had to do for one of my sisters."

It was an awful feeling—knowing all of us were hurting so much and me making my "complete transformation" into a visible cancer patient. For all these months, it was easy to pretend I didn't have cancer; I never physically appeared any different. I was the same person I was on my twenty-eighth birthday. Now it was impossible to deny my sickness because it stared back at me in the mirror.

I spent the rest of the night trying to get used to the "New Me," constantly feeling my scalp and how tender it felt when I rubbed the stubble.

Kath had finally removed the guard and gave me the closest-thing-to-a-Bic shave without actually getting out the shaving cream. I kept staring into mirrors and darkened windows, constantly reminding myself that the "G.I. Jane" looking back was *me*. I tried on all my borrowed scarves from Kath, finally settling on a red, white, and blue one in honor of Election Day. The scarves were so much more comfortable to wear than being bald, but they were so much harder to look at. I always wondered why my friend Heather wore obvious wigs when everyone knew she didn't have hair due to her chemo. Now I realize why: it was so comforting and less jarring to see and feel hair than to look at yourself bald. *Now* I understood.

Kath said I was still beautiful and had a PRETTY bald head (no bumps or weird spots). It was hard to feel beautiful without my "crowning glory" that I took so much time to care for, that I was so proud of.

At least, Obama won the election. I called Justin to say we did a great job voting. He told me to say hi to my family, even called back to leave that message. Kath and Shel both loved him and would like to see us back together. I didn't think that was what *we* had in mind.

NOVEMBER 5, 2008

The next morning, Mom smiled and took in my new haircut quietly. Pete and Brit were both scared of my bald head and waited for me to put a wig on. Dad happily smiled at my new 'do and decided, during my wig fashion show, that he liked my long blond wig on me. I was glad I shared that with him. I needed to just show him I was still doing okay, so he would worry about me a little less. He, of all my family, was still taking my cancer the hardest, and I hated to do this to him. He was my dad, and I just wanted him to be proud of me.

Grocery shopping after hitting up the pet store with Pete today, I caught a woman staring at me. Since there was nothing behind me to look at, I assumed she could tell I was wearing a wig. Hopefully, it was true; otherwise my paranoia of people seeing the "Cancer Me" was already taking a strong hold of me. Kath and I were interested to see what Mark's reaction would be to the hair. Since he had a hard time adjusting to the short bob look, what might he think when he had to see me bald? How would he feel about kissing a bald woman? Would he even want to? And why did I always fear for the worst in others?

I even received an e-mail from Andy today, saying, "I heard about your hair. You'll always be beautiful."

Umm, what?? What a random e-mail.

NOVEMBER 7, 2008

Mark was great about the hair. I knew it would be hard for him to get used to, but he was great about not making me feel unattractive. It was a relief to still feel beautiful on the outside too. I was still hesitant to boldly wear the baldness around him, but time would help me with that too.

I was up to 390 cc's. Wow, was my chest pretty! I loved how big they were, but I decided I was nearly done filling them. Just one more small fill next week and I'd be ready for my final implant surgery. Dr. Garino said "Absolutely not" to the implant surgery during full chemo because of the high risk of infection, so I realized that I'd have to wait for a four-day break after January 20. Until then, I'd get to wear Alison's old 34D bra. I loved having a large chest! It definitely made the cancer reward list, not to mention the chest made my waist look smaller too—bonus.

I met Andy at Wells Fargo to notarize the quitclaim deed, officially signing the house over to me. First thing out of his mouth: "You look great!"

I thanked him and told him our notary was waiting. Of course, I came prepared with the forms from the last time we quitclaimed together after my married-name change, just to make sure I was getting this signed correctly the first time. I *really* didn't want to see him again—for any reason. I also asked him to talk for a minute, and immediately he burst into telling me about how bad things were at work, that he wasn't in any rush to get back to work that morning.

I just *hmm-ed* him and started talking about our settlement. On a piece of paper, I drew an outline of what we'd agreed upon, starting with his settlement, minus the money he owed me: $800 from our Ireland trip "refund" since Orbitz only refunded $800 from the $3200 we paid, $1000 to take his name off of two mortgages and release him from that responsibility, $630 for the lawyer fee, $12 from the last Comcast cable bill, and $30 for the quitclaim filing. He was furious to see the paltry amount he had left coming to him. He questioned why he needed to pay me for the trip, after I'd already told him that I wasn't going to be out any money from skipping the trip I would have taken alone, but he'd wanted to get a refund ("I have to pay you half of the trip we paid for together?"). He questioned the lawyer fee ("Wasn't it supposed to be $800 total?"), the mortgage name removal ("Will you send me proof when it's done to show me how much it really cost?"), and the postage ("What's that for?").

Seriously, do *you* want the cancer?

Must he always be so petty? Wasn't this one check easier than him cutting me one too? Sheesh, you try to be nice to someone....

So of course, he didn't want the cash I offered but a check, saying if the IRS questioned it, he could prove it wasn't income. He was still hiding his tips, not claiming them as income but hiding it in his apartment. (In hindsight, why was I so stupid to give him a check with my account number on it?)

The best part of the meeting was how his eyes kept burning holes into my new breasts; I caught him looking more than a few times. He added twice more some remark about how good I looked.

I just thanked him again, got into my car, and said to myself, "I know." Funny how he was still driving his brother's car, the one without the whiskey plates.

Some things never changed.

In the evening, I drove to Willmar to meet up with Justin at his job then hang out for the night. We stopped by his brother's house, where he was staying, and it was so surreal to be back there after four years. I was even able to enjoy some beer during bowling, relishing the fun of relaxing with him. It was a flashback to all those years ago. It was nice to have his male perspective on the divorce, especially from someone who had recently left his ex. After bowling, we watched *Hostel*, and holding back from grabbing his arm during the gory parts was hard. I didn't want to cross any "friend boundaries" and feel like an idiot.

The next morning, after sleeping on the couch with my wig on because I didn't want him to see me bald, we sat watching TV and drinking coffee. I can't remember how long it had been since I'd spent a day like that. I didn't want to leave, especially after we sat on the couch and he kissed me. How weird was that! It felt so good, so normal, so fun, but so wrong if I was still dating Mark.

I had a lot to think about on my way home. Was I ready to date again?

NOVEMBER 9, 2008

I tried to make Mark breakfast, but he was so particular about how he wanted his breakfast burrito prepared. I had to follow his prescribed regimen of how to cook the eggs, how to warm up his salsa, how to melt the cheese. I was taken aback when he freaked when I put the tortilla on the counter before I had the egg cracked.

Wow, since when did I become the calm one in a relationship? I understood being anal—I'd been there before—but I felt like nothing I did was good enough for him. I was so upset that I was ready to go home, and all he kept doing was justifying why he liked things done a certain way.

I tried to explain how insufficient he made me feel, but he wasn't listening to a word I said. I knew I was not perfect, but I did try to please him when it was not that big of a deal to me.

NOVEMBER 11, 2008

Last night, Mark again made me feel insignificant, not letting me give him even a small kiss in front of Tracy and Jason. How much these things bothered me. I went to see my counselor Ardith, and she said that when I felt that way, I needed to catch myself from feeling angry. I also needed to reduce my number of sleepovers with him because I was feeling anxiety from not being ready to be in another relationship. I was feeling suffocated, as if losing my independence and rushing into another domestic role. Talk about hitting the nail on the head.

Most importantly, she said that if someone wanted to help me, to just let them. For example, when my dad offered to buy me a wig (that I vehemently refused) I needed to just let him because it was the only way he knew how to offer comfort to me. He would feel like he was helping me out somehow, because he couldn't express in words how he felt.

Damn, I wished I had just let him get it for me!

After Kath and I dropped Justin off at the airport, I was half an hour late for getting to chemo. The chemo nurse Becky had actually called Gail to see if I was okay, since I was not there yet. How nice was that—she called to check up on me. Of course, in my excitement to have Kath with me and to see Justin, I forgot the Lidocaine, and the needle stung going into my port. Even worse, Becky couldn't get any blood to come out of the port, so she needed to readjust it without removing the needle first. Double ouch. They also drew blood for my P53 test, the rare genetic cancer test that Medica finally agreed to cover at 100% after much pestering from the genetic counselors.

The P53 test made me think deeply about how Mark said I might have caused my cancer since my genetic tests were negative. Not only did I feel guilty about how I'd lived my life in the past, I worried about how much I'd need to change it in the future.

NOVEMBER 12, 2008

I went to Gram's in the morning to learn how to bake her famous bread, but since she didn't know I was coming, we didn't have time to get it all done in one day. Instead, I helped her hang plastic on her windows. She said her guardian angel sent me to help her. How proud I was to be there to help her. How often did I get personal one-on-one time with her, and how much time might I have left to get more chances like that?

FROM CARINGBRIGE.ORG,
THURSDAY, NOVEMBER 13, 2008 4:01 PM, CST:

Shaving my head made my situation all seem real to me...the diagnosis, the cancer, the chemo. I finally felt like a cancer patient; it was now staring me in the face. It was easy to hide behind my hair and deny that things weren't really happening, but now it's a constant reminder to those around me and to myself of what I'm truly accomplishing here. I'm surviving this, even without hair. I'm still the same strong person I was before I knew of the cancer, before I lost my hair.

It is still weird to get used to, feeling nothing when I "wash my hair" or sleeping with nothing on my pillow, but I can't tell you how nice it is to not have to style my hair. It's great to throw on a scarf or wig and run out the door. I even think the stubble is already growing back. Sheesh, follicles...make up your minds! Either you stay or you don't!

Not much new for side effects other than being sleepy all the time, the reaction to the Herceptin, and the nosebleeds came back a little this week. The Claritin is helping control that. I will have my third round of full chemo this coming Tuesday, but I'm no longer wondering what will happen this time. I feel like a pro already, and all of the chemo nurses on Tuesday know me and my side effects well.

My next surgery, the final reconstruction, will now take place after I'm done with the full chemo (which ends in late January). Since I will have a high risk of infection, my oncologist said, "Absolutely not" to my request of surgery before I go back to work in December. Darn, but I completely understand and agree. I'll wait until spring break in March for my four-day recovery time needed. I can't wait to go back to work already! I'm a little nervous about having a difficult reaction to the chemo and needing a few days off when I return (I have one full chemo in January while I'm back at work) but I have a few days to take off for just this one treatment. I haven't been this excited to go back to school since...September. I'm the person that is always excited to go back to school. This year, I get to do it twice. Aren't I lucky?!

NOVEMBER 13, 2008

It was nice to pick up Justin from the airport and have time to talk to him about life. He completely understood my fear of dating again, knew how it felt to want to share your life with someone, but he also understood that it was tough to know who is the best one for you. No one in love had ever *not* had a broken heart, and if I wanted love, I needed first to give it away to those around me.

NOVEMBER 14, 2008

My TMJ appointment went well, after the twenty minutes spent updating my medical history form. I so fondly remembered the days of *no* medical history, those distant yesteryear days of…June 2008.

Harrington told me my chest was too hard/stiff to make any more injections. Damn. I was hoping for at least one more small pump up. I needed to wait until January to see her and schedule my final implant surgery for the first week of March—spring break. The best parts of the appointment were Kathy congratulating me on my updated last name and Harrington saying, "Whoa, mama!" when she saw my breasts.

NOVEMBER 15, 2008

A truffles party at Mom's with Manda, Kath, and Sheila. I hadn't laughed that much in such a long time. Mom made reference to me not having to babysit my "6'5" lump" and I could just enjoy myself. [Note: with that comment, my mom actually inspired the title for my memoir of my "three lumps." Two of the lumps were my breasts; the third was Andy.]

Part Five
BACK TO WORK

NOVEMBER 18, 2008

Dr. Garino said I should be okay to go back to work on December 15 with no problems. Fatigue would always be an issue for me, but I knew I could handle it. I kept impressing myself with how great I was doing. She also told me that my face rash was probably caused by the dexamethasone, not the Herceptin. Thank goodness. I would be done with that one soon.

Full chemo #3. Becky the nurse told me how my dosage was formulated: Taxotere was based on weight/height; Carboplatin on height, weight, kidney function, blood counts, and sex (male/female, not whether I was "getting any"); and Herceptin on height/weight. Counts today: WBC: 11.71, RBC: 3.54, HGB: 11.1, PLT: 164. Gotta keep up on the iron, apparently.

Justin also told me that he was willing to give "us" a shot again. I told him that he was a great, perfect guy, but he still lived almost two hours away from me. We didn't work the first time due to distance. He said this time we were both mature, and he'd move closer to me if we both wanted that. Oh, so different from the Justin I knew in 2003. I was still not ready to rush into a relationship when I was clearly not ready to committedly date someone. Even my family was voting on "Team Mark" and "Team Justin" (though it was not much of a contest with the vote at 10-1 in favor of Justin).

Let it go, folks! I was NOT looking to become a Missus. Cuddling was just fine for me for now.

NOVEMBER 19, 2008

A family secret was revealed to me; today I learned how to bake Gram's bread. She had been such an inspiration to me. At almost eighty-seven, she worked tirelessly at home and on their farm. She had the energy of someone decades younger, even more energy than her granddaughter today.

I had to take three short naps when I was there, feeling instant remorse after waking up, knowing I'd lost that time with her. What little time we had together went slipping away. How I wished these side effects would stop stealing so much of my life.

The metallic taste in my mouth was now worse than ever, making eating a rough chore rather than enjoyable. Brushing my teeth hurt too, not only the brush on my gums and tongue, but the toothpaste and mouthwash *burned*. At least I was not having mouth bleeds or mouth sores.

NOVEMBER 21, 2008

The *Twilight* movie release! Rachel and Dan came over for dinner with Mark and me beforehand. As I got my plate to go to the table, Mark sat in my spot, assuming that I was serving him. Rachel and Dan even got their own plates. He sat disinterested during dinner and our movie chitchat, and even took my can of juice for his own.

I thought I would not opt for "Team Mark" anymore. We were just too different. I felt nitpicked for so many insignificant things, and I didn't like being the calm/rational one in a relationship, not that I was otherwise a crazy, organized freak. I began to wonder if this is how Andy saw *me* when we were together and how I would vow to learn from this and apply it in the future.

I also learned how my half-glass of Riesling tasted absolutely awful to me. I used to love sweet white wine. Smoking also made my tongue burn and lips ache, like small needles poking my lips every time I took a puff. Did I need any more inspiration to quit drinking and smoking?

FROM CARINGBRIDGE.ORG, MONDAY, NOVEMBER 24, 2008 9:19 PM, CST:

My sister Victoria posted a great question for all of us on our family's website: With Thanksgiving only a week away...what are you thankful for this year? Vic is thankful for her gray hairs, though she wishes she would be brave enough to shave it in solidarity with me. (What a sweetheart!) Here is what I wrote:

I am most grateful for my wonderful family. I was sad to lose three years of being closer to everyone, and I had a good wake-up call to remind me how lucky I am to have such great folks around to love and support me. I thank God for all of you often. So many people are battling cancer alone or with no support, and I am blessed to have my parents and sisters (and extended family throughout the US) with me every day.

I am also thankful for my health, believe it or not. Even with all of the chaos of cancer, the doctors were able to get it all, and with chemo, I have a ninety-five percent chance of having a breast-cancer-free future! I am thankful for those odds.

I am also thankful for health insurance, which makes all of my treatment fiscally possible. Go, Medica!

I am lastly thankful for Suerte, my little pal and roommate. Without her, I'd be resting on the couch alone.

MONDAY, NOVEMBER 24, 2008 9:24 PM, CST:

With the holiday approaching quickly, I am sure glad that I had full chemo last week. I spent the rest of the week taking so many naps, being constantly tired no matter how much I slept. I already feel much, much better this week. Working out today was more difficult than usual, my whole body feeling sore with the easiest of moves. I am going to take it easier tomorrow. I wish it were warm enough to take walks outside, but my videos at home will need to suffice for now.

The nausea is easier to manage now, too. I have to eat when I feel the least bit hungry, skipping foods that haven't been so nice to me in the past few months. Cereal, yogurt, and apples have been good (bananas and peanut butter, not so much), though chocolate tastes metallic; can you imagine the horror of finding out your favorite comfort food makes you ill? Shudder.

My heart has been strongly palpitating irregularly off and on since the pneumothorax, worse again since I started chemo. I think that caffeine is a big culprit, so I begrudgingly started cutting down on coffee and Diet Coke. I can't give up the DC, because that is also helping with the nausea. Everything in moderation, I suppose.

I'm starting to get used to the baldness, slowly starting to wear my hat outdoors rather than a wig. I can imagine that soon I can just proudly wear the baldness altogether, getting used to the stares that are inevitable. Still cannot wait until the regrowth process can officially start.

I also volunteered at the Maple Grove Library today for the first time. I spent four hours checking in reserved books and shelving them. How fun to spend all that time organizing! Makes me sound a little neurotic, but the constant organizing is good for me. With my "chemo brain" alive and well, I have trouble focusing and remembering things. Not to mention, this gets me out of the house. I will be returning soon, since their mountain of reserved books grows every day.

To all of my great friends and family, have a great Thanksgiving. I love the reminder of all that we have to be thankful for (and the thousands of delicious calories I'll be consuming on Thursday).

NOVEMBER 25, 2008

I went to Mark's to tell him how I felt about wanting to end things between us. It was awful. I tried the excuses Tracy and I came up with to try to make it seem like I was the one with the issues, the "I'm not ready to date" and even the "I can't punish you for Andy's mistakes," but all he did was become silent and refuse to talk to me. When he gave me back some gifts I had given him, I started to cry. He didn't want any reminders of me around.

So much for ending things easily.

FROM CARINGBRIDGE.ORG, WEDNESDAY, NOVEMBER 26, 2008 8:19 AM, CST:

Another reason to be thankful: great friends! Jason and Jessica, college friends, took me to see the new Bond movie (great movie, by the way). My date, their son Victor, spent a good portion of the movie cuddled up with me. Now that's love. He's such a peanut; how any three-month-old can spend two hours in a theater without crying is beyond me.

Heather, another great college friend, came to spend the time at chemo with me yesterday. She chatted with me and the nurse about how the process works and wanted to make sure that I was doing okay. Afterwards, we enjoyed our endless soup bowls and a little shopping for Christmas presents before heading home. What a great day with some amazing people. Again, how can I be down with all the fantastic people I have around me?

Symptoms are still the same; irregular heartbeats, the metallic taste, and the fatigue are the biggest culprits, but they are joined by more nosebleeds. Darn! Still looking forward to a great holiday weekend, and not even these symptoms will keep me from completely loving and enjoying my favorite holiday.

FROM CARINGBRIDGE.ORG, THURSDAY, DECEMBER 4, 2008 6:48 PM, CST:

What a great Thanksgiving weekend! My amazing family all went into the "office" (the back bedroom of my parents' house) and put on head-scarves to surprise me. I about cried when I saw them all come out with them on.

Chemo this week was pretty easy again. I spent the entire time on the phone with Medica arguing over yet another claim. On the bright side, not only did the time pass quickly but the claims were in my favor. Another small victory. However, I didn't get to try the Nutella cookies I'd baked and brought with me. Darn.

I also received a great early-Christmas present last night—a trip to the Orpheum to see Wicked with my Aunt Laurie. She also gave me a copy of the soundtrack to enjoy in my car. It was an incredible show and I am so lucky that my Uncle Gary gave up his ticket so I could go. I am also glad that our tickets were not amidst a huge crowd and I easily avoided the masses before and after the show (fear of infection and germs). We snuck out quickly afterwards and Gary picked us up at the door. I couldn't have asked for a better evening with my extended family.

On a sadder note, though, I have been forced to make another difficult decision regarding my leave. Since my side effects have been getting worse as the full chemo treatments progress (awful fatigue, nosebleeds, nausea, etc.) my oncologist recommended that I stay away from crowds (namely, work) until full rounds are over in late January. I have been anxious—okay, paranoid—about getting an infection or a high temp that would require a hospitalization when I return to work, and I have no sick days left to cover yet another absence. My blood counts were even lower this week, not a good sign, so with all of these factors, I've modified my leave yet again. The poor folks at my disability office, clinic, and school district are about sick of hearing from me, making so many calls to get things in order again. New D-Day: January 26, 2009. By then, I'll be out of full chemo for a week; that better be enough time to be able to return. Coincidentally, it's the first day of the second semester at work—a nice time to get back in. Here's to hoping that all goes well, with my health and approval for disability. Best to err on the positive side— all will be fine! (gulp)

DECEMBER 7, 2008

What a couple of weeks! My nosebleeds have become my "second week ritual," coming the week after a full chemo round. I got a big one on Thanksgiving that never seemed to quit. Rachel sat patiently with me and doctored me up. The fatigue this time was nothing like it was on the full chemo weeks; I could function relatively normally. My hair was growing back oddly, but my head resembled a half-furry kiwi fruit.

I could not wait to have a normal head of hair again.

I kept my friend Heather's chemo hair and post-chemo-three-months pictures close by, and they gave me hope and helped me look toward the future. The other side effects, like the metallic taste specifically, got much better the farther I got from full chemo. This all had become my "normal" way of living. To go back to where I was before all of this mess, if even just in terms of the side-effects, to feel "regular" or "normal" or like a healthy and strong woman…To feel less like a science project...*Ay, algún día...* Someday...

Last week, my counts were getting very low, which freaked me out. They had never been that low before: WBC: 5.48, RBC: 3.47, HGB: 10.9, PLT: 101. I'd been trying to bulk up on the leafy greens and red meat, just in case that actually helped, but I was paranoid that my counts would drop so low that I couldn't get back to work by my projected date.

Now I was trying to date both Mark and Justin at once. Apparently I couldn't make up my mind. I had such a great time with Justin, just being relaxed and not being judged all the time. But with Mark, there was something about him that clearly got to me every time I saw him. I knew I was opening up a dangerous can of worms. I was now tearing my heart in two, but I understood I could not give my heart to anyone if it was already left in pieces. I felt that I was cheating on both of them, but neither relationship was official. The stress was killing me!

Relax, Gwen.

I made the mistake of logging into Andy's Facebook page to see what he was up to (and no, he still hadn't changed his password, so I didn't have any problems doing so). I saw picture after picture with his arms around many young women, with a big smile on his face. There were quite a few pictures of him with a female bartender he worked with, and slowly the pieces fell into place. The long nights at work, the overnights at this female bartender's apartment, seeing the way they were smiling together.

I felt sick. Nauseated. How could he be so happy away from me? I was sick to have trusted him. I was sick to have trusted her; she was supposed to be my friend. I was sick with myself for even wanting to see where he was, and even more sick that he could still hurt me so much.

Clearly, I had some more letting go to do.

Over Thanksgiving, I picked up Mom's copy of *For One More Day* by Mitch Albom. There were two parts of the book that really affected me. One, "['Divorce'] comes from *divertere,* which means 'to divert.' All divorce does is divert you, taking you away from everything you thought you knew and everything you thought you wanted and steering you into all kinds of other stuff." This "other stuff" was happiness, inner strength, peace, and the love and appreciation for all the blessings I had.

Yeah, it made divorce sound like a *good* plan when I looked at it that way. I'd take this diversion in a heartbeat rather than stay miserable in a loveless marriage. The second part that got to me was, "Now you know how badly someone wanted you. Children forget that sometimes. They think of themselves as a burden instead of a wish granted."

After reading this, I burst into tears and went over to where Mom was sitting in the living room and held her tightly. All I could do was keep that one thought running through my head, *I was a wish granted. I am never a burden to my mom.*

For these past six months, I'd felt like a horrible burden to my family, a drain on their own lives, a wild albatross that required so much attention and care. Albom's perspective offered a great reminder that I was not the burden/drain/albatross that I envisioned myself to be. Many people saw me as a wish granted. As long as I could live my life the best way I could and always show my loved ones how much they meant to me, I would be blessed to get their love in return.

FROM CARINGBRIDGE.ORG, WEDNESDAY, DECEMBER 10, 2008 12:29 PM, CST:

Round Four of full chemo done! These infusions were the quickest of all the rounds so far, only two-and-a-half hours from start to finish. However, I spent the rest of the day on the couch. Nausea hit me harder than usual this time, and I did my best to avoid foods that made it worse. My white blood and platelet counts were good this week, but red blood and hemoglobins were low. I looked up online what to do for falling red blood and hemoglobin counts, and I hit the red meat and leafy greens as hard as I could. All the meat and greens made me nauseous, though, so Mom said I had to get creative in how I prepared them. I couldn't wait to attack the beef stew she made for me when I got home on Sunday.

Of course, rest is the other component of bringing up the counts, so I'm getting over the Catholic guilt of feeling lazy by spending so much time on the couch. Good thing my friend Angie lent me her Season 1 DVDs of Grey's Anatomy. *I'm addicted now! Good thing to sneak in between all the naps I've had in the last two days. I get in a good half an hour of house chores before I need to rest again. Even making oatmeal for breakfast takes so much out of me. It's weird to feel so out of commission; I'm usually so active and it's hard to take it down a million notches.*

I'm just grateful that I have the health I do have and for all the wonderful people that continue to support me. Even when life and/or fatigue get me down, all I have to do is remind myself of all the good things I have and what wonderful things are yet to come.

FROM CARINGBRIDGE.ORG,
MONDAY, DECEMBER 15, 2008 12:56 PM, CST:

Whew! Was that a rough week. I was really nauseated for the rest of the week, not so tired this time. I dropped five pounds in five days...good for a weight-loss plan, bad if it keeps coming off or if I don't get my appetite back. I'm getting back on track this week, still eating well when I can and avoiding anything too greasy or fatty (oh, so yummy, though...) Still queasy, but it's nothing like how I felt all last week. Thank goodness for small favors.

I'm looking forward to a quick Herceptin round this week for a few reasons: Rachel is coming with me (yea!) and no awful side effects. She and I are heading back to St. Cloud afterwards to volunteer with Mom and Victoria at the Place of Hope, a homeless shelter, making dinner. I plan to stay in the kitchen as much as I can—no germs for this one!

FROM CARINGBRIDGE.ORG
WEDNESDAY, DECEMBER 17, 2008 9:45 AM, CST:

What a humbling experience last night, making dinner at the Place of Hope. The cooking itself went smoothly (thanks to Mom and her uncanny sense of when potatoes aren't baking fast enough), but it was hard to see the people coming through the line. I was at the juice station, next to Aeron at the milk station and Rachel at the desserts, and it was hard to say that we had to limit the amount of beverages they were allowed. Clearly, the people needed as much juice and milk as we could hand out, but we were on a mission to serve as many people as we could. We ended up serving eighty-five, including second helpings and PoH staff. That, for me, embraced the true meaning of the holidays—being able to help others. I left feeling extremely grateful that I have a warm place to sleep every night, and I always have food available in my refrigerator. Every day is a blessing for me.

New–Side–Effect News Flash! (Insert cool audio effects and light show here) I knew that the Neulasta shots were to boost white blood cell counts by stimulating bone marrow to produce more cells and could cause "bone pain," but I had no idea what that would feel like. Who knew bones could hurt?! Oh, how quickly did I learn that on Monday. It is a pain that I cannot explain well, a sharp ache that feels like a stabbing that comes and goes in waves. I have it mainly in my lower back and hip bones, but I can feel it almost everywhere. It is definitely enough to make me take myself out of the TaeBo circuit for now, but I hope that it subsides relatively soon. Nosebleeds have also joined the bone pain in keeping me company. I'm such a fun little ball of side effects. In a sadistic way, it does fascinate me to record and watch. It also adds an element of surprise to my life— which side effects will I get today? The surprises never end!

DECEMBER 19, 2008

It's been another rough couple of weeks with chemos. Mark came with me last week for a full chemo treatment. It was über-awkward that morning, because as Justin was leaving from spending the night, Mark was coming over to bring me to chemo. Justin was sad that he wasn't coming with me, that another guy would accompany me instead. I couldn't blame him for running off so fast.

Mark came over bearing a $400 stand mixer, a situation that was also very awkward. Since we weren't really dating, why would he give me such an expensive gift? I tried to give it back to him, but he really wanted me to have it. "Some things you shouldn't have to wait for," he told me when I said I'd wait to get one someday. Even the chemo nurse made things more awkward by asking if he was my significant other.

The whole thing with Mark—or anyone else—probably confused me the most. I would love to be in love again, but I didn't want to screw up another relationship. Another life goal here: I will not get divorced again. I refused to figure out how to sell another wedding ring.

Yeah, *that's* a positive way to look at marriage. Clearly, someone was *not* ready to date again.

Counts this week: WBC: 6.91, RBC: 3.26, HGB: 10.4, PLT: 150. A new one that I have to watch out for: Neutrophils (NEUT). I was at 4.92 this week, and 1.80 – 7.80 is normal. Okay, so all the leafy greens/red meat weren't helping me. What's a woman gotta eat to get her counts up? I had to ask my chemo nurse Cynda what would defer me from chemo; God help me if I had to be put off schedule from finishing this crap! She said my WBC or neutrophils would have to be below 1.5 or platelets below 75. I had to realize what my body was going through, and that maintaining my counts was a huge accomplishment.

Leave it to me, the constant overachiever, to want to exceed what was "normal"! Geez, Gwen, let it go. Sometimes average or even below average would be sufficient, as long as I was trying my best.

The week after full chemo was the full week of nausea. *Nothing* sounded good, and anything that did tasted like feet afterwards. Yea, five pounds lost in five days. The side effects were sure getting worse. The bone pain was a shocker though. Thought I was able to skip that one, but December 5 through 17 was Bone Pain Central at my house.

For this week's chemo, Rachel came with me. I was the most popular person at this place! I felt so loved. Counts: WBC: 7.42 (and that's after a Neulasta shot! For $5000, I expected better results, darn it!), RBC: 3.10, HGB: 10.0, PLT: 176, NEUT: 2.67. Best to keep up on that iron intake.

I got a great rate on a mortgage, so I refinanced at 4.75% on a conventional thirty-year loan. Hurray on so many levels. First, I took a huge step all on my own—being a big girl—and negotiated all these financial dealings without the help of a husband or my father. I found the rate, contacted my mortgage broker and haggled with him on the closing costs. Then I used my large savings account—that I'd worked tirelessly to accumulate—to take care of a large portion of what I owed on this place. Second, I was paying off the second mortgage to avoid paying private mortgage insurance, leaving me with $138,000 owed on the house and, in turn, lower monthly payments. Third, I wouldn't have to worry about refinancing an adjustable rate mortgage in 2011. And fourth, Andy would be off of the mortgages, cutting my final tie to him.

Finally, I was rid of him in every way possible, well, except for what emotions I still fought to get over. I sent him an e-mail telling him about the refinance, then asking him to end all contact with me.

It was difficult to write this. I've wanted to say it for a long time, but actually coming out and saying it required all the strength I'd slowly rebuilt. I quickly hit the *enviar* (send) button, to make sure I wouldn't go back on it. It felt freeing to send it, but as soon as I did, I felt nauseated with the thought of him responding to it. I kept fearfully refreshing my inbox all afternoon, just checking on that fear. Sure enough, just after I'd lost that fear and resumed normal erratic inbox refreshing, he replied.

Why was it that we were divorced and *now* finally fighting about money? Ironic.

I now feared he would get an attorney to sue me for the money he lost. I had rationalized it out for the both of us why I kept money from his settlement, and he continued to feel I was trying to screw him out of money. I'd been more than honest with him with everything, much to my greedy-side dismay. He also liked to forget that I'd been out of work since September, had lost $20,000 in salary and had thousands of dollars in medical bills. These weren't the reasons I kept money from him, of course, but I wished he'd remember these three facts when squabbling over the money he owed me. I just didn't have patience for that crap.

Sheesh, I thought, just use your illegal unclaimed tips.

Still, if he wanted to sue me for $2500 and lose most of it in legal fees, I could always call Uncle Sam about his tips.

God, please just let him drop it without us having to exchange more checks.

In his reply, he brought up good memories that he had about us, "because the other ones hurt too much," such as Valleyfair in the rain on my birthday. But all those did were rip open my healing wounds, ones I'd earned through countless tears and hug sessions. I spent the following two days replaying the thoughts in my head, to the point of missing those moments with him too. Fortunately, I'd worked past them, and I was stitching up the cuts once again. However, I was still keeping the e-mail as proof that he'd promised he'd drop the financial questions, requests, and threats to go to a lawyer.

I'd also completely FUBARed all relationship connections with Justin and Mark. I tried so hard to keep my distance from both of them, to maintain more of a "friend" status, and that had worked well—if I did NOT hold my friends' hands or kiss them with reckless abandon. I'd drawn the line in the sand of restraint and pranced beyond it without a thought. So much for not wanting to date anyone; now I was dating two great men. I had more support, hugs, kisses, and random acts of kindness than I could handle. Actually, it was really great, in a guilty, selfish way.

Okay, so here was my rundown on each of them. Justin was wonderfully chill and relaxed, could handle my neuroses, loved movies as much as I did, and was incredibly patient—especially with knowing how I was in the past. Mark was very handy around the house, loved attending church with me, was very much into eating well and fitness, loved finance and was smart with money, and had a way of looking at me that drove me wild. Both men would throw themselves under a bus for me, would be great fathers, would stick with me through anything, and made me feel beautiful and special, even without my hair, and with nausea that kept me from having fun, constant medical updates, nosebleeds and bloody tissues, teenager-esque acne, and lumpy fake breasts with fading red scars and no nipples or areolas.

I was reading *Eat, Pray, Love* by Elizabeth Gilbert. She realized after six years of marriage and being over thirty and not wanting kids that she was painfully unhappy and wanted out of her marriage. She decided to take a year of her life to travel to Italy, India, and Indonesia to find herself and her pathway to spirituality. She realized that she was afraid to be alone and that she clung to relationships to keep from feeling lonely. During her time in Italy, she realized what she was doing wrong: "So be lonely, Liz. Learn your way around loneliness. Make a map of it. Sit with it, for once in your life. Welcome to the human experience. But never again use another person's body or emotions as a scratching post for your own unfulfilled yearnings."

I realized that I did the same sad thing. I was afraid of being lonely. I hated going to bed alone, of cooking for myself, of shopping for myself and my cat, of having no one I could rely on when days seemed impossible. But I also used other people when I was lonely, especially men. Realizing this, I began to wonder when I would change from using someone as my scratching post to just trusting and caring for someone in an honest-relationship way. When would I go from preventing loneliness to openly enjoying someone else's company without guilt? In the meantime, I needed to "let go and let God." Letting my trust lead me to Him would bring me some inner peace in the meantime. I needed to remember that, for now, I was on *my* journey, but enjoying stops with others along the way.

Random thought for the last week or so. My left eye had been twitching sporadically. Was this yet another side effect, or was I just losing my mind with the twitches?

DECEMBER 20, 2008

I found these two quotes by Gina Ogden in *Women's Health* magazine from October 2008. Both spoke volumes to me in two different ways.

"You're at your most vulnerable—body, mind, and spirit—when you're naked with a man. If you're afraid of that kind of intimacy, you're going to subconsciously avoid sex, and you certainly won't have a desire for it."

"Everyone is different, but for some, it can be very therapeutic to do things that remind you that you're alive, that reconnect you with the joys of life."

DECEMBER 21, 2008

I found out that Luis died yesterday. He was an adopted barn cat from Sheila, who lived most of his young life with my parents. (My poor parents—how we love to leave strays at their house too often.) Luis had contracted a fatal and cat-contagious disease somehow, so I made sure to leave my own little Suerte at my house. He'd looked like he was drunk, staggering around the house barely coherent, and snuggling up to anyone who'd give him the time of day. Mom "put him out of his misery" by feeding him the rest of his antibiotics the vet had prescribed.

We weren't even that close, he and I, but we were the little sickies, sharing in each other's suffering together on the couch. We'd cuddle each other, almost like enduring our hard times together. Hearing he was gone forced me back into the loneliness of my illness, no one else relating to my daily reminder of being sick. All I could pray for was that this wasn't an omen that I was next...

FROM CARINGBRIDGE.ORG, TUESDAY, DECEMBER 23, 2008 6:06 PM, CST:

What a day. Days like these remind me of why it's so difficult to work and have cancer/chemo at the same time. Thank goodness I had Rachel there to keep me in good company. I started off the appointments with a meeting with a genetic counselor regarding the results of my P53 test. (P53 is another cancer gene test of a rare type of cancer strain). Finally, I'm not in the "gray area" of results—I'm negative for this gene. Who hoo! What that means to me now isn't much. I have one of three possibilities: 1) My variant of my BRCA 1 (breast cancer gene 1) may be a cancer-causing strain, but they aren't sure, with the limited information the doctors have on the gene; 2) I may have a cancer-causing mutation of a yet-to-be-identified-or-named BRCA "3;" or 3) the cancer I have could have been completely sporadic, a "freak of nature." I'm hoping for option three, as it will create less risk or pressure on my mom or sisters. That is the last thing I'd want: to scare my family into fear of increased risk of experiencing for themselves my infiltrating ductal carcinoma. All of these options have nothing to do with treating my current cancer, and there isn't increased risk of ovarian cancer yet either. Whew, more good news.

I also had my second MUGA (heart activity) scan at Mercy after the genetic counseling. I'll get those results next week at my check-up appointment with Dr. Garino.

Finally, I had Herceptin treatment #12. Hard to imagine that I'm already this far in, and I focus on that rather than think of the forty I have left. My blood counts are "very good for a chemo patient," according to Jenny, my chemo nurse today. All the nurses in the office also loved my sassy little black wig I flaunted there today, at first not recognizing who I was. It is a cross between Elvis Presley (according to Vic) and Pat Benetar (according to me). All I know is that I feel like singing "Hit Me With Your Best Shot" every time I wear it.

My nephews Alec and Luke aren't as positive. "Take off your black hair, Gwenna!"

Not everyone is a fan of the black, I guess.

Another Christmas Eve at "Hurricane Rosha" tomorrow, filled with delicious delicacies, carefully-wrapped presents under the small tree atop a small table, and rowdy and sleep-disrupting games of Pit and trivia. My parents' house struggles to accommodate all twenty-two of us, but we wouldn't want it any other way. To be with all of the hugs and memories to be made makes for a wonderful holiday.

Merry Christmas to everyone who has followed me through the last six months of mayhem. You are my blessings, my strength, and my happiness. Thank you for being in my life. You are in my prayers for an enjoyable, safe, and healthy holiday break.

DECEMBER 23, 2008

My counts for the chemo today: WBC: 11.31, RBC: 3.31, HGB: 10.8, PLT: 110, NEUT: 7.78 Not bad, eh?

Another freak-out from my genetic counseling appointment today. My BRCA 1 variant indicated that I was not at a huge risk of ovarian cancer right now. However, the risk could grow with time. At thirty, I would have a zero percent risk. At forty, a three percent chance. At fifty, it grew to twenty-one percent. Through the years, I could get a CA-125 screening and ultrasounds for precautions, but if I ovulated again someday, ultrasound exams might give me some false positives. Again, best not to add more freak-out risk with my mom and sisters; they'd already need additional breast cancer screenings from now on. Mom and my sisters over thirty should consider MRIs, and sisters under thirty should consider mammograms or MRIs (if requested). Denise, my new genetic counselor, offered her help in getting my family scheduled for MRIs if they'd want them, if their primary care physicians weren't willing to give them a referral for one. She seemed very knowledgeable and helpful, especially since this was our first meeting since she "adopted" me from Jessica Greenberg.

My nose ran—another chemo side effect. My toe hurt—a

chemo side effect. My weight gain—another side effect. Cracking, dry hands—yet again. Trying to determine what was a true side effect and what wasn't had become a constant pull on my sanity. I didn't need to pull the "I have cancer" excuse on myself to gain sympathy, but it would be nice to have that clarity.

Finally completed another book to add to my 2008 reading list: *I Am Not My Breast Cancer,* thanks to the Hennepin County Library. I saw reading this book as a pseudo-support group that I needed to attend, relating to so many other breast cancer survivors. It was my introvert/antisocial way of bonding with others. The book really frustrated me again in a few ways, even to the point of tears. First was the thought of having kids. Funny how once you've decided that you want kids, that is when you find out that they may never be possible—*ever.* I had no idea that having kids would increase my risk of recurrence. The elevated estrogen levels when pregnant increase the risk. Oh, great. Now I would be forced to be selfish in any child-bearing decision that I made. Would I be selfish and make my own health as my number-one priority and avoid the extra estrogen (but never have my own kids)? Or would I be selfish in wanting to have my own children, only to leave them behind at a young age? And to make it all the more difficult, I might never even have to make these decisions if my fertility didn't come back.

This didn't even resemble *fair.* Hadn't I already been through enough? Why should I have to lose this too? Why couldn't my reward for all this cancer crap just be to hold my baby without the fear of leaving him/her?

The children concern brought up another fear from reading *I Am Not My Breast Cancer:* my mortality. Even with constant cancer reminders in every moment of my daily life, I never thought of an early death from BC as an option for me. Darn it, I refused to let go of life. That was the one refusal I'd make while accepting cancer. Denial, perhaps? Sure, but I'd live in that denial without guilt. This was just a large bump in the loooong road of my life.

A few questions that *I Am Not My Breast Cancer* brought up for me: *metastasis and bone mets.* So many women mentioned those; what the F were they?! Using the American Cancer Society website, I learned that a metastasis is a recurrence of cancer. They came in three varieties: a local metastasis: my cancer recurring in the original cancer site; a regional recurrence in the vicinity of my original cancer (such as, for me, the lymph nodes); a distant/ metastatic recurrence: anything further out than the breast or, for me, lymph nodes. That was where bone metastasis (bone mets) came in—if my breast cancer would spread to bones. Knock on wood, no worries for me on that!

Relationship update: I was leaning toward having a relationship with Mark. (It was frustrating to constantly pull and push myself toward and away from these two. I had way too much time alone with my thoughts, so I blamed that for my constant fluctuation. That, or the chemo. I could always blame it on the chemo.) He'd been so patient and wonderful these past few weeks, giving me all the time and space I needed. I felt so much more comfortable in my own skin, leaving me able to enjoy the time I spent with him. With every step I took towards him, I felt less like "jumping ship" and running far, far away. Much to Tracy's concern about him stalking me, since he was calling me and stopping over unannounced, he was making me feel great about myself. He was so incredible with Syd and Haley when we went ice skating, even playing Twister with them afterwards. He met Manda and Vic, and then worked on a puzzle with Mom in the kitchen. All of them really seemed to like him, though so many sisters were still on "Team Justin." Just as Justin said his relationship with his ex seemed "comfortable," that was what he seemed like to me. He was incredible, a great partner match for my personality, but it became impossible to have a relationship with him when my heart was elsewhere.

I also closed on my mortgage refinance! What a huge accomplishment for me, making a $30,000 payment and still having $25,000 in the bank. Was I a big girl or what? Yea me!

FROM CARINGBRIDGE.ORG, WEDNESDAY, DECEMBER 31, 2008 6:48 AM, CST:

Great news! I was approved for LTD until the end of January. What a relief knowing that I will get back some of the lost wages. I felt like a "big girl" again, being able to deposit money into my account.

Full Chemo Round #5 completed. It feels amazing to know that I have only one left. Who hoo! It was also an appointment with Dr. Garino that answered so many questions for me.

One, I will definitely not need radiation, due to my small tumor size, clear margins around tumor site (after mastectomy), and no involved lymph nodes.

Two, my hair will start to regrow six to eight weeks after the last full treatment on January 19.

Three, my MUGA results were excellent at seventy-five percent, up from seventy-three percent from the first scan. Garino also told me that if I were to show signs of congenital heart failure, it would happen in the first three to six months of Herceptin....I'm in the clear!

Four, my chance for metastasis (recurrence) is very low. I am doing chemo to get rid of any cancer that bypassed my lymph nodes, but if it were to occur (God help me) it would likely show up first in my bones, lungs, lymph nodes, skin, or liver.

Five, after full chemo is over, my cancer screenings will include a physical and blood counts every three months, in which they will also check my bone density and ovulation. No more mammograms for me. Now, that alone is something to celebrate, and anyone who has already had the pleasure of one, you know exactly what I'm talking about. I shouldn't need MRIs, CAT or PET scans often either, unless my body is in pain later on in life, causing me to need additional screenings.

Six, I can begin the last phase of my chemo, an estrogen-receptor-blocker hormone treatment pill called Tamoxifen, a month after my full rounds are over. I thought I would have to wait until I was done with Herceptin to begin, and that's about a year and a half from now. Since I'll be on Tamoxifen for five years, I'm elated to get that started and out of the way.

Garino said there have been many studies in the last ten years with BC patients and pregnancy showing there aren't the risks that

I had feared, so I won't have to concern myself with any future problems. Thank God for the relief of my fear. Even after I fought so hard to conquer cancer, I thought that I had lost what I now hold so close to my heart. Even if kids aren't on the horizon now, it is so good and comforting to know that they aren't a lost cause.

Side effect-wise, I'm doing okay right now. I'm tired, probably since I couldn't fall asleep until one A.M. I was feeling nauseous from the treatment and steroids, and falling asleep in that pain scared me into staying up longer. I tried that once, and I was up every fifteen minutes.

I was really hoping to ring in 2009 with a glass of champagne to celebrate—the end of a rough year and the promise of better days ahead—but I will abstain from alcohol for a while. Any thought of liquor of any kind makes me sick to my stomach. I'll be pleasantly content just being home, being warm in front of the fireplace with Suerte, maybe being with friends for a few minutes, being enthralled in a great book, being engrossed with refreshing the page for my watched auctions on eBay, being eternally grateful for all that I have, being alive.

Happy 2009 to all of my fantabulous family and friends! Enjoy a safe and memorable night, beginning your new year in good spirits and looking ahead to great times.

DECEMBER 31, 2008

Chemo #5! Counts: WBC: 12.08, RBC: 3.22, HGB: 10.6, PLT: 140, NEUT: 11.16. Cynda asked me about the cute guy with me. (It was Justin.) He was looking pretty darn cute. We played some cards and had a movie marathon that night, and he stayed up until one in the morning with me, since I was afraid to sleep from my nausea. I felt awful that he had to drive to Litchfield for work the next morning.

Garino's Q&A session with me helped a ton, and I was so grateful that I came to the appointment armed with a million questions. She eased my deep fears of future pregnancy woes; a pregnancy with all its hormones would *not* cause a recurrence! What a relief. There would be nothing like holding a little one in my arms someday. Sure, my cat was cuddly, but she wasn't a baby. I looked forward most to the hair regrowth that should start six weeks after full chemos end. To feel like a real woman again should become complete with my own hair back on my head. I expected to feel like a teenager again when my periods restart, three to six months after chemo. I also hoped to keep up the hemoglobin levels, because if they dipped below 9.5, I might need transfusions or Procrit injections to bring them back up.

What a day of information overload.

Hurray on the approval for LTD. Oh, joys and hurray! Even better, along with the approval letter was a check for my late December—January 26 leave salary (for $4200!) Oh, to have money coming in again. Hopefully, this also meant I would have my sick leave bank money on the way now. Ardith was right; best to err on the positive side of things.

Well, it's the official end of this year. I remembered well back to the day when Carrie and I were thinking, "Won't it be great to look back on 2008 someday and think, 'Wasn't that a crap year?'"

I felt that more than ever today. I'd been through so many twists and turns, bumps and bruises, smiles and laughs, hugs and tears that the lower level of drama that 2009 might bring would be well-worth the stress I'd been through. I looked forward to seeing what my new "normal" might look like, to regaining my "real" life and growing ever stronger with each passing day.

I could barely remember what life before cancer was like, but I did remember that I was sad and weak emotionally. I'd learned so much about what life should be like, full of happiness and love, despite all that life throws at us. Even without hair, with fake boobs and teenager acne/nausea/constant unsolicited cancer updates, men could see past all that and find me beautiful. I was so much stronger than I thought I ever could be, facing the Big C and the Big D simultaneously. I was surrounded by many people who cared about me—family and great friends—that I would never have to feel alone, even if I was single. I'd learned that being a great daughter/sister/aunt/friend meant more to me than ever, and I refused to let go of trying to show them how much they meant to me. I'd learned to focus on what *really* mattered in life: LOVE. Without love, life was meaningless. Love made every waking moment worthwhile.

I learned that I'd settled for far less than I deserved in my love life, and I eagerly awaited finding a real, true love and partner someday. I learned to focus on *me* again, thinking about *my* happiness and future, and realizing that the insanely strong, driven, and optimistic Gwen was still there, just waiting to be rediscovered.

Here's to an alcohol-free New Year's Eve and to the beginning of all the wonders that are to come. God be praised for all the blessings in my life!

FROM CARINGBRIDGE.ORG, FRIDAY, JANUARY 2, 2009 4:39 PM, CST:

Happy New Year! I pray that everyone's night brought fun for all and brought you home safely. I spent a quiet night at Tracy's and had a great time without having drinks. See, Gwen? It is possible! Kidding...

Wish I could report that the side effects are a thing of the past, but I'd be lying. The nausea is pretty awful this week, and I feel the bone pain coming back already, too. I am so glad that I can curl up on the couch and enjoy just being there. Suerte is keeping me great company through it all. This may not be the most pleasant way to ring in the new year, but the thought of being done with all this monkey business by this time next year makes me let go of the frustration of today. Thank goodness I'm almost done!

JANUARY 4, 2009

The start of a new year. It was difficult to be joyous with the gift of each breaking morning (for which I was grateful, every day) and not to rush through them like a horse blazing across the finish line. I desperately wanted this whole episode in my life to be over. I was sick and tired of being sick and tired. For once, I was just going to be honest with myself and complain about life for a while.

This whole week post-full-chemo had been awful. I'd been so nauseated for six days and the end wasn't really in sight. All I wanted to do was curl up on the couch and watch TV or sleep, but I couldn't even do that. I couldn't tolerate the combination of being sick in any position I sat/lay in and going stir-crazy from being cooped up in my house. Then when I was finally in a comfortable spot, I felt too hot, then too cold.

I went to Victor's baptism this morning, but I was too sick to stay long. I was so sick that I felt like a social puddle when I tried to see friends. Carrie also moved in today, hoping to "take a break" from her marriage. Glad I was dealing only with side effects rather than that. Side effects go away; bad marriages are harder to fix. Yep, I'd rather be me right now.

I had dinner plans with Mark before church tonight, and we'd planned on making it together. Since I'd prepped a lot of the food at home beforehand, I was ten minutes late getting to his house. He'd just started working out when I got there, so I made dinner alone.

Okay, no big deal.

Then his friends he'd invited to church came over during dinner and he talked only to them.

Okay, no big deal.

Then he chatted with them throughout church and ignored me.

Okay, now I was frustrated.

Finally, after church, the truth came out: that he felt I wasn't putting enough into our relationship anymore.

Okay, forget this. I went home.

When I got home, I talked briefly to Carrie, and then decided that I did need to keep trying harder, so I drove back to his house. I was going to give it a shot.

But was I making the right decision?

It certainly felt right sleeping in his arms that night.

FROM CARINGBRIDGE.ORG, MONDAY, JANUARY 5, 2009 11:18 AM, CST:

Praise Pepto-Bismol! The worst of the nausea is finally over. Finally I am back to feeling relatively "normal," or at least not feeling ready to vomit at any given moment. I'm even ready to try basic, non-cardio exercise today, after a five-day hiatus, just because I feel the need to be as "normal" as I can manage. (Side note to readers on the Pepto: before you throw the bottle into your bag to leave the house, please make sure the cap is screwed on tight. Some of us learn these lessons the hard way.)

Still can't eat much. Don't get me wrong, I am still eating small meals throughout the day, but the types and kinds of foods allowed by my stomach and nasal passages is slim to none. For example, my "breakfast" today was acorn squash, dried-out leftover turkey, and an English muffin with a smear of PBJ. All the delicious leftovers that I prepared as meals make me sick to my stomach, although only a week ago they were wonderful. Anyone up for Mediterranean Couscous or Wild Rice with Venison? Stop by my house! I am still grateful that I have food to eat, even if I don't want to eat it, and I am proud to have made it unscathed through one more tough round of chemo.

Happy First Day Back to Work to all my teaching friends! I'll be there to bug you soon enough.

JANUARY 5, 2009

I spent a fun night with Justin in Willmar, although I tried to keep it more platonic. We cooked dinner and had a Clue tournament. Okay, so when I was *with* one guy, it was harder to make decisions in the other's favor. Couldn't I just morph them into one perfect guy, or would I be stuck with the "bad" parts of the combo?

Dating continued to frustrate me.

FROM CARINGBRIDGE.ORG,
TUESDAY, JANUARY 6, 2009 4:08 PM, CST:

Whoa. Talk about a rude awakening today at chemo. I got my normal blood count test, but the results stopped me in my tracks. My whites were at 3.03, normal is 4.3–10.8. I haven't been below 7 at any point this far in the treatment, and after a Neulasta shot last week, I expected them to be over 10 this week. Even scarier were my neutrophil (a type of white blood cell, more info on neutrophils: http://en.wikipedia.org/wiki/Neutrophil) counts: 0.99, normal is 1.8–7.8. I was warned about this count—if it dips below 1.5, I will be deferred from full chemo until the counts are back up. I have my return-to-work date already set with the stipulation of being done with full chemo by then, and I don't want to even think about pushing that date back yet again. Oh, please let that count come back up by next week!

I asked a nurse if I could still go home to my parents' house today, and she asked if anyone was sick and how many people go in and out of there in a day. I started to cry, knowing that multitudes of people passing through the Roshas' door have been battling the flu. It's been two weeks since I felt good enough to go home, and I was so excited to finally go home again. Jenny the nurse gave me facemasks and said that not going would decrease my quality of life, and I need that to be higher than ever right now. She said just to wear the masks, avoid seeing people that are openly sick, and wash my hands constantly. Happy with that thought, I'm taking it easy at home tonight, going home in the morning armed with masks, soap, and hand sanitizer.

Red counts were low but decent, and hemoglobin was actually right in the normal range, abnormally high for me. Yay, finally all the iron I've been ingesting is paying off!

I also had a check-in with Dr. Harrington this morning about my final reconstructive surgery. I'm scheduled for the hour-long procedure on March 3 at 7:30 in the morning. Not the way I'd prefer to spend my spring break, but I'll take it just to be done with another step. By next fall, I'll be done healing and finishing up all the details with her. Another yay! Another note for readers: if you're bored, have a good time online researching saline v. silicone implants. You'll find a ton of info out there to keep you busy.

So many steps closer to being done. Another productive day in Gwen's life.

JANUARY 6, 2009

Harrington decided this morning that I didn't need any more expanding, that my full Cs will be great for my surgery in March. After my research, I decided on silicone implants rather than saline, and Nurse Kim concurred. She said they look and feel more natural, and if they rupture, they're now made more solid, like a "gummy bear." I was glad to know that modern technology has made silicone implants more durable and less of a health risk. I was also on a "Ninety-Day Warranty" with them for rechecks and revisions after the one-hour surgery. Bits of my mastectomy scars would go to pathology, just to make sure I was still cancer-free. I'd get my nipples in the summer and my tattooed areolas in the fall.

Sheesh, when can I finally get comfortably naked again?

JANUARY 9, 2009

I decided that I needed some good chatting time with Carrie, but I offered to Mark that he could stop over. He assumed I meant he could spend the night, and didn't catch my "stopping by" part of the offer. He seemed upset that I wanted my girl time, but all I felt was that I was being smothered. I was peeved by him not understanding why I felt the need to be there for my friends who were there for me. I felt frustrated from spreading myself too thin.

Even Justin was disappointed that I spent the time with Carrie and that I wasn't coming to Willmar sooner, but he understood that I needed my time to talk with her. Now *that's* what I hoped for—understanding.

I drove up late Friday night, spent Saturday with another *Clue* tournament and too much beer, and we ended up having more fun than I'd planned on. Maybe it was just that, or just an enjoyable weekend with him, but I finally felt my wall-of-keeping-my-distance crumble. What's the worst that could happen if we dated? We'd break up? The best thing, we'd be happy? Hmm.

JANUARY 12, 2009

Mark wanted to make me dinner tonight, so I decided this would be a good time to tell him that I needed real space. He slammed his wine (rare for him to even be drinking) and he seemed to want me to leave. I mentioned that to him, and he countered that he wanted me in his arms, to share his life with me. Seeing how hard he was trying (and even after making me chocolate-covered strawberries using the contraband *microwave)*, my plan to stay strong was wavering. I did leave, and e-mailed him the next morning to tell him that I was staying strong even if it was tough.

Even if he seemed wonderful sometimes, we were just too darn different. ("Round peg in a square hole" was a perfect description of us.) I might like that round peg, but I just couldn't make myself into a round hole so we'd be a good fit. I first needed to figure out what shape I was, all by myself.

FROM CARINGBRIDGE.ORG, THURSDAY, JANUARY 15, 2009 7:55 PM, CST:

Hurray for Neulasta shots! My counts at chemo this week were back to a great level for me to get my full round on Monday. My WBCs were at 9, and my neutrophils were at 7, much higher than they needed to be for chemo. It was also great to be done with the surgical masks in public, enjoyed thoroughly at dinner tonight with the ESL crowd from Northdale Middle School. [Note: if anyone is up for amazing Mediterranean/Greek food, check out Big Marina Grill and Deli in Columbia Heights: http://www.twincitiesfun.com/Big-Marina-Grill-and-Deli-ID002443.html]

I am more than ready, excited actually, to be done with my last full round. Full treatments of chemotherapy—the Taxotere and Carboplatin—will finally be gone, but certainly not forgotten, but it was a great step to be cancer-free and moving on with my life. Bring on the pixie cuts, the nights of being able to enjoy a glass of red wine, of feeling "normal" and returning to work!

What I will honestly miss, though, is the time I was blessed to spend with my family. This week was the last time I'll be able to visit them for a few days during the week, at least until surgery in March. In the last seven months, I got to spend more time with them than I have in the last four years. I went from being the aunt that my young nephews didn't recognize when I came over (and they actually cried when I went to greet them) to Cool Aunt Gwen that baked cookies with them, made dinner, or played "Rock-a-Bye Petey/Luke." I learned what it was like to feel truly loved and supported by all of my family members and to truly love and support them back with all my heart. Cancer was definitely not a gift, but these "side effects" were a great experience. It was bittersweet leaving home today, knowing I'm finally at the end of this awful treatment, but also at the end of all the extra quality time with my mom, dad, sisters, brothers-in-law, nieces, and nephews.

However...

Here's to a happy beginning to the rest of my life!

FROM CARINGBRIDGE.ORG, THURSDAY, JANUARY 15, 2009 9:39 PM, CST:

Before the chemo brain kicks in again, I'm taking advantage of a brief moment of clarity and updating the side effects status too...

I feel pretty darn good this week—no nausea, but I'm tired often and I have some burning in my stomach (but the Mediterranean buffet had nothing to do with it!) I'm also proud of my avoidance of one common side effect: I have not lost my eyelashes! *knock on wood* My random head-hair scraggles have been hard enough to deal with, but losing my eyelashes would have been the hot fudge on my cancer sundae. Thank goodness for small favors, right? I'll take what I can get!

One last thought. Keep repeating my mantra, "Spring is coming, spring is coming...!"

JANUARY 13-15, 2009

The Final Trip at home. I spent the days helping Mom clean out her closet (literally) and enjoyed my final coffee and Petey-time before leaving Thursday afternoon. I couldn't be more grateful to have all these months with my family, but I was also grateful for my future return to work and "normalcy." I felt blessed to have rediscovered my family connections, to feel so loved and supported, to realize how truly lucky I was with my life. There wasn't a luckier girl out there, even with all my hard times. Hurray for a great future ahead...

JANUARY 16, 2009

Justin came to Maple Grove for the weekend. I invited Tracy and Jason over for soup, beers, and board games. Jason had been having a hard time finding a job and the stress was hurting them both. We all had a great night with snacks and games, but waaay too much beer. We all needed a night of relaxation like this. I felt sick that night, though, and it continued on to Saturday. I spent the day vomiting constantly, with my skin sore to the touch, and with explosive diarrhea. Poor Justin had to spend an awful day with me. He was very sweet and went on a Gatorade/McDonald's run for me. Finally, Sunday brought salvation. I went to church in the morning, even felt good enough for a Mall of America trip that afternoon before heading to Rachel and Dan's for dinner. Finally, a weekend resembling "normal" again!

While at Rachel and Dan's, Mark called and wanted me to go to church with him. I called him back, saying I'd already been to church and now I was making dinner with my sister before heading back to my house to meet Kathryn. He called back again, asking if something was wrong, and I said no. (True) He called *again* to say all he wanted for his birthday was for me to attend church with him, to ask Kathryn to just let herself into my house and wait for me to get back.

The last time he called, I didn't even answer the phone. It was feeling a little obsessive, but really, I was bringing it upon myself. I'd been giving him so many mixed signals that I'd be confused too.

In the meantime, I upset Justin too. He'd overheard me say I went to church, and that now I was at Rachel and Dan's, but I'd failed to mention that I was with him. In trying not to hurt Mark's feelings, now I'd hurt Justin's. I ended up showing him my Gwen/Justin journal and how I'd said that I wasn't afraid of moving in together with him. I tried to show him that I really cared about him, that I was moving along in my apprehensions, and it seemed to work well. He left in the morning.

I was happy to see him leave so I could have my sister-time with Kathryn. Had I known that more bad news and times were about to come, maybe I'd have felt differently...?

JANUARY 19, 2009

I wore my new "Warriors" panties from Victoria's Secret to my final full chemo, ready to kick some Taxotere/Carboplatin ass. I was on top of the sunny world, so glad to be heading to the end of my Chemo Era, to finally move on with my life. Then they took my counts. WBC: 8.45 (great), RBC: 2.97 (decent), HGB: 10.1 (good), NEUT: 6.62 (great), PLT: 72. Uh oh.

FROM CARINGBRIDGE.ORG, MONDAY, JANUARY 19, 2009 12:26 PM, CST:

Here's what's on my mind: *@#%!@&$!

Here's why: I was deferred from my last full chemo round this morning. I was so careful to keep my counts up, but my platelets dropped to 72; I need 75 to get full chemo. If I did try for the chemo, my risk of internal bleeding is increased and I could actually die from not being able to clot like I should, due to low platelets. My oncologist was paged and she held me off for a week, until the counts can be redrawn and hopefully rise high enough by then. I was able to finagle another blood draw for this Thursday, hoping that I can get the darn counts up by the three measly points and get the Taxotere and Carboplatin. If that fails, I will try again on Friday. If that fails, I have to wait until early next week and try again.

Cynda had overheard me mention to Kathryn my drunken

antics from the past weekend, and said that it must have been too much for me. She paged Garino, who deferred me (held me off) for a whole week. GD! F! S! SoB! WHAT?! *Deferred?!* For three measly points? I still got Herceptin 16. Whoop-de-doo. All I could do was feel awful for being so stupid on Friday, and I cried like a baby. On the brink of freedom, only to see it slip right through my fingers. Oh, please God.

I promised Him that I'd quit smoking if he could get me my full chemo on Thursday. *And I meant it.*

Now, I have contacted my school, will contact the district office to let them to know I can't come back for another week, try to keep my sub for another week, reapply for LTD and try to extend the leave, kick myself for not keeping up my counts, feel bad and awful for a good while, then move on. I hate thinking that I'm letting so many people down—work, family, and myself. The chemo nurse (and Kathryn, who came with me this morning) told me that there was nothing I could do to keep them up, nor is there anything I can do to bring them back up (that was confirmed by an extensive Google search), so I am just letting myself feel bad for now, then I'm quickly back on to fighting off the negative feelings and trying to rest up enough for the platelets to "do their thing."

Here's the new (and hopefully last) D-Day for returning to work: February 2, 2009.

Here's what I'm NOT going to do: keep complaining, have a beer to calm my nerves, wallow in self-pity, put off more paperwork, eat a grotesque amount of chocolate or ice cream, or keep wondering, What if...?

Here's to praying for the best for the week to come. Thank you to everyone who is thinking about me or saying a little prayer for the best. You are my strength!

Mark came over when I got home with a *Congratulations!* balloon and candy for me (and on his birthday, making me feel even more awful for not making that a bigger deal for him). I had to tell him to hold the congrats, and he gave me a big hug. He'd also included a soundtrack from the movie *Fireproof* and two versions of the letter he'd written for me. The first was short and sweet, yet hurt a little. He said he wasn't a DVD player where I could push "play" and "pause," so he was giving me my space. He said that he loved me, and goodbye.

The second was a list of why he liked me, how much I meant to him, that he got a state reffing job, that this was where inspiring me ended for him; he loved me, and goodbye.

I'd made Mark cookies to bring to him at work, but first, I talked to Kathryn. She admitted to me that she saw me as a person who needed to have someone in my life, and I cried again, telling her how I used to be that person, but now I really *didn't* want anyone. I needed this time to deal with my own life, not to add more stress with dating. I had made up my mind after dealing with Andy's leaving me that I didn't want to date and complicate my life.

But, of course, when you stop looking for something... Time to put my faith back in God. I needed to put my strength where it would bring me peace—my family, God, work, my friends.

Lord, please give me strength.

The best part of this day came when I got to go back home

again! Embarrassing to go into the snowy ditch across the road from my parents' house (while I was texting), but oh so peaceful to be around my parents for another time while on leave. I needed to get my lesson plans together again. "Back to work" mode, whether I was there or not. *I needed to feel normal again.* Please let it be soon. Lord, please give me strength.

JANUARY 22, 2009

Sitting here so *impatiently* at the cancer center. 9:16 A.M. For the last four days, I've avoided bad food, caffeine, alcohol, and got plenty of rest and exercise to bring up my counts. Not that any of these were supposed to actually help, but I continued hoping. I was desperate. I'd also been praying nonstop, asking God for any extra points I'd earned. He must know I was serious about wanting to be done if I was willing to quit smoking cold-turkey. As much as I'd love to quit and never light up again, actually quitting would be tough. Even in the back of my mind, I kept imagining vignettes of me sneaking one outside, but I honestly promised to keep at it. Really, it was all for my better health, so I was being selfish even making deals with God. Again, I was a desperate woman.

There was not much I wouldn't do if I was desperate.

Needle attached to the port, counts almost ready...

FROM CARINGBRIDGE.ORG, T HURSDAY, JANUARY 22, 2009 12:49 PM, CST:

Gasp...

Platelets were at 156! (I feel like Elle Woods announcing her

LSAT scores. I was able to get the FINAL Taxotere/ Carboplatin infusions this morning. Don't know how I doubled the platelet count in four days, but I'll take it happily. I tried everything from being overly-hydrated, eating nothing but salads and oatmeal, skipping coffee (ouch!), soda (darn!) and alcohol (no biggie). My friend Heather also told me that she'd heard that running up and down stairs beforehand might bring them up too, so I was up über-early at 5:30 this morning for a good healthy dose of Tae Bo. A ton of prayers and a bargain with God may not have hurt either. Whatever the case, I screamed in Chemo Room Two loudly enough for all the nurses to hear the commotion and congratulate me on reaching the end.

I also realized that I have been waiting for this day since Election Day, the day I lost my hair. That was the turning point for me in the cancer race, the moment that the sickness was staring me in the face. I've been waiting to be done so I can regrow my hair, to have that constant reminder of chemo disappear and finally begin to feel "normal" again. Well, in six to eight weeks, I can blow the dust off the "nice shampoo" that I had stored away since October and enjoy whatever hair color or texture I'm given.

Free at last! Free at last! I can now use the lesson plans that I have drafted for February 2 and take the first step back into the working world.

Muchísimas gracias to everyone for all the notes and prayers on Caring Bridge, Hotmail, and Facebook that I've received over the last week. I don't know how I would have gotten through this stress without all the great support. You are the best family and friends that a girl could ask for. We did it!

Now, bring on the nausea. Darn it, I'm ready!

Official counts: WBC: 10.13, RBC: 3.07, HGB: 10.5, PLT: 156, NEUT: 8.93. Oh, the joy of finally being at the awful finish line! So many beautiful things to look forward to, so many memories to banish. Lord, thank you for my strength.

Side note, completely random: I e-mailed Mark last night to say thanks for the balloons, that I hoped he'd had a good birthday evening, and to say congrats on his state reffing job. I must be having Mark withdrawals. I had a hard time not calling him Tuesday night. No wonder the man's confused.

Kath and I also talked yesterday morning. She'd taken notes on what she wanted to say too, always the great student. The teacher in me was so proud. She said that the only feelings she was concerned about were mine, no boy's, and she was only here to support me. "If any man wants to be with you, he'd better be ready to be treated like a DVD player."

I love my sister. Such a great feeling to have that constant love and support. I just hope I can show my family that I'm okay without a guy in my life, that even alone, I'm strong and capable of taking care of myself. I've done it before, and if I can make it through chemo, I *can* do it again!

How ironic that Irene Cara's "What a Feeling" popped up right then on my iPod.

FROM CARINGBRIDGE.ORG, FRIDAY, JANUARY 23, 2009 1:09 PM, CST:

Day One Post-Full-Chemo! Man, was I tired this morning. I slept in until 10:00, pretty rare for me nowadays. I'm still feeling good enough to eat, though many foods are already not sounding very tasty. My highlight so far today was giving myself my first intramuscular injection of Neulasta. Figured that it was about time to try it myself, so I YouTubed some videos, took some deep, cleansing breaths, and did it as quickly as I could. For years, I've detested the sight of needles, especially needles going into my body, so what great steps for me! First I watched the needle going into my port yesterday, and now I'm giving myself shots. What's next, performing my own implant surgery? Kidding.

The nausea is coming, but I'm welcoming it with the thought of being done. But I will still have a great weekend. I'm going to stop out to dinner with some fabulous Costa Rica alums tonight, then enjoy the January/February Birthdays Celebration at the Rosha House on Sunday.

Enjoy your time too, and try to keep warm! It's a great time to stay indoors and enjoy a movie marathon.

JANUARY 23, 2009

What a mixture of emotions. First, I was *so* excited to be done with my full rounds of chemo, to be done with this chapter of my life. To know this was *finally* over, to know that this illness was finally moving on, really helped me to be ready to step forward with my life. I'd been at this awful stalemate, just *waiting* to move on with my life. Never before had I waited for life to keep moving; I'd made my own trail and blazed along. I hated having this awful outside force keeping me back, keeping me from making my own decisions and being who I wanted to be. However, this outside force had brought a new level of patience to my life. I'd learned that not everything had to happen all at once, that sometimes the best life had to offer came when you're waiting for other things to happen. I couldn't have been luckier to have these uninterrupted months with my family. To return to where I'm most loved and comfortable brought me closer than I'd ever have experienced otherwise. I couldn't be sad about losing the years with my family since I'd been given something so much better. I felt then and still do today so eternally blessed to have such great people in my life. I'm such a lucky woman.

On the flipside, the nausea officially started again. I was also *very* cold sitting around my house today, compounded by my lack of activity. My boredom with sitting around (not much to do when it was six degrees outside and I was sick to my stomach) kept me smoking too, cardinal sin number one when I'd promised the Big Guy that I'd quit. I resolved to force myself to smoke through this pack, get even sicker to my stomach than I already was, then *not* buy any more.

Well, at least, I knew I was strong enough to do it. Now I just had to show myself.

My nails began to bother me more and more. My toenails didn't bug me as much, since they were always covered, but they were brittle and breaking, surrounded by dry, flaky skin, exfoliating the other day! *Yuck!*

My fingernails were also brittle and discolored. The top half appeared yellow, filled with vertical, dry-looking lines, ready to crack. My left pinkie nail had broken off to the quick and continued to disappear. It was still breaking off, and I just waited for it to fall off. Yuck again! The lumpy, bumpy, breaking nails would soon grow out, just like the hair stubble I daydreamed of.

Being this sick, I was happy to pack up all my crap and crash at Mom and Dad's for the weekend, if not longer. I was excited to cram in all the family time too.

FROM CARINGBRIDGE.ORG, MONDAY, JANUARY 26, 2009 8:37 AM, CST:

Oh, so sleepy! No normal person can pass out on the loveseat in the middle of the Rosha living room during a Sunday birthday gathering. Of course, yesterday, I was that person. I haven't been this tired since starting the entire chemo run. I am awake for an hour or so before needing a nap again. Forget sleeping in my bed, I've taken to couches "just to rest my eyes," but I wake up there hours later.

The side effects continue to amuse me. I wake up with no idea of what today will bring, so I enjoy noting which ones come and go. I am grateful that the nausea isn't as bad this round—knock on wood—but food still doesn't sound good to me. I am totally enjoying the McDonald's runs, knowing full well that this is one of the rare times in life that I can eat there every day if I want and get away with it. I could eat their cheeseburgers for breakfast, lunch, and dinner.

One week until work! I have my plans ready for Monday, and I'm enjoying the last week of "sick-person schedule" to its fullest. Now, if I could only make it a good thirty degrees warmer outside too...

JANUARY 26, 2009

One word: sleepy. I felt awake for about an hour before needing to nap again. I tried a half-hour of Tae Bo this morning, and it was darn near *impossible* for me to finish! Sheesh, thirty minutes and I was done? I *must* be tired. I was awfully sleepy at Mom and Dad's yesterday too. I couldn't have got enough of the "osmosis" of family time, though. I could have sat there all day "resting my eyes," just absorbing all the voices and sounds. I had invited Justin to stop by (because I felt bad that I'd backed out on our Willmar plans the day before), but I tried to warn him I'd be sleepy. I appreciated that he came and drove all that way to hang out, but I really wish he hadn't come. Not only was I a crappy host, it felt way too awkward with him visiting—too much like we were dating.

To make the day even more difficult, Vic kept bringing up Mark. I knew she really, *really* liked him, but hearing his name all day made it even harder *not* to think about him. I then thought about him all day, how he'd fit into our family, whether or not I'd have to "babysit" him all day as I had to do with Andy, if he'd be able to hang out and relax with me coming home like this on a random Sunday.

With all the pressure from not smoking and all the thinking about Mark, I ended up driving home to Maple Grove and attending church, just hoping I could see Mark. I called him on the way to see if he was going and to meet up with him, and he agreed. Why did I keep getting drawn to him? What did I really enjoy? Was it being with him at church? Was it knowing what a great person he was?

Awkward leaving at the end of the service. I had brought some games, just in case he was interested in hanging out afterwards, but he seemed pretty disinterested (or trying to keep his distance, one of the two). I drove home alone, grateful that I hadn't let myself be all over Mark or make any quick relationship decisions. I spent a lonely (*very* lonely, since Suerte was still at Mom and Dad's) night huddled on the couch, trying to keep warm and not feel nauseated for the cigarettes I'd bought on the way home.

I gotta stop sleeping on the couch!

Chemo today went well. All counts were still high (WBC: 13.91, RBC: 3.35, HGB: 11.5, PLT: 187, NEUT: 12.47) and I got Herceptin 17. Then I found out that my every-third-week Herceptin treatments (that I could have started today) would be triple-dose treatments. I hoped that meant I could have three times fewer treatments…? I would gladly trade twelve treatments left to the thirty-six I thought I'd have!

Suppose my oncologist would have told me that. No wonder I was not her biggest fan. I decided to use that anger to self-advocate tomorrow.

Side effect check: hot flashes! Man, they were driving me nuts. Hot, cold; freezing, sweating, huddled in front of the fireplace, sitting in a tank top and shorts. *Enough already!*

My hat was getting quite the workout: on, off, on, off. I'd fall asleep fully clothed with a hat and scarf on under a mountain of blankets next to a heater and still be freezing. Then I'd wake up drenched in my own sweat. I'd move only an inch or so, freeze again, but mercifully fall asleep, only to wake up in sweat later on.

Bring on the menstruation again. I'd be happy to take periods over hot flashes any day!

More side effects. The metallic taste in my mouth returned again yesterday. Nausea subsiding. Extremely tired *all day long*. Pounding heart apparently caused by dehydration…? I'd been drinking liquids without caffeine all day, but the heart pounding hadn't settled down. My eyelashes and eyebrows were getting thin; please let them hang on until the end! They'd been such brave little toasters, holding on this long. The last week of all this nonsense, though. Who hoo!

I had to figure out how to fit my chemo schedule around my work schedule. Did I want to go every Monday at 4:00 P.M. until October, just so I didn't have to take any sick days to get there on time? Or might I prefer every third Monday until October, taking half-days at work to get there on time? No worries until I even knew what my options were—after talking to administration about that.

FROM CARINGBRIDGE.ORG, TUESDAY, FEBRUARY 3, 2009 7:15 PM, CST:

I drove to work yesterday morning reveling in the fact that I was driving towards the sunrise horizon, finally heading to the place where I needed to be. It was a wonderful first day back at work! I waded into another supportive sea of pink worn by my incredible coworkers, and I was welcomed warmly with so many hugs. It was most definitely like riding a bike, taking only a snap of the fingers to be right back in "teacher mode," even with being so nervous. It was a blessing to be around so many smiles and chatter. I felt right back at home. I was tired getting up so early, even with all my "training" trying to get back into that schedule, but I even had energy to come home and make dinner after chemo.

Chemo went well too, just a quick round of Herceptin. I'm working desperately to schedule the upcoming triple-dose rounds to be after school, so I don't have to take a half-day off from work to go every three weeks. The latest I can be scheduled is 3:30 to be done with chemo by 5:00 when they close, but I can't leave work until 3:30. Even my back-up plan of getting outpatient chemo at Mercy Hospital after hours won't necessarily work, since they don't always have staffing for chemo administration. I'll be working on that tomorrow again with Gail, Garino's nurse, and my school administration.

The less time I have to spend away from work, the better for me. I hate being away from students so sporadically; it's not fair to them to have so many guest teachers coming in and out.

Just as I suspected, my second day back was much harder than the first. I was so tired this morning that I skipped Pilates and went straight to work. The cup of coffee and Diet Coke before first hour kept me going throughout the day. I can tell that my body is adjusting well to the work schedule, though; I was able to tutor after school today, and I still feel good. Time to sneak in Pilates before I read myself to sleep with The Shack, the book circle selection of Victoria, Rachel, Mom, and me.

Being back to my work routine is the best medicine I could mentally give myself. There's nothing like getting my life back, the one that was put on pause with treatment. Time to move upward and onward!

Resolve to be thyself, and know that he who finds himself loses his misery. -- Matthew Arnold. What an appropriate quote-of-the-day phrase from my calendar.

FEBRUARY 9, 2009

I don't mean to feel guilty about being so perky at work, but honestly, everything about being there excites me. The meetings, the paperwork, the lesson plans, the late nights finishing up work—at this point, it's the best mental therapy I could ask for. Being around everyone, people so genuine and helpful, excites me every morning. (Well, every morning after I have a cup of coffee!)

There was a happy hour gathering this past Friday after work, and to see so many people come out and celebrate my returning to work made my heart burst. I am truly lucky to have such great coworkers in a job I love. A huge thank you to everyone who could make it, either in person or in spirit!

My students have been great, still curious to see what my bald head looks like. I've decided to use it as motivation to do better on spelling tests; if they all score 100%, I'll take off the wig for that class. So far, after three spelling tests from three separate classes, no newly-darkened scalp scraggles have seen the light of day. Maybe this Friday will be better for them!

I started the triple-dose Herceptins today. Thankfully, I also have supportive admins that allow me to leave ten minutes out of my seventh hour class to get to treatment on time, and incredible coworkers that offered to cover my class (thanks Julie, Julie, and Jeana!) My infusion of this dosage takes an hour and a half, stretched out so I don't get nauseated from all of the drug infused so quickly. So far, so good on the side effects. Now I don't have to return to Mercy until my next triple dose on March 2, the day before surgery. Hurray for spring break and getting so many medical steps out of the way so I don't have to take more days off.

Also started this evening was the Tamoxifen, the anti-estrogen hormone therapy. I've been reading through the Patient Education guide that comes with the pills, and I'm interested to see which of the possible side effects may hit me. (http://www.cancer.gov/cancertopics/factsheet/therapy/tamoxifen)

Again, so far, so good. Gail, the oncology nurse, recommended that I take the pill at night, so if I do have side effects, I'll sleep through most of them. Sounds good to me. Any way to reduce side effects sounds great!

FEBRUARY 9, 2009

Ironically, my last full treatment led to the least bothersome side effects. The hot flashes, the really bothersome ones, lasted only a good week or so. No awful nausea or fatigue. Even my face seemed to be clearing up quickly. It broke out again in the last two days, though. My nails, nearly all of them, were "receding," the beds getting smaller and smaller. I just cut them all very short to prevent more breakage. It didn't hurt. My hair "sprouts" (what were left, nothing regrowing yet) were *dark,* dark brown/black. They gave me an idea of what my regrowth would look like. One random hair by my right ear, about one-and-a-half inches long, was very curly too. Just that one, though. My coworkers were fascinated with my variety of wigs; which one might I wear next?

I'd hit the ground running in my first week back, determined more than ever to prove that I was doing okay. I thought I did a great job with all I was taking on, showing them that I was stronger than ever.

I was designated ESL department leader and staff development chairperson too. I was so proud of myself to be able to call myself both of those. What an accomplishment for my second year in the school district. I'd become even more hopeful for my job next year, as Julie S. decided to resign. I didn't feel happy that she was leaving (much to the contrary; she's amazing!) but with one full-time teacher leaving, I took a position higher on the totem pole.

Oh, please bring me a job for 09-10!

Last week was my last weekly Herceptin. Counts were decent. WBC: 10.45, RBC: 2.79, HGB: 9.7, PLT: 133, NEUT: 7.28. Cynda told me that it would take a few months for the counts to come back up. My first triple dose took almost an hour and a half to infuse, and that was even rushing it at the end. I was elated to visit Mercy only once every three weeks; it was another big step in moving forward. I was not worried about my triple-dose side effects, which could be nausea again. My next MUGA would come in a few weeks, after my second triple dose, to see how my heart was doing.

Reminding the schedulers that I work full-time now grew tiresome, but once they understood, they made every effort to schedule me for more convenient times. Thank God for small favors.

I wanted to avoid possible side effects of my Tamoxifen by taking it at night, so I could sleep through them, if any occurred. My greatest fear of Tamoxifen side effects was that I'd get fat or have an even lower sex drive.

More cardio and/or porn could make for some interesting evenings at home. Ha!

Oh, boys. Justin sent me flowers at work to congratulate me on my first week back. Why could I not like him back "that way"? He was wonderful, patient, fun, easy-going, and adored me. What was my deal? Was this why we broke up so long ago? And what was the deal with my masochistic relationship with Mark? We argued all the time and I ended up crying ninety percent of the time we were together. Yet there was something about him that I couldn't get enough of.

Seriously, I just needed to find someone new, a delightful mix of everything I enjoyed about both of these men. Until then, I would enjoy my exercise and porn. Seriously.

FEBRUARY 16, 2009

I started the Tamoxifen. Painlessly. None of the side effects bothered me: no hot flashes, vaginal discharge, irregular or lighter menstrual cycles (still no periods, though), weight loss, or diarrhea. Good thing I was not worried about getting pregnant any time soon. I still needed to use a barrier type of contraceptive, since I was not aware of any non-estrogen birth control pills available. (Note to self for the next Garino appointment). Tamoxifen can also cause harm to a fetus (good to know) and the drug can be excreted into breast milk, though I have no worries there.

Still no hair regrowth, but I watched for this daily. No other crazy side effects anymore either. Hurray! Even my energy level was wonderful, even with a full day's work. I found myself spending longer hours at work than necessary, not to avoid going home but just because I felt I could stay. I didn't have to go home and make dinner or clean or spend time with a husband that would rather be at work.

Wow, that sounded harsh, but it was really liberating, freeing, to know I could be on my own schedule. It would be nice to come home to someone special again someday. Someday.

Justin continued to be thoughtful. My Valentine's Day present was a wine and chocolate pairings tasting. Does he know me, or does he know me? He was wonderful. Still didn't feel "that way" about him, but darn it, I should. Mark, on the other hand, had finally pushed me to the brink. I asked him if he liked me for who I am, and he said, "Most of the time."

Yeppers. Done with him now.

So what did he do? Ask me out on a date. I had to e-mail him and tell him I only wanted to hang out with people who liked me for me.

The only response I got back from him was, "Good luck."

Ouch.

Good time to cut my losses. I had to decide whether I really needed someone who liked me only when I conformed to who he wanted me to be. No thanks.

FROM CARINGBRIDGE.ORG, FRIDAY, FEBRUARY 20, 2009 10:32 PM, CST:

Week-3 back to work also successful. I enjoyed parent-teacher conferences last night and my first "real" paycheck since September.

Too bad I was docked for over half of my salary from medical leave, and the government took the rest; but hey, it was a check! Can't complain about having a job I love.

I keep looking in the mirror every morning and every evening, just waiting for the day that I will see the slow regrowth of my hair. Still nothing more than what I had left, but I notice that what is left is still very dark. Does this mean the official beginnings of Gwen as a brunette? I look forward to finding out! (PS: none of the classes have "won" the wig removal yet, but my ESL III class came close last week. There were only two points missed by the entire class, and they were heartbroken that they came so close. I had to remind them to keep the scores private. What a great bunch of students.)

The rest of the side effects are down to not a whole lot. I think the Tamoxifen does give me a little bit of a stomachache, but it's a good thing I take it at night so I sleep through most of it. I still have the energy of a student teacher, which comes in handy when I stay at work late. I'm grateful to be able to function as I did before I started treatment. The road to recovery is getting much easier to navigate from here.

Part Six
LEARNING TO LIVE AGAIN

FROM CARINGBRIDGE.ORG,
FRIDAY, FEBRUARY 27, 2009 6:13 AM, CST:

D*um...dum...dum! DA-DUM! (I'm imagining the timpani-drum sound when something big is happening) You'll never guess what I discovered last night. While working out, my head felt different—less skin, more fuzz. I honestly thought that I was just wishful thinking, but I WASN'T! Behold, the golden splendor of new hair growing! Yes, golden. It resembles a small, glowing halo atop my head. I can't get enough of the newfound fuzziness, and I rub my scalp like one would rub a Buddha's belly for luck.*

Imagine that, the second I stopped watching when my hair would start to regrow was the very time it did. Just like the cliché suggests, a watched melon never grows hair.

FROM CARINGBRIDGE.ORG,
SATURDAY, FEBRUARY 28, 2009 10:05 AM, CST:

Wooo! Spring Break 2009! Like any normal spring breaker, I started the weekend with a pre-op physical, which I passed with flying colors. Carrie and I then enjoyed the State AA Gymnastics meet, where I dreamt of more flexible days of my own. I'm filling my three doctor-free days with a Pampered Chef party at my house, shopping with Rachel, movie trivia at Champps with Jenni and Amanda from work, and dog shopping tomorrow with Julie G. Julie thought it would be quite ironic if I bought the hairless Chinese Crested pup she has picked out for me at the Humane Society, just as I'm getting my own hair back. Quite humorous when I thought about it. The dog is a darn cutie, but am I ready for dog ownership? My cat is nearly neglected.

First stop in the week-long spring break adventure: Plymouth, MN. Tuesday is my final reconstructive surgery, where I'll finally be rid of the painful skin stretchers and be healing with the "gummy-bear" silicone. Second stop: Clearwater, MN. I'll be recuperating at my parents' house for the rest of the week. Since Dr. Harrington promised that it's only a "long weekend" recovery, I will be back at work on March 9 as planned.

Sure, these aren't typical spring break plans, but I can take care of yet another recovery step without taking time off from work. I'm more than ready for the three days of fun and a week of skipping workouts.

MARCH 2, 2009

I needed to keep up on this journal, because "chemo brain" and my genetic CRS syndrome (Can't Remember Shit) kept overtaking me. It was nearly unbelievable to realize that I'd already completed four full weeks back at work! Days were full and productive, still continuing to eat all of my daylight hours.

I'd been fighting myself to go home at a decent time so I could actually enjoy my evenings, not just go home and go to bed. Work had served as an escape for me, a break from living alone and being reminded of it every night when I returned home. I'd finally become happy with living alone again, reveling in the joy of cleaning up after myself and myself only.

And wasn't that just how life works, that once you're happy with your new life, the heavens send you what you were looking for? (Such as, you'll find love when you least expect it.) God sent me Mike, my new roommate, who was moving in this month. He seemed like a decent guy, early 40s, computer website techie. All his references checked out just fine, and his e-mails had been very entertaining and witty. Still, I asked Carrie to come over and "water the plants" when I stayed at Mom and Dad's recuperating this week.

When Mike told me things, I believed that they were indeed the truth, and hey, I could sure use an extra income. I put it straight into savings. Still not sure if I'd have a job next year, so I saved all I could.

Always a planner, I am.

I told Justin last weekend that I could only be friends, that I felt I was holding him back from finding a new, real relationship. I had no idea if/when I'd be ready for a commitment again, and I truly felt it was unfair to give him false hope. He wasn't happy to hear that, but we still tried to spend Sunday together. When he said he felt like it would be the last time we'd hang out, he started to get sad.

Then there was a knock on the door. Mark.

I'd finally had to tell Mark I didn't even want to be friends. He turned *psycho*, stopping over that night three times before I even came home, sending me random forwards all week, calling twice (even at six A.M.), sending the craziest e-mail mid-week. It was a "journal entry" for the five previous days, outlining how he couldn't understand me, how he "loved me unconditionally," how maybe I'd miss him if he ran into a cement wall.

I was so glad that whole situation was finally over; no need to beat that dead horse any longer.

FROM CARINGBRIDGE.ORG, FRIDAY, MARCH 6, 2009 9:20 AM, CST:

It must be all the time spent relaxing with family and friends, all the Tae Bo I endure, and good thoughts sent my way, but I am sure blessed with recovery time. Surgery was a breeze this round! Even after I was discharged Tuesday morning, Mom and I went to lunch. I slept the rest of the day away, from the anesthesia and Percocet, but by Wednesday morning, I was on to Tylenol. By yesterday, I didn't need any pain meds. How weird is that!

I have a follow-up with Dr. Harrington this afternoon to take off the ACE bandage holding me together, but I can already appreciate the implants versus the skin stretchers, just from what I can see. I feel much more normal, comfortable with how I look. I'm not horribly uncomfortable and stiff anymore, and that is a gift in itself. When the stitches come out, I'm heading right to Victoria's Secret for some much-needed retail therapy.

It's been an odd spring break, but I have enjoyed this week immensely. It was great to spend the time at my parents' house again—baking more cookies and playing with the nephews, sipping coffee with Mom, watching Days of our Lives replays with Brit at night, visiting Gram and sharing quiet moments together. It was very easy to go back to the time-off mode, but now I'm ready to tackle the spring!

MARCH 8, 2009

A day that I'd been waiting for since October—I busted out the "good" shampoo yesterday! My head scraggles had finally made it to a stage when it seemed necessary again. I'd never been so fascinated with my hair. I enjoyed nothing more than the feeling of fresh fuzz beneath my eager hands and fingertips. It looked like a thick five-o-clock shadow. It still appeared darker than my usual blonde hair, but I honestly welcomed *any* hair I could grow! I was much braver to sport the Sinead O'Connor look than don a scraggly wig. It felt less painful for *myself,* because I could now wear my cancer proudly. I'd accepted it, now that my hair was regrowing, of course, and I felt displaying my shaggy head was a way to show others what I'd overcome.

I WAS a face of cancer, and it wasn't such a bad idea to show people what it looked like, what my life was really like.

There was other hair regrowth as well. My leg hair came back in full force, but very soft. No underarm hair yet (who hoo!) My eyebrows, especially the right one, were even thinner, no regrowth there, but it was so easy to fill those in with an eyebrow pencil. My fingernails were breaking like *mad*. Five were now short, beyond the quick, and my hands looked dry and cracking. I'd thought about acrylic nails, but I was hesitant to destroy what little I had left.

Suffer through this ugliness, I guess. Another red badge of cancer.

Yay, final implant surgery complete! The night before surgery, Mom and I had a fun night of dinner and a movie at my house. We sat up in bed together late, chatting. It was a fun but painful reminder of this summer. It hurt to relive some of my summer memories but so nice to have Mom so close by again. We arrived at West Health at 6:30 Tuesday morning. I found it funny that they had me wear a hair net for my fuzz, but I proudly wore it into the operating room, along with my TEDS thigh-high stockings. I loved the "Dr. 90210" feeling of the surgical room; I'd never actually been awake for that part before. The anesthesiologist painfully stuck the IV in my right hand, and I hadn't fully felt the meds until all at once they hit me. I even squeaked out, "Ok, there it is," and then the next thing I knew, I was fighting to regain consciousness in the recovery room.

After a cup of Diet Coke, two cups of coffee, and a slow walk to the car, we stopped off to get Suerte before heading out to lunch. Yes, folks; I went to lunch immediately after my surgery.

Who does that? Who honestly feels well enough to go gallivanting around town after a major surgery? ME!

I made it through lunch and a cigarette (sigh) before falling asleep for the entire ride home. I took one more Percocet at two in the afternoon when we got back, then slept the rest of the afternoon. I woke briefly when Amanda and Alison stopped by Mom and Dad's later that day, then passed out again after that. Wednesday brought only two Tylenol three times all day, and Thursday was pill-free. What a quick rebound! All the better to enjoy my family time with everyone, including Gram. What a great spring break.

However, Dr. Harrington could tell on Friday that I'd been overdoing it on the movement, since my incision sites were very red. Busted. I was scheduled to get my stitches out next Friday, and in three months, I could go back to discuss nipples. Sure, it would be easier to forego them, but I desperately wanted to feel good naked again. So gimme the nipples and tattoos!

The breasts themselves already felt incredible, so much softer than the skin stretchers. They looked smaller, but so cute and natural. I *loved* the 500 cc implants! Great call on the silicone too; it felt and looked very cute.

I was dying to hit up Victoria's Secret as soon as the stitches came out. I couldn't stop staring at their reflection or touching them. Already, I felt more beautiful on the outside.

Boy update: still no word from Mark. Whew! I also decided that I either had to stop seeing Justin or date *only* him. Spending the day with him and his family just further cemented the wisdom of focusing on a good thing right in front of me. He was incredible in so many ways, we were more than compatible, and he treated me like a princess. I reminded myself to proceed slowly, but I knew I really needed to make up my mind one of these days soon. I was driving myself crazy with *not knowing* what to do. How could a woman be so consistently confused? Enough already!

FROM CARINGBRIDGE.ORG,
MONDAY, MARCH 9, 2009 8:59 PM, CDT:

More great news today! My genetic counselor called with more information about the gene variant that was found on my BRCA I gene. Myriad, the genetic testing company, gathered more information about the variant from other families that were found with it, and through further investigation, they determined that my "variant" is nothing more than a "favor polymorphism." (See Resources section for more information on this.) That's human-speak for "no cancer gene detected." Jolly fabulous news! This new discovery means nothing for my current cancer or treatment plan, but it does make a world of difference for my mom and sisters. Rather than have increased risk of infiltrating ductal carcinoma from the former "variant," they will just keep a precautionary increased-screening regimen.

This is just what I wanted to hear, that I was a freak of nature and that I wasn't raising risk for my beautiful sisters or mother. I was so glad to call and e-mail everyone with a positive test result (positive = favorable and good, not positive = cancer). What a great way to start a Monday after returning from break.

FROM CARINGBRIDGE.ORG,
MONDAY, MARCH 16, 2009 4:24 PM, CDT:

What every breast cancer patient longs to hear at an oncology appointment: "You're cured!" or "Congrats for making it through the rough part!" What we never want to hear at an oncology appointment: "So, have you given any more thought as to what you want to do with your ovaries?" Oh, yes...on Friday, I was asked if I want to keep my only shot at bearing my own children. To Dr. Garino's question then, I gave her my best blank stare and said, "Uh, keep them...?" I'm so proud of myself; I've done enough research about BC and fertility that I know that I have a great chance at pregnancy without increasing risks for cancer metastasis, not to mention the fact that I can advocate for my own health without relying solely on the opinions of my specialists. I can even support my views with research that I've read, even more impressive to myself. I've sure come a loooong way since the doe-eyed woman who started this path last summer.

I also had a MUGA scan and blood count tests on Friday. I eagerly await those results. I'm hoping to maintain a seventy-five percent on the heart scan and that my red/hemoglobin counts have increased since January. I'm not at any infection risks, since my WBCs were just fine, but I need to increase to compulsive hand washing; since I've returned to work, I've been sick twice with a cold/congestion.

This afternoon was also my first day hatless/wigless at work, which would have caused anxiety if it weren't for the hot flashes that made it necessary. It is so much more convenient to skip the melon-cover when I need to pull it off every few minutes. My friend Michelle asked, "Isn't it freeing [to skip the hat]?"

"No, it's just cold!"

No, really, it is freeing to be able to show my real self to everyone. I had one person to convince that this is what cancer looks like: myself. Once I made it through that, I've been delighted to realize that I was indeed the only person who made a big deal out of not having a full head of hair. Even the stereotypically-immature sixth graders simply shrugged their shoulders and went back to work on their poetry projects.

The old adage is true: things often turn out better than what you'd feared. Never ceases to amaze me how true it really is.

MARCH 18, 2009

Loooooooved the new breasts! It might have been probably borderline self-molestation how much I enjoyed looking at them, seeing how great I looked in a bra, brushing up against them with my arm, hugging others now without restraint, hearing the compliments, and yes, touching myself in a completely "platonic" way. I couldn't get aroused by that anymore if I tried; I had no sexual sensitivity in them, especially since I possessed no nipples. I was enjoying the sexual awakening they'd given me, how I felt so feminine, pretty, finally—a woman.

I was regaining that feminine part of me with each hair that regrew on my head. How my stubble gave me confidence!

I needed a new oncologist. At my Garino appointment on Friday, she didn't remember my case at all, not even a quick pre-appointment brush-up with my rather large medical file. I had to debrief her on my status, my meds. The worst part was when she asked me what I'd planned on doing with my ovaries. Damn!

Really? Did she even have to ask? It seemed all too easy for her to put on her doctor hat, or even her "I'm-already-a-mother" hat, and assume that, *Of course, I'll give up my ovaries!* will come out of my mouth. I was so damn proud of myself to be able to come back at her with my "favor polymorphism" reclassification, negating my increased risk of ovarian cancer.

She quickly dropped that part of the conversation.

I asked her about new birth control options for me, and the only one she recommended was a copper IUD. Even the Mirena IUD contained progesterone, also not recommended for me. My days of the ol' birth control pills or Nuvarings were over. Luckily, the IUDs were meant to last up to ten years. Now I would just hope that they didn't puncture my uterus.

Now wouldn't that be funny.

Ha bloody ha.

I had also been reading up on Tamoxifen, and I wasn't all too convinced that, as a pre-menopausal woman, this drug would be really effective. Garino seemed to get haughty and said there were many studies that proved it was.

Umm…okay? I was still not all that convinced. I'd be doing more research on that. Apparently, I would need to take it the full five years for the medication to be effective. If I decided to quit halfway, to have kids, it would be like I'd never taken the drug at all. A thirty-three-year-old mother? Weirder things had happened.

After thinking about the whole Tamoxifen fiasco, I asked Justin if he'd father my children. I was mostly kidding. Who was I to have kids with a "good friend" at this point in my life? He said he'd need more of a commitment first, and he seemed serious about that. I agreed but felt the need of a wedding ring to do that. I *needed* to have a stable partner to father my children.

This conversation with Justin spurred a few more things: an enjoyable evening with the lights out and a commitment talk.

Honestly, I had come to a realization—Justin and I were two peas in a pod that enjoyed each other's company as much as we enjoyed board games, great coffee, and naps. Now that Mark's confusion was gone from my life, I was so much *happier*, free to be me and enjoy my life. We became officially "boyfriend/girlfriend" that night, though the terms made me feel as if I was again in middle school. It was more than strange to have a boyfriend after being married, to feel like I was just starting to date for the first time in my life. Odd.

Mark's drama continued. On Friday, he called me three times during the day. He even called my school's head secretary twice—once in the morning to see if I was at work, then called back in the afternoon to find out that I had already left for the day. I arrived home that afternoon to find two bunches of flowers, two bottles of wine, two tickets to his hockey game that night, two cards that went with each bouquet of flowers, three pages of a thank-you card, and one angry Justin on my front step.

Apparently, Mark had also called Tracy's Jason to ask if he'd deliver the flowers for me (so they wouldn't freeze in the cold), to which Jason told him that he was on his own. (Thanks, Jason!) I was both angry and freaked out after all this stalking; I prayed that it was finally over.

FROM CARINGBRIDGE.ORG, TUESDAY, MARCH 24, 2009 6:15 PM, CDT:

I'm so glad I've finally come to a point in all of this that I don't have much to report. I'm still growing my little hair sprouts, giving them more sunshine than ever at work. I started taking prenatal vitamins to help the hair and nail growth, since so many people have told me that they work wonders with speeding up the growth (I'll take whatever help I can get; it's just weird buying and taking prenatals when I'm not near pregnant.) The Herceptin-only treatments are still nothing compared to what I was going through. My energy level is wonderful, I'd even say better than what it was before I had the diagnosis. Maybe the optimism helps more than I give it credit for.

The one negative I have is that my MUGA scan from two weeks ago showed a drop in my heart function. I went from seventy-five percent, my normal rate, to seventy percent. It wasn't enough to stop me from taking the Herceptin yesterday, but if my body knows what's good for it, the drop stops right where it is.

Yep, that's a threat!

Even my blood counts were all in the normal range again except the RBCs, and that's without any drugs or treatments to keep them higher. Apparently, my vitamin B12 and folic acid levels are very high, but that still doesn't mean I'm deferred from any treatments (nor do the higher levels of these two mean anything to me, literally. Rachel tried explaining it to me, but I didn't get what the fuss was about).

Can't tell you how great it feels to NOT wear the wigs every day, and the hot flashes are getting much easier to deal with while wearing only a hat. I'll enjoy the spring showers and sleets, especially when it means that warm weather is indeed on the way. Ahh, to wear only jackets again...

MARCH 30, 2009

I was living in the Land of Indecision, where I was now the mayor, governor, and representative.

Seriously, I couldn't imagine why Justin put up with me, sometimes. Not even a full week after the Commitment Talk, I had a week of second-guessing spurred by uninspiring phone conversations with him. I honestly felt that we were incompatible and had nothing to talk about. I got bored and bailed.

Yep, not even a full week and I jumped ship.

But whenever we're together, we have a blast. This past weekend, I thought things were perfect, fun, relaxing. Was I just being caught off-guard and thrown off by the actual conversations I had with the good-looking art teacher? I really didn't like trying to find someone I was as compatible with as I once was with Andy. I was trying way too hard to make something seem RIGHT in my mind.

Facebook. The joys and the horror, all in one. I received a FB message from a friend from college, Joe. It was crazy that he'd find me on there after nine years of no contact, but it was nice to see that he looked happy and was doing so well. We reminisced about funny times we had years before, when we'd hung out for a few months (back when I was still hung up on my high school boyfriend).

Then came the morning I was checking my e-mail at work, when I received notification of a message from his wife, Jayne. I read the message in complete shock. She said she'd been reading his messages to me, that she was deeply disturbed by the one he'd sent to me the night before, that, to be blunt, she wanted me to stay away from him.

I had no idea what she was talking about! I'd remained completely platonic with him in my messages! Oh, how odd.

Then I saw the notification that I'd received a message from Joe, the one that Jayne was referencing. In it, Joe said that I was the one who got away, that if I had stayed with him, his cute kid could have been mine.

Oh. My. God.

Now I understood what she was talking about.

That night, I sent her a reply, explaining what I saw of things, that things were completely on a friend level, that my husband had left me for another woman, that I'd never do that to someone else. I told her she could trust that I'd never have contact with him again, and that I hoped she'd understand my perspective.

I think Jayne must have invoked fear within him, since he'd messaged me back just gushing about how great she was and how lucky he was to have her.

(She might be reading his messages still, perhaps?)

I never responded, but I never received another message from either of them.

Can't a woman just move on with her life without more drama?

I had my Herceptin triple-dose last Monday. All went well, with the exception of my latest MUGA results showing, as I've already reported, that I dropped from seventy-five to seventy percent. The nurses didn't seem too concerned about it, since they let me proceed with treatment. Counts: WBC: 5.95, RBC: 3.55, HGB: 12.9, PLT: 189, NEUT: 3.08. Apparently, my folic acid and B12 levels were also quite high, not that Gail really told me anything about whether I should be concerned.

No new side effects, unless you count *amazing* hair growth! My scalp was wonderfully fuzzy! I couldn't stop playing with it. My eyebrows were now also a dark stubble, but my eyelashes were very thin. Always a trade-off with the hair-growth game. My leg and underarm hair was also coming back strong. Surprising how soft they were, though, not wiry as I remembered them from so long ago. It was hard to know when to shave the underarms, since I couldn't even feel the hair.

Well, good thing I didn't get naked much.

I went to the *Look Good, Feel Better* class a few weeks ago. It was a unique bonding experience with the three other cancer survivors over a table full of free cosmetics for us. Oddly enough, the blush, foundation, and makeup tips gave me a renewed sense of self-confidence. I felt beautiful again, granted through pounds of carefully-applied makeup, but it didn't matter to me. All I needed was to see those huge blue eyes surrounded by mascara and a twinkle of sass and spitfire.

Ahh, the old Gwen—the best parts of her—were back.

I was disturbed by an e-mail I received from Jessie (high school friend/fellow breast cancer survivor) last week. She recently got married and the couple were now desperately trying to conceive. Like me, she was surrounded by her nieces and nephews, making the wait for her own that much harder. Her step-mother was making her feel guilty and upset, even blaming her for their infertility.

It freaked me out to think of being in that same boat. It might be hard to conceive at thirty-three, after chemo and five years of Tamoxifen. I thought: if it was difficult to deal with my short fingernails, how would I deal with telling a future partner that I was barren? How could I ask someone to give up his chance at fathering children?

I knew how that felt: like part of my future was ripped from beneath my feet. I felt like damaged goods, trying to knowingly sell myself to a wonderful man, but asking him to ignore all of that.

Sheesh, would life ever get easy again?

QUESTIONS FROM A CANCER MAGAZINE:

Write about a tree that was part of your childhood and why it was important to you. Out in the pasture at my parents' house, there was a large tree on the edge of the "forest." It had beautifully strong and broad branches that gave us hours of shade and playtime enjoyment. Out there, we played "Thundercats" and "Goonies," each of the sisters choosing their role and playing them out with our memorized lines from the shows. I was "Mouth" from the Goonies, even then being the loudmouthed rebel. I always wanted to be "Andi," the pretty and popular cheerleader, but my beautiful older sister Amanda always had that role. I just loved the countless warm, sunny hours and days spent with my tight-knit sisters.

How has cancer changed you, and how do you feel about the changes? I believe I've spent pages upon pages answering that one already, yet the answer changes every day. Now, I am grateful for every day that I am given, and finally, I have the peace and happiness that I've always wanted in my life to spread to others.

FROM CARINGBRIDGE.ORG, MONDAY, APRIL 20, 2009 9:32 PM, CDT:

I am so grateful for Young Women Breast Cancer Survivor support groups. I went last Thursday to my first meeting since August, and I am so glad I went. It is so inviting to know I am surrounded by women who face the same problems I've faced, and they get it. Amidst the alphabet soup of acronyms and firsthand experience with the side effects and fears, I was welcomed and supported in a room of strangers-recently-turned-friends. Not only can they offer support, they can offer a wealth of oncology knowledge that they never wanted to have.

Again, I could relate.

I got the name of a great oncologist at Virginia Piper, whom I called today and I will hopefully see sometime soon. I need a doctor who can help me through my rough spots and not leave me with another list of questions to Google when I get home (or call Rachel...again.... Soon she won't answer the phone when I call).

I also learned of a blood test—CYP2D6—that my oncologist can order to see if my body metabolizes the Tamoxifen well, meaning, if the Tamoxifen is actually useful in preventing recurrence. I am scheduled for that test when I go in for my next chemo round in two weeks. However, the results may be a double-edged sword; either it works and I am still forced to take Tamoxifen daily for the next four years and ten months, or it doesn't work well and I am back to keeping my fingers crossed and hoping my cancer doesn't metastasize, hoping that surgery and chemo were good enough to "cure" me. It's very similar to knowing my genetic results; either I'm carrying the gene, or I am a freak of nature that had a sporadic case of cancer. Either way, is it really good news?

My "haircut" continues to grow slowly but surely. I've been complimented so much on this pixie that if I didn't love my hair long, I'd keep it this short. Even with the cowlicks and bed-head, it's still so simple to style in the mornings when I'm running late. Even my eyelashes and eyebrows are now filling in, more small steps to feeling beautiful on the outside.

My favorite update: now I really do have to reschedule my chemo/oncology appointments in the third week of June, because I will be in Paris! My wonderful friend and coworker Dawn and I are heading to France for a week filled with the Louvre, the Eiffel Tower, walks along the Seine, and pain chocolat. Thanks to her amazing planning, we will enjoy the one week I have off this summer, and I will bring back some incredible pictures and memories. Bonsoir!

SUNDAY, MAY 17, 2009

After eight months of "dating," four months of more serious dating, and two/three weeks of being boyfriend and girlfriend, I hit a wall with Justin. We had such a great weekend together, Friday night with wine and fun, sleeping in, errands, dinner with Laure and Marty Saturday night, and a relaxing Sunday with a movie and a jog. Before we left for Laure's birthday party,

I asked Justin if I said "I love you" too much. Hesitating, he said no, but it was the hesitation that truly gave me my answer.

I'd gone and done it again, giving my heart away too quickly. I'd fallen head over feet in love without reservation. Sure, I'd had a ton of reservation after losing my husband, and Justin had definitely paid too much for what Andy left me with, but I knew that when I was ready for a relationship again, it would be one I would want forever.

I honestly felt that forever-commitment would be possible with Justin. We'd been through so much together that I thought, by putting myself out there, I'd have what I was really looking for when I got married.

Man, it killed me to know that I felt too much, that I put too much out there. I didn't mean to scare him off. I knew that he wanted to be with me, but to be told that I say "I love you" too much? Was I expecting too much? He was the first one who said the love word. I was trying desperately to just let it go and not overanalyze too much, but my heart was guarded, fearing rejection again.

Speaking of rejection, I had a sickening thought this afternoon. I was wearing the tank top that Andy had found. I remembered him telling me he found it in his car and he thought it was from my ex-sister-in-law or her friend. As I sat and thought about this from the divorced, hindsight-is-20-20 perspective, I finally realized that Andy had been cheating on me way back then, after we'd been married only a year. Why on earth would there be a random tank top in his car?? And why did it take me this long and all of this experience to finally GET it?

Jesus, how awful to feel so stupid and rejected.

Why would I want to trust someone again after that? I was so much better off NOT knowing any of this. My ignorance was indeed bliss, and I could have gone the rest of my life not knowing that.

I threw the shirt in the trash. Too bad. It looked great on me.

I was really hoping for the best with the CYP2D6 test results: that I couldn't metabolize the Tamoxifen at all and I wouldn't have to keep taking it. I feared that I'd be in the gray area of results, that I would weakly metabolize it and it wouldn't help much at all. But no, darn it. For once, things worked as they should for my recovery and I metabolized it very well. There would be five more years of pills to take and five more years of putting off getting pregnant (if I even could). That meant that I couldn't have kids until I was at least 33.

Yes, that was still young, but sheesh, having kids that late in life would be difficult, and I'd be a much older mom than I'd like to be.

I realized that in all of this I was darn lucky to be alive and a bigger plan for my life was dawning. It was damn hard to let go of my decision-making and control of my life to forces unseen.

Seeing Lexie and many other babies this weekend was damn tough. I couldn't get enough of cuddling up with a little one, but it was difficult to hold them and look into their smiling eyes, knowing, at this point, that having my own children was nearly impossible.

I really hoped that the saying "you always want what you can't have" didn't reflect the reason I looked forward to being a mom.

Deep down, I knew that wasn't the case. I'd have to be patient and wait.

FROM CARINGBRIDGE.ORG, MONDAY, MAY 18, 2009 10:03 PM, CDT:

I heard once that after cancer, you never have a bad hair day (thanks, Linda B. at work) and darn if that isn't true. My hair is finally long enough to style again, and I'm taking full advantage of it. I've been using "surf wax" to work the messy look, and at dinner last night, I actually gave myself a "faux-hawk," the pseudo-Mohawk. Can't help but smile and giggle with reckless abandon with the giddiness of having real hair to play with again. Thankfully, I'm still not using the blow dryer or flat iron, but I can't wait until that comes back too. I keep hearing that I should keep it short, but I think everyone can also understand why I'm working towards the Crystal Gayle look. Kidding. But long enough to curl would be nice.

As I was doing my hall duty last week in the eighth grade hallway off of the North Commons, I was surrounded by the chatter of before-school excitement. Silently observing all of the laughter, drama, and loner's silence, I just smiled to myself. I cannot begin to be more grateful for having a job that I truly love and am blessed to have (and for the upcoming year too—another woo hoo!) How great it is to be one of the few that can actually say with a straight face they love their job.

Finally, a random thought...the best part of spring is a warm day with the scent of lilacs drifting through the dusk air. After every winter, there is a spring.

TUESDAY, MAY 19, 2009

I'd been deliberately sabotaging the relationship with Justin, just so I would not be the one hurt again. I'd been punishing him for Andy's mistakes. What had I learned about moving on from the past, that what was done was done? Not much. I'd been so upset with Andy and the tank-top realization, and Justin was the one feeling my pain from it all. What had he done to hurt me? Nothing.

What did I do when I knew I'd been hurt but didn't know what to do about it? Run away.

I was no better off than Andy. What a great day to get this bible quote: *Do everything in love.* (1 Corinthians 16:14) To truly move on and be the person I knew I was, I needed to walk away from the pain of the past year and step into the happy existence I knew and loved.

There was no doubt in my mind that I could spend the rest of my life with Justin and be happy. I knew him, he knew me and loved me in spite of and because of everything I was. When I was with him, I always felt happy—when I stopped analyzing everything excessively—and there was nothing he wouldn't do for me. I loved this man.

I talked to Sarah and Amanda in the office today, and they were amazing. I didn't know what I'd do without my second-hour therapy sessions. It was so reassuring to know that they felt the same way I did about my ex and that they could offer advice and sympathy. We jokingly decided that I should log on to Andy's Facebook page one last time, change a lot of the info, and hope he saw it and changed his password once and for all. I had a list of things I wanted to change: marital status to married, his hobbies *(cheating on his wife, leaving her when she has cancer, getting drunk and getting DUIs, dating his servers at work)*, and anything else I could come up with on the fly.

I came home last night ready to do it, but I prayed instead. I prayed that God would help me to be strong enough not to become a vindictive person, that I would feel His true purpose for my life and just let the negative parts of everything go. I found so much comfort and strength in prayer, and I was glad that my strength kept me from changing his Facebook page.

Now, with all that willpower, why couldn't I quit smoking??

After my summer school training session, I talked to my dearest friend Garnet again. I told her about the rough few days I'd been having, that I struggled with analyzing what I did wrong in my relationship with Andy and how I could have done things differently. She told me about something she tells her students in her "Teen Issues" class: make a list of all of the things you didn't like about your ex. Now go over the list and think about those things one by one and think, would you date someone with that issue? Would I want to date someone with two DUIs? Would I want to date someone who left his wife at the weakest point in her life? Would I want to be with someone who puts more effort into being a college-aged-mentality person? Would I want someone who doesn't treat me well? Would I want someone that runs at every precipice of adulthood?

Of course not!

Then, why oh why would I want to keep hurting myself,

believing there were things I could change about myself to make things better, when he was far from someone I'd want to spend my life with?

Thank God for Garnet. What would I ever do without her?

FROM CARINGBRIDGE.ORG, WEDNESDAY, MAY 27, 2009 10:23 PM, CDT:

Via the Young Survivors Coalition, I received an invitation to submit a story of who or what gave me hope during my experience with breast cancer. Though I have an extensive list of all of the fabulous people who know, love, and support me, immediately one person came to mind. This is what I submitted.

"Hope is what I see when I look into the eyes of my three-year-old godson and nephew, Alec ("Pete"). After my cancer diagnosis and a divorce, it broke me down to see Pete run away from me in tears. Since I spent so much time away from home, he didn't even know who I was. Spending my time on chemotherapy leave with Pete and the rest of my dear family renewed my bond with all of them, and Pete now runs to "Aunt Gwenna" and shares my love of baking cookies. We spent countless hours reading books, playing with trucks, and taking naps together. In the tender and innocent smile of someone who truly loves me, I feel the hope of better days ahead. His hope is what keeps me going, since he showed me what the true meaning of life and happiness is—being with the ones you love most."

I really needed this reminder of what is important to me, especially with these last few chaotic weeks of school looming. Through lesson plans, nights tutoring, helping out friends, making travel plans, and being exhausted, I needed to picture his little face smiling up at me.

If I needed more reminding, I can just look at the picture of him—hiding behind the rocking chair at Mom and Dad's—that is always on my dresser. How wonderful it is to love and to be loved.

FROM CARINGBRIDGE.ORG, THURSDAY, JUNE 25, 2009 5:03 PM, CDT:

Summer is well underway, and I'm just getting into the swing of things. I guess that taking off for Paris the last day of school, getting back a week later after a completely full week of sightseeing, going to two weddings and a Father's Day gathering, then starting summer school—all within ten days—can take a LOT out of a woman. I'm glad that I've stayed healthy (knock on wood) and I've even started getting a little bit of a healthy summer tan. Hurray for half-days at work so I can walk down to Weaver Lake and enjoy the beach and more sunshine. Summer school has also started and is keeping me busy. I have another great group of kids, and the shortened schedule is great for catching up on reading time. I have already finished The Kite Runner *and am almost done with* The Shack.

I am beyond blessed to have maintained my health throughout all the traveling, germs, and Herceptin. Even my latest heart scan came back at seventy-six percent, six percentage points higher than last time. Thank you, Billy Blanks and my bike. Dr. Garino said that I'm doing extremely well, but she's being proactive in my return-to-"normal" process by scheduling a bone density exam for me. Since the menopause hasn't reversed yet, my bone density could decrease as a result. I'll be stocking up on cheese, oh darn. Only a small handful of Herceptin-chemos left; then I can get rid of the port. I physically feel fine, though, no fatigue or nausea of yesteryear (well, of January). It's impossible to have a bad day when the sun is already coming up at 5:00 A.M.

Oh, how I've missed you, summer...

FROM CARINGBRIDGE.ORG, TUESDAY, JULY 14, 2009 2:53 PM, CDT:

One year later. Three hundred sixty-five days since having life change completely from how I knew it. Fifty-two weeks of learning what my new normal looks like. Twelve months of laughs, tears, new experiences, knowledge gained, and appreciation for life. One year since starting my life over again.

So, how does a one-year survivor celebrate? With a surgery, of course! I went in for continued reconstruction the day after my twenty-ninth birthday, with my loving mother at my side again. The two constant variables in all of my surgeries: my mother and me. Damn, am I lucky to have her.

How completely weird to be conscious for the entire surgery. I could feel all the cutting, prodding, tugging, but without any of the pain. Not only did I get some reconstruction, I asked Dr. Harrington to remove my port. That was an experience I'll remember for a while. All the pushing and tugging to get that darn plastic thing out from all of the scar tissue it was buried under, then finally the deep breath in and out...voila! I asked to keep the port so I could show my students, but I think I'll be more fascinated by it than they'll be. It indeed became such an important part of me and my recovery, my lifesaver. I don't think I'll frame mine as Sharon Osbourne allegedly has, but I'll keep it with my mementos. All clean, it's interesting to look at!

I know that I still have six chemos left, but I can't tell you how liberating it is to NOT see the permanent bump on my chest. The incision from that was what actually gave me the most trouble afterwards; it hurt like heck for a few days. I skipped the Percocet this time and relied solely on Tylenol; hindsight—maybe a bad idea? It is weird to have about fifty stitches covering my skin, but it is one gigantic step into feeling more feminine again, not just a science experiment.

Not having the port wasn't that bad yesterday at chemo. They just used a "good" (nice and juicy) vein in my right forearm, and in no time, it was over. Just like having the port. There are so few oncology nurses I recognize at Mercy now. Since converting from HHH Cancer Center to Minnesota Oncology, I found few familiar faces I looked forward to seeing. Those nurses grew to mean so much to me, like sisters that were always there to comfort me. How odd that I feel I'm proceeding without them now. Like a graduation from chemo, almost? Only five more chemos left until I really can toss the pink mortarboard up into the air!

Twenty-nine is indeed much, much better for me than twenty-eight.

TUESDAY, JULY 14, 2009

Wow, could life change in a course of two months off from my journal! In June, I successfully completed my sixth year of teaching. Six years of changing students' lives and, hopefully, making a positive mark on their futures. At least, I knew that they'd had a positive effect on mine. I felt so blessed to have a job that I love.

The last day of teaching duty for the year brought me to my colleague Dawn's house after work. From there, we whisked off to Paris for a week. The sights, the culture, the food, the people, the museums, the wine, the lights. It was truly incredible. For never wanting to go to Paris, I fell in love with Parisian life. I dreamed of getting an apartment near our hotel, of falling in love with the adorable waiter from the restaurant on the corner, of learning fluent French and staying for the rest of my life.

Funny how with every travel I take, I end up wanting to move there. Even funnier how I can't wait to get home and see my family and friends and resume "normal" life.

Right off the plane that Friday when we got back, I changed into my cutest clingy green dress, put on my new purple heels bought in Paris, and drove to Paynesville to meet Justin for his friend's wedding reception. From Paris to Paynesville in one day. What a change, driving on the open road in my car rather than taking the dark Metro to another new location.

We had a great evening, dancing the night away, enjoying the first time seeing each other in over a week. I knew I had a pretty darn amazing boyfriend. The next day brought us to a wedding for my coworker, Jess. We had a great time at the wedding and at the dinner, but then the drama of the reception hit us hard. Justin had a horrible week at work, FDA audits and picking up the pieces after a stressful week, and he was overwhelmed with all that he went through that week. As incredible as my week was, his was the exact opposite. He was quiet all through dinner, and refused to talk about anything, even after I kept asking him about it. We ended up going home early that night, and he finally opened up to me about how much stress he was under and how he was ready to leave his job on Friday.

It felt wonderful that he'd opened up like that to me with something so heavy on his thoughts. We talked, had a quiet night at my house, and enjoyed the rest of the weekend.

The drama made for fun making up later on.

He came to Maple Grove on his birthday, June 2, for a dinner that I cooked for him. As he put it, I was no longer robbing the cradle, well, at least for another month.

I went to a conference in Minneapolis my first week back from Paris, and who did I run into but my old principal Ray. The principal who'd fired me two years ago. Instantly, I felt nauseated and wanted to cry. That smug look was still on his face, and it brought back to the forefront all the same fear.

I decided that I needed to move on from this pain and to confront him when I went back to the conference two days later. I was proud that I got up the confidence to go near him that morning, but in actuality, I went up to the assistant principal sitting by him at breakfast and started talking to her. Ray did come back to his spot, and I smiled at him sweetly and maintained a happy disposition. I played the part perfectly, and I walked away from that with a newfound strength. I regained some of the strength that I'd lost working for him, part of the strong woman I used to be.

Confident and walking on air after that, I decided to chase away more demons in my life. Hey, I *was* in Minneapolis, and I might as well make the most of it, right?

I drove over to the bar with the eeriest sense of familiarity, over the new I-35 Bridge, down the reconstructed exit to University Avenue SE. I parked out front, put my quarter in (for twelve minutes on the meter) and walked into the same musty-smelling bar I used to haunt only one year prior. I saw Andy instantly, walking from the back end of the bar. He turned to go into the kitchen, not recognizing me standing there, so I was forced to find my voice and call out to him. The look on his face, upon second glance and recognizing me, was shock. He came right up to me. "I thought I'd never see you again."

Well, I wasn't planning on seeing him ever again. What the hell was I doing there? Did I really need to do this? Wasn't just knowing he was a jerk enough for me to move on? Apparently not.

I asked if he had a minute, and he asked if I wanted to go outside to talk. I said no and quickly moved on to reasons for my visit to this place. After a big sigh, shaking visibly like a leaf in a hurricane, I said, "A lot has happened this past year. I just wanted to tell you that I am happy for you."

With all the nerves, unease, nausea, and fear, I even started to well up uncontrollably.

So did he. He hugged me.

It felt sickening to be in his arms again. What was I doing, letting him touch me?

I ended it there, and walked out. Less than a one-minute-drive-by meeting. I got into the car, thinking I'd feel better. I didn't.

Justin and I were going camping that day in Winona. When

he got there, I told him about Ray and about seeing Andy. He was obviously surprised by what I told him, but he was very supportive, saying if I needed those confrontations so I could move on, he was proud of me.

At first, I was proud of me too, of my courage to face my ex after all this time. Again, I was wrong. All Friday night and Saturday, I thought endlessly about Andy. Not about all the reasons to be happy that he was gone, but about all the good times we'd had. About how he surprised me with a candle-lit dinner one night after I worked out. About all the little things we'd say to each other. About how needlessly I picked apart things he did and stayed pissy with him for hours.

Instead of being overjoyed that I could move on, I thrust myself back into the face of the storm, into the middle of my guilt and sadness.

I got drunk on the wine we picked up at a winery down there, and I foolishly started to freak out on Justin. I was angry and struggling with my feelings for Andy, not my feelings for the one man who had never let me down but had always been there for me.

I started to bawl and called Carrie to talk about the sickness I felt about what I did. I was at the point that if Andy had called me and wanted to get back together, I would have said yes in a heartbeat.

Yes, I know, I *know!* I was drunk, okay?

She talked me into going back and telling Justin my frustration, to focus on the good person I had in my life, and to call her later if I needed to.

Justin and I got into a big argument, thanks to my

belligerence, and I started to pack up the camping equipment, removing the tent stakes. Thankfully, I fell asleep in the tent and woke up early the next morning, finding Justin sleeping in the driver's seat of my car.

The official next morning, we talked. I got out all the anger I felt for Andy, telling Justin I was obviously not over what my ex did to me. Sure, I was over *Andy*, but I was still hurt by how things ended. I realized that rather than try to be the good little Christian and just pray for Andy's happiness, I needed to give in and get *mad*. Angry. Furious.

Damn it, I skipped over that part of my recovery. Like my breast cancer, I needed to get it OUT.

So, at my teacher's conference in San Diego, I took time during the week to make notes on all of the things I'd been dying to say to Andy since last summer. Jenni E. was incredible, helping me through all of those nights of whining about it. I got home with my notes and wrote Andy a letter. I texted him to ask if he'd meet me for coffee, and he agreed.

I met him in Maple Grove the following Tuesday and read it verbatim. I needed to see his reaction to my words. I wasn't, by any means, nice to him.

It took me aback that he remained devoid of emotion. No sadness or anger. Nothing. I would have put money on it, however, that he'd get up and leave in the middle, but darn if he didn't stay the entire time. When I was done, I thanked him for coming and for listening.

He said he'd kept up on my website, since people asked him how I was doing. He asked how I knew he was happy with his life (Hello, *Facebook?* Mutual friends that post pictures of him? New kissy-kissy profile pictures of him and his new girlfriend?) Most disturbingly, he asked if I'd like his new phone number when he changed it in a few weeks.

I easily declined that. Of course, he mentioned that his new girlfriend wouldn't be happy with his staying friends with an ex. Wonder why…could it be that he cheated on me with her?

I came home, at first happy with myself, but soon was back in the middle of wrestling with all the emotions swirling around me. How easily my judgment could be clouded with doubt and frustration.

I knew how much better my life was without him. I'd again become the person I could be proud of, the strong woman he'd met back in southern MN. Sadly, I'd let myself become someone I didn't know how to be—a wife—and he acknowledged that he was never the adult he had to be to be committed to our marriage.

However, I was proud to be back to who I really needed to be. With Justin, I didn't have to pretend to be someone I was not. I was with a person who truly showed me what it meant to love and be loved unconditionally, to be there in sickness and in health. I saw myself having a future with Justin, even if I refused to trust in that, and I knew we were great together. Although we were similar enough to think of ourselves as two peas in a pod, we were also so different that we brought out the best in each other. I could see actually being married again (though I still struggled with the name change thing…again), having kids, enjoying owning a house together, retiring to the lake.

Even his brother asked him if he was going to propose in August, when we were going to Italy. The romance of that would have been pretty, but I didn't think we were ready for that. Every day was a new step in the right direction.

Hurray, the final reconstructive surgery! This time, I was conscious for the entire nipple-creating ordeal. I felt the tugging and ripping of my skin, the stitches being carefully applied to each side, the port being removed from the scars that surrounded it. Seeing and feeling the new nipples felt crazy. They were huge! Thank goodness the swelling would go down. Even five days out, I was still sore, yellowish bruises covering the entire area surrounding my nipples. Some fifty stitches lined my old scar and the newly-formed circles on my breasts.

The day after surgery, since I'd refused the Percocet prescription, I took Tylenol and tried to clean up the areas and apply new Bacitracin. Didn't understand why, since it didn't hurt, but I instantly felt nauseated. I got sweaty, my vision got blurry, and my hearing started to go. Yep, I started to pass out, all by myself at my parents' house. It was a good thing no one was there, however, since I had to lie on the living room couch, topless, and try to maintain consciousness.

I recovered about twenty minutes later, finished up quickly with my first aid, and got dressed to visit Gram.

Those lovely nipples were still oddly nice to have, even with the stitches and black permanent marker and dried blood/scabs lining the incisions. Who knew I'd be so proud of them?

Even weirder than being proud of my nipples was becoming a woman again on Sunday. I'd been waiting in vain for months for my period to come back. For the last few months, I'd been having menstrual-like cramps every four weeks, but still no official menstruation. The hot flashes ended, and with the cramps starting, I was beginning to get excited. Sunday after church, I found blood. I was so confused, checking about four times to see where it was coming from.

It was like being thirteen again, finding it for the first time, and getting scared and confused, then telling Mom about what happened.

Mom laughed when I told her that story, comparing the twenty-nine-year-old self to me of sixteen years ago. Even if I was not supposed to have kids for another four-and-a-half years, just knowing that the possibility existed felt so damn good. Not every part of the future that I envisioned was destroyed. Now I might have a chance to have a family with someone I knew was going to be there, be a great father, and be an amazing partner for me.

Could it be too much to be so lucky at this point in my life?

FROM CARINGBRIDGE.ORG, MONDAY, AUGUST 3, 2009 9:46 PM, CDT:

I've been agonizing about it for weeks. I'd already talked myself out of it countless times, getting it almost committed into my planner, then resisting. It really wasn't necessary, yet I was compelled to do it. Finally, this afternoon, I timidly walked through the glass door and strode purposefully to the back counter.

I proceeded to get my first professional haircut in over a year.

I came armed with my pixie-cut picture of Alyssa Milano, stating more than a few times how I was growing it out, how I just wanted to get it cleaned up, how important these post-chemo sprouts were to me. The hair stylist told me her mother had alopecia and she'd cut her mother's patches for years; she understood.

She carefully trimmed up my mess, and for the first time since last October, I had a true shampoo, cut, blow-dry, and style. I sauntered out of that place puffed up like a Saturday-Night-Fever John Travolta, feeling darn cute, even with my workout gear on and my right arm in a sling.

Oh, yes. The reason why I'm typing with only my left hand...

I finally invested in a good pair of inline skates, so my friend Garnet and I suited up and hit a Maple Grove trail on Saturday morning. What a difference real blades made. I now flew down sidewalks and through the trees. However, I never mastered stopping with them. A family with a baby in a stroller was coming around a corner of the path, so I took a running jump onto the side grass to avoid taking them out. Noble, right? I hit the grass with my right eyebrow/sunglasses and with my right wrist. One look at my wrist, and I knew it wasn't good. After six hours in urgent care and the ER, I found out that I'd broken both my radius and ulna, now splinted up until I have surgery on Wednesday afternoon. Justin and I will have an interesting trip to Italy next week, since he broke his left wrist over a week ago at softball. We already get a lot of awkward stares and questions about what happened to us.

It's weird to notice the changes now in my medical treatment. Every time I need my blood pressure taken, they have to use my calf, since the left arm is off-limits from lymph node removal and the right is now splinted up past the elbow. Now I have to get chemo in my right bicep (ouch!) since my port is gone and my juicy vein is under wraps. I have a lengthy story every time a new nurse asks, "How has your health been?" or "Any surgeries in your history?"

My most interesting physical change: my hair is now either very wavy or curly! My stylist confirmed my suspicions today. My hair is still blonde, just no longer stick-straight. I'm very intrigued to see what develops as it continues to grow. It's past my second knuckle now when I measure it with my fingers, so I guesstimate that it's about two inches long. Yep, highly scientific, my measurement methods.

Curly, straight, short, long...I'm just glad I have some!

FROM CARINGBRIDGE.ORG, SUNDAY, AUGUST 30, 2009 9:06 PM, CDT:

As I sit here shivering in front of my laptop, I couldn't help but wonder, where did the summer go? I start workshops already tomorrow morning! I've been running around Minnesota (and the world) since June, and now I will start running around school again, seemingly after only a few weeks of summer.

I am so glad that I took the past week to spend my last few days with my family, just like I did last year during my medical leave. It was like I never left. My "bedroom" in the library of my parents' home was prepared for me by my incredible mother, I spent the days sipping coffee with Mom and wrangling little kids, and I enjoyed the late-night recaps of Days of Our Lives on SoapNet. The biggest difference for me between last year and today was when I left; I held Mom for a long time, but this time, I had no tears.

It's incredible to see how strong I've become again over the last year. I can't wait for September 11, the one-year anniversary of being cancer-free, just to celebrate yet another milestone.

Not much new on the cancer front. HURRAY! I completed another round of Herceptin on Monday, and now I have only two sessions left. That alone is exciting for me, only two more steps to finishing my year of chemo. This news came from my new oncologist, Dr. Bloom. I switched oncologists to have one I was more comfortable working with. Dr. Bloom came highly recommended from other Young Survivors Coalition members, and I was so grateful that he was as wonderful as everyone made him seem to be. He was the first doctor I've worked with who actually took the time to find out who I am, not just what my cancer looks like. He emphasized that he wants to treat my cancer as best he can, but he also wants me to have the highest quality of life treatment will allow. Through his humor and comments about his own life and cancer journey, I met the man I will walk with through the rest of my cancer path.

Dr. Bloom also wrote everything we talked about in the form of a letter to me, a service he provides to all his patients (not just the ones that have casts on their writing hand). I knew he was great when he started the letter off with: "Gwen: Damn. You have (had) cancer."

I am not even concerned with having to drive to south Minneapolis and pay for parking at Abbott to see him. He's incredible, and now I am one who also highly recommends him.

On a happier note, I adored my trip to Italy! Justin and I spent three days in Rome, then two days up in Cinque Terre at the beach, then three days in Florence before heading home again. The gelato, the sights, the picturesque views, I loved it all. I became quite good at explaining—in Italian—why we were both wearing casts, as we *were quite the spectacle over there too. Even with the metal plate in my wrist, I fortunately had no problems getting through security checkpoints.*

Note to future visitors to Italy: consider a month other than August. One, the entire country is on a holiday, leaving little other than areas around tourist spots open. Two, it is HOT! You have to bring a water bottle and drink more water than you ever thought possible, and just accept the fact that you will sweat from sunrise to sunset.

Even with these two setbacks, I was in awe of how incredible it all was.

I will be up early to enjoy a morning Tae Bo session, then a hot mug of Italian coffee, then a day of starting back to the best job in the world.

How lucky can one woman be?

FROM CARINGBRIDGE.ORG, TUESDAY, SEPTEMBER 8, 2009 10:03 PM, CDT:

Day One of my seventh year teaching completed! Man, does that make me feel older. What a great day of issuing lockers, lunch pins, new binders, and "Hey, this is a one-way!" warnings. It's a great feeling to know that I'm in it for the long haul this year and not taking a leave. Not that I won't miss the leisure of medical leave, but ending the chemo is a blessing.

Karen, a friend/coworker, told me this afternoon that someone close to her was just diagnosed with breast cancer. The plague hits again; that is the third person this week to come to me with that same comment. She asked me what she could do to help her. My first reaction, I've now realized six hours later, was the best response I could have given: lots of hugs.

The best remedies and sources of hope for me were hugs and time with family and friends. Keeping myself surrounded with all of the positive energy kept me from burying into a hole of self-pity. That is some of the best advice I can offer to caregivers and friends.

That, and chocolate-flavored anything will cure every other ailment!

Thank you again to all of the incredible folks I am blessed to be around, at home and at work. You are what saved me, and for you, I am grateful.

The Final Chapter
IT ALL COMES TOGETHER

SEPTEMBER 17, 2009

After months of struggling with Justin, and even a trip to Italy, I couldn't lie to either of us anymore, and I told him that I needed to gracefully end our romance. For months, I'd already known that he wasn't The One for me, that I was wasting his time to find the right one for him. I'd been torturing myself with forcing the feelings that I'd had for Andy, but I'd never had for Justin. I was in my own self-inflicted personal hell, knowing how wonderful to me he was, yet I was walking away from being treated better than I'd ever known.

I was sitting at my computer in the west office again, slowly plugging away at my never-ending to-do list. A special guest teacher, Gene, sat near me, enjoying his well-deserved lunch break. When he asked me if I had any weekend plans, on a reflex I turned to my planner to see what I was up to.

I paused then said, "Yes, but what I really need is a weekend away, a place where I can gather my thoughts, to be alone."

Instantly, he replied, "I have just the place for you: Pacem in

Terris." I jotted down the name in my planner's margins and thought, *Yep. That place does sound nice.* Remembering that I was at a computer, I Googled it. Gene and I briefly looked over the basic information about it, and then I found some pictures. This was *exactly* what I needed: a small hermitage away in the woods, far from the daily pressures of life.

I wrote down the number to call later but realized, *What was I waiting for?* I dialed the number and asked if the following weekend was available. To my disappointment, it wasn't. Nor was any weekend until the end of October. I felt such great disappointment, knowing that I desperately needed this time away.

By the grace of God, however, they had one opening for *this* weekend, and immediately I booked it. This was a sign I was hoping for, that He would lead me to the only available days at Pacem in Terris, but that He also knew how much this time meant to me.

My pal Jenni E. was afraid for me to be out in the woods alone, and my friend Laure was afraid I'd be eaten by a bear. Not a positive way to start out the weekend.

SEPTEMBER 18, 2009

Friday, 4:00 P.M. Through a detour on Highway 4, I carefully and observantly drove up to St. Francis after work. Upon "check-in," I was briefed by a kind staff member on what Pacem in Terris was all about. The experience was based on a book, *Poustinia*, a time of quiet solitude away from all distractions in life. The hermitages were designed for a one-person stay, stocked with a basket of breads, fruits, and cheeses, a small gas burner with a teakettle to make supplied tea or coffee, a bible, and a copy of *Poustinia*. These were the only items I'd need for the weekend, along with any personal items I'd brought.

In my "trying to relax" fashion, I'd also brought a book to read—a copy of *Don't Sweat the Small Stuff* for my reflections—my cell phone, and my iPod. I knew, especially from the great sense of love and comfort I felt swelling up inside my heart, that this was where I needed to be.

The staff person brought me to my hermitage—St. Peter—left me with a tour of the hermitage, and I began my time of solitude. Well, no. It would actually start after dinner in the main house with the other hermits.

7:00 P.M. After dinner and the closing prayer, I excused myself to take the "long way" back to my hermitage, a five-minute stroll through the primitive trails. I happily "got lost" on the trails winding around the property, and I was somehow drawn to the boardwalk out to the lake. I'd wanted to see and experience the water's edge at some point this weekend, and I was led here on my first night. After walking the boardwalk, I settled into a metal chair placed at the end of it, put my feet up on the matching ottoman, and *just was.*

It became an inner struggle with myself to focus on the silent solitude in God's presence. I was swarmed with life thoughts of my Saturday plans with Heather and Josh, my break-up with Justin, my need to go to the bathroom, remembering I missed my daily workout, how I was being eaten alive by mosquitoes, how I already planned on coming back to PiT though I had *just* arrived, thought of volunteer tutoring at school, and a few other thoughts that eluded me.

I retraced my steps and walked back to St. Peter. I washed my face, put on my glasses, and lay on my bed. I looked out the picture window, out over the treetops, at the setting sun. I realized how emotionally and physically tired I was, and I closed my eyes.

SEPTEMBER 19, 2009

6:00 A.M. I woke early, just to see the light beginning to fill the morning sky surrounding the woods. I fought the urge to get up and start my reflecting, knowing I was on no schedule to accomplish any to-do list. I comfortably nestled back into my twin bed and fell peacefully back to sleep.

8:00 A.M. When I finally rose, it was because I couldn't hold my bladder anymore. After I took care of that, I relished my morning muffin from the basket and a pot of coffee. Rather than freak about how many calories the muffin had, or how I needed to work off said calories later, I sat peacefully enjoying the walnut halves atop the prune-flavored jelly that covered the top of the bran muffin. That alone was a breakthrough for me, to release my mental food fears and to remember that this moment (and muffin) was feeding my soul.

Coffee in hand, I grabbed my provided copy of *Poustinia* and headed out to my screened porch to read the recommended chapters one and six—on true solitude and the hermitage experience. Already, at 9:00 A.M., I felt at peace. God's love filled me with the rest I sought, and I refocused on His agenda for my life. I needed to remember I was on His time, not to rush my plans or future because I felt I was not accomplishing anything or that I was missing out on where I thought I should be. I concentrated on my love of my family, on my purpose of helping others (including volunteering to help my students). I focused on the calm presence of the nature around me and fought the urge to get my mental to-do list in order. Finally, peace.

2:00 P.M. What a serene day, away from the hustle of day-to-day living. I thought about how I could do this at home too, but it would never be the same. At home, I knew I would scurry around with ten concurrent projects of cleaning, chores, and errands, while trying to also pay attention to Suerte. I'd have a movie on in the background and I'd check e-mail and Facebook incessantly. Here, I could follow God's will—enjoying coffee and fresh bread, already partaking in two naps, and I'd just covered every trail on the property in a forty-five minute walk.

Oh, the beauty of this late summer day! About eighty degrees outside, blue sky peppered with fluffy white clouds. I'd love to drop a blanket down on the prairie and soak up the sunshine, but I forgot my swimsuit. God forbid I get tan lines from my "I am Loved" t-shirt and jean shorts.

I'd successfully fought the urge to turn on my iPod, even to listen specifically to my Christian music. The peaceful silence fed my soul much better than the music could right now, and I'd break the serenity if I stopped on a Lady GaGa song (even though I loved them). During my walk, I carried my map of PiT in my pocket, just in case I got lost. I also fought the urge to take it out "just to see where I was." I kept my faith in the Lord (and in my keen sense of direction) and of course I found the way right back to my cabin. It was a great reminder that even when I felt lost, or when I needed to double-check on where I was going, God would continue to walk with me and show me the way.

I picked up a rock on the trail to commemorate my first trip to PiT, wanting to find a pretty one to remember my time. Out of nowhere, I found a small blue one with a small "plateau" growing out of the center on top. I envisioned my little rock as my life: how I was a small part at the center, but also a piece of something much bigger than myself. I proudly held my rock all the way back to St. Peter.

4:30 P.M. I'm sad to think I have only one hour left, some of which time will be spent preparing my hermitage for the next hermit. I felt myself relax in the arms of God here, a place where I was protected from my fears and frustrations. Maybe part of me also felt I was in hiding here from going back home to where I had to face head-on the same fears and frustrations. I even did a mental calculation of what it would cost to live here, and sadly, it was not possible on a teacher's salary.

I was stronger than the broken teacher who had arrived here yesterday, the one who was (just before arriving) texting her ex to spend the following weekend with her. I'd already proven to myself I *could* be alone, even completely alone in a hermitage in the woods with no electricity, iPod, no TV, and minimal cell phone use; now I just needed to do it at home.

For once in my adult life, I needed to be alone—no

boyfriends or random dates, no signing up for online dating, no set-ups from well-intentioned pals. With all I'd been and lived through, I knew I was far from weak. I was very much the opposite, and much of that came from the love I received from my family and friends. I'd faced cancer and divorce, all within the same year, and I'd emerged on the other side as the confident woman I used to be before marriage. I'd faced trials and challenges many women my age would, I hoped, never experience in their long lives, and I'd successfully coped with each one. How could I fear the unknown of my future when I'd conquered the nightmares of my present?

Besides, it couldn't get any worse, right? :D

Epilogue

FROM CARINGBRIDGE.ORG,
TUESDAY, OCTOBER 6, 2009 9:37 PM, CDT:

Dum, *dum dah dum dum dum, dum dum dah dum dum...
(Okay, so just imagine the graduation march in your head...)*

*I am now a graduate of Chemo College! One year of poisonous
infusions is finally over. I went for my final Herceptin treatment on
Monday with my hot date (Jenni from work), dressed up in my cap
and honor cords. My tassel proudly read 2009—borrowed from my
sister Rachel—and I wore one cord for each of the chemo drugs I
lived through plus one for the hormones that I'm still taking. I have
never been so excited in my life to be stuck with an IV needle. It was
so bittersweet to leave, knowing it would be the last time I saw the
wonderful nurses who have helped me through so much. I wanted to
take pictures of all of the nurses I knew, but I didn't want to seem too
weird. I left with the pictures that I hold in my memory.*

*I did leave a final batch of chocolate chip cookies and a hug for my
nurse Jenny.*

It is surreal that I don't have to go back in three weeks. It was nice to

293

have these months to "wean myself" off the treatments, getting used to not going weekly. I look forward to my once-every-four-months checkups with Dr. Bloom rather than the infusions, and with every checkup, I'm closer to being officially in remission.

Technically, I won't be in full remission until I've been cancer-free for five years, so that will take a while.

I was also elated to see that Dr. Bloom was rated as one of the best oncologists in the Minneapolis area, making me even more confident in my decision to switch to his care.

Through these past two months, I've been as far from being a "cancer patient" as I could ever imagine. I'm proud of how far I've come and how much I've learned and grown. I'm now stuck in a new reality, though: the "after-cancer, now-what?" life. I went from being a wife, to being a full-time patient, to being a poster child for breast cancer, to where I am now. I wrestle with trying to figure out who I am now and where I want my life to go. Even without the answers I'd love to have, I'm blissfully happy with having the greatest family and friends. I have a job that keeps me on my toes and makes me smile every single day. I'm living with the thought of having a fabulous cancer-free future, no matter where I end up.

I hope to never lose this optimism...

FROM CARINGBRIDGE.ORG, FRIDAY, NOVEMBER 13, 2009 8:30 PM, CST:

More great news! I talked to my oncologist this week about stopping the Tamoxifen, and he agreed that it would be okay, since the drug does so little to actually help me anyway. Not that the additional pill was awful, but it's one less reminder of the past year.

He also brightened my week by telling me that my every-four-month checkups would be my only cancer screening from here on in. No more MRIs, no more blood tests. I just have to be aware of my body and anything that may seem off. That will be my greatest indicator to how well I'm doing.

It still chilled me to the bone, however, when he reminded me what recurrence really does mean for me. If my cancer actually resurfaces, it is no longer curable. They would focus on helping me live as long as possible, that I lead as good a life as my health will allow.

Yep, I'm still mortal. Check.

Good thing I'm not allowing recurrence to happen. Take that, cancer cells!

My fundraiser for the Pay it Forward Foundation went very well. I sold "Cancer Sucks" t-shirts to raise money for the foundation that graciously helps women going through cancer treatment with their living expenses. I was a part of that group last year, and I know firsthand how that money was a blessing. I am proud that my family, my friends, and I could be a part of truly paying it forward to someone else in need. In the future, I will remember to order more L and XL shirts and fewer S. I should have known that larger shirts are just more comfortable. I will donate my extra smalls and mediums to the Cancer Resource Center at Mercy, so they can either give them away or get more donations from others.

THANK YOU to everyone who supported the fundraiser! It was so humbling to receive so much selfless support.

I love being a full-time teacher again, living every day filled with activity and laughter. I truly appreciate how wonderful my new "normal" is.

FEBRUARY 5, 2010

It seemed funny how I left the hermitage committed to being a strong, single woman; then the next day, I went on my first date with the man I would spend the rest of my life with.

My Kern was and is the combination of all the things I've always wanted in a partner—strong, supportive, makes me laugh, comforts me when I'm down, and loves more than anything to cuddle and kiss me. How lucky I was to have found him when I did, when I was back to being me, when I was finally ready for someone good to share my life with.

In these past few months, I'd done many things on the list of life goals I wrote for myself while sipping coffee on the screen porch of St. Peter. I'd completed a fundraiser for the Pay it Forward foundation. I'd made plans to take another trip abroad this summer. I'd had at least one "date night" a week, even if just with myself. I'd helped almost all of my students pass all of their classes (though some were proving to be greater challenges than I'd banked on). I'd written my memoir.

When I'd have the days that seemed to knock me down, I needed to read only a few pages here, and instantly I became grateful for every blessing, every day, every experience, that I didn't think I had two years ago. So grateful.

Resources

The following section is just a starting place for finding invaluable resources for cancer patients, their families, friends, neighbors and caregivers. Please feel free to visit my Facebook site for live hypertext links, ongoing updates, additions, etc.

American Cancer Society: http://www.cancer.org/

"The Bible" of all things cancer-related. There is everything from information about types of cancers, keeping a healthy lifestyle, finding support and treatment, research around cancer topics, and how to get involved in fundraising for the ACS. A reliable website with great references! It also has a search feature that will allow you to discover resources in your area, such as ACS offices and local events. There is even a Youth Scholarship Program for cancer survivors who were diagnosed under the age of twenty-one. (I'm all about free money for furthering education.) Also in Spanish and Asian Languages! Also available any time by phone: 1-800-227-2345.

Finding and Paying for Treatment
http://www.cancer.org/treatment/findingandpayingfortreatment/index

Caregiver Support
http://www.cancer.org/Treatment/Caregivers/index

Children and Cancer
http://www.cancer.org/Treatment/ChildrenandCancer/index

Virginia Piper Cancer Institute
http://www.allinahealth.org/ahs/anw.nsf/page/vpci

In the Allina Hospitals system, Virginia Piper is one of the leading cancer centers in the country (in my opinion). The link to clinics will give you an extensive list of oncologists and their clinics in the metro area. The Minneapolis clinic is one of the top in the state.

Mercy Cancer Center

http://www.allinahealth.org/ahs/mercy.nsf/page/cancercenter_home

This is where I received chemotherapy from my first oncologist. A link to Patient and Family Resources will put you in touch with a social worker that can help you with support groups, financial support, patient care programs, and counseling. My social worker also put me in contact with the Pay It Forward and Angel Foundations (both of which paid for a month of my bills).

Dr. Stuart Bloom, Oncologist, Minnesota Oncology Minneapolis

http://mnoncology.com/your-team/physicians/stuart-h-bloom-md-msc/

The best oncologist you could ask for. Not only does he treat the cancer, he primarily treats the patient. He understands that there's more to life than treating your illness, and he works to help you have the best outcome for you. In his "former life," he was a stand-up comedian in New York. You can tell; he's hilarious! But, more importantly, he is a determined and successful doctor. He has also been rated as one of the top oncologists in the Twin Cities by Mpls St. Paul Magazine. His nurse is always available and willing to go the extra mile to help you out.

Dr. Jennifer Harrington, Harrington Plastic Surgery

http://www.harringtonplasticsurgery.com/

Voted multiple times in the Mpls St. Paul Magazine as one of the top plastic surgeons in the Twin Cities, Dr. Harrington is one of the best medical professionals I've ever worked with (and I have my fair share of experience now). From the first day I met her, she took great care to learn who I was, not just as a patient, but as a person. She supported and guided me through months of reconstructive surgery. I am blessed to have her expertise displayed forever. Her skilled staff, Kathy and Kim, always focused on me and asked me questions about my life. They all genuinely cared about me and my care.

Dr. Dana Carlson, Specialists in General Surgery

http://health.allina.com/providers/159

The first doctor I saw in my cancer treatment that showed me what a great provider looks like. She is a skilled and caring surgeon who did an amazing job with my bilateral mastectomy.

Mayo Clinic Breast Cancer Page

http://www.mayoclinic.com/health/breast-cancer/DS00328

Starting with a definition of breast cancer, the Mayo Clinic follows up with comprehensive information about symptoms, causes, risk factors, preparing for your appointment, tests and diagnosis, treatment and drugs (including clinical trials), alternative medicine, coping and support, and prevention. You can also sign up for their "Living with cancer" newsletter via e-mail. (AND for all you social networking fiends like me, they are on Facebook, Twitter, and YouTube.)

MC's Breast self-examination
http://www.mayoclinic.com/health/medical/IM01782

Mayo Clinic Cancer Center
http://cancercenter.mayo.edu/?mc_id=cancercenterpilot&placement=bottom
The MCCC is a National Cancer Institute-designated cancer center with three campuses: Phoenix, AZ; Jacksonville, FL; and Rochester, MN. Their magazine, Forefront, is full of their research on the topic.

Mayo Clinic's Breast Cancer Treatment
http://www.mayoclinic.org/breast-cancer/rsttreatment.html
Straight from this web page, "All diagnosis and treatment options for breast cancer described on these pages are available in Minnesota." The clinic's Breast Diagnostic Clinic provides treatment and follow-up care for breast cancer patients. In addition to their oncologists, there are genetic counselors, nurses, and psychologists who provide care. "Mayo Clinic in Rochester, Minn., and in Jacksonville, Fla., are ranked among the Best Hospitals for cancer by U.S. News & World Report." The clinic is also committed to providing access to new patients within 48 hours to meet with their health care team and develop a treatment plan.

National Cancer Institute at the National Institutes of Health
http://www.cancer.gov/
With a domain of .gov, you know that this has to be a reliable resource for all things cancer. Their link headings include cancer topics, clinical trials, cancer statistics, research and funding, and news. You can look up any type of cancer with their hotlinks, including an A to Z list of all cancers, cancers by body location, childhood cancers, adolescents and young adults, and cancer in women. There are also links on clinical trial information and cancer topics, such as definitions, treatment, prevention, genetics, causes, screening, testing, coping with cancer, smoking, NCI Fact Sheets, and a Physician Data Query (PDQ). The PDQ has cancer information summaries, a dictionary, lists of clinical trials, and genetic services directory.

Dictionary of cancer terms
http://www.cancer.gov/dictionary

NCI Drug Dictionary
http://www.cancer.gov/drugdictionary

NCI Dictionary of genetic terms
http://www.cancer.gov/cancertopics/genetics/genetics-terms-alphalist/

NCI Vocabulary Services
http://www.cancer.gov/cancertopics/cancerlibrary/terminologyresources

NCI en español
http://www.cancer.gov/espanol

Caring for the Caregiver
http://www.cancer.gov/cancertopics/coping/caring-for-the-caregiver/page1

Young Survival Coalition
http://www.youngsurvival.org/
One of the best resources I found as a young patient and survivor. This put me in contact with other young patients/survivors, people I desperately needed when going through diagnosis and treatment. These women could relate to exactly what I was going through and gave me so many tips on treatment, clinics, and living with and beyond the "c-word."

CaringBridge
http://www.caringbridge.org
A lifesaver in sharing my story and adventures with my family and friends. This is a free website that allows you to blog. I added the disclaimer on my site that it wasn't to dissuade anyone from talking to me about my story, but it was a quick way to keep everyone informed.

Chemo Chicks
http://chemochicks.com/
A fun spin on cancer resources, "with style, humor, and dignity." This includes articles, fashion, cheer-ups, and resources. I especially loved the shopping ideas; it made being a cancer patient fashionable!

Minnesota Cancer Resources
http://www.mncancerresources.org/
Offers resources and information for Minnesota cancer patients and caregivers. Resource categories include cancer types, caregiver resources, education resources, financial assistance, legal assistance, medical assistance, and support groups.

CancerCare
http://www.cancercare.org/
Free, professional support for anyone affected by cancer: patients and survivors, caregivers, and healthcare professionals. Being a caregiver has to be harder at times than actually being the one in the chemo chair. I can't imagine how helpless someone would feel not being able to take their loved one's pain away.

Caregiving support
http://www.cancercare.org/tagged/caregiving

BreastCancer.org
http://www.breastcancer.org/
Specific information relating to breast cancers. Includes research, cancer and life, treatments and side effects, lowering your risk, and discussion communities.

Café Press
http://www.cafepress.com/
Search "cancer" and your world to cancer clothing is opened. Everything from cancer awareness, cancer sucks, Stand Up 2 Cancer, and chemotherapy, there's a t-shirt for everyone on your Christmas/Kwanzaa/Hanukkah list. I'm a big fan of the "My oncologist is my homeboy" shirt.

Breast Cancer Awareness Association
https://bcaamn.org/
This Minnesota-based group has links to events and news, resources for cancer facts and links, and their annual conference held in Minneapolis in October every year. The conference has a plenary speaker, two break-out information sessions, a luncheon, and a "Sense of Style Show," a fashion show sponsored by a department store and fashions modeled by breast cancer survivors themselves. (I've been invited to model twice, but they seem to lose my name every year.)

Susan G. Komen for the Cure Minnesota
http://www.komenminnesota.org/

Every Mother's Day in the Twin Cities, the Susan G. Komen Foundation sponsors a Race for the Cure. Participants can register as an individual or as a team (a team would be more fun, since they come up with the silliest and most inspiring team names) to raise money for Komen's breast cancer research. There is also a link to other fundraising events in the area and fundraising partnerships with other companies (such as Warners' Stellian, Yoplait, and the Minnesota Lynx). There is another link to grant recipients, an application for Community Grant Requests, and even a mammography facility finder.

Susan G. Komen for the Cure
http://www.komen.org/

Hope Chest for Breast Cancer
http://hopechest.us/

What an amazing foundation! Since being founded in 2001, they have provided more than $1 million in support to more than 2,000 breast cancer patients and their families in the Twin Cities. Their financial programs are financial assistance with rent/utilities/other needs, "Delivered Meals that Heal," and early detection and screening programs. Their funds are raised through donations of upscale furniture, accessories, and women's clothing at one of their two retail stores (Orono and St. Paul), individual or corporate donations, and fundraising events. One of their fundraisers is "A Year of Hope" calendar for sale each year. The months are filled with stories of hope from cancer patients and survivors.

Purchasing a calendar
http://hopechest.us/year-of-hope-calendar/

University of Minnesota Masonic Cancer Center
http://www.cancer.umn.edu/research/programs/wc.html

This Women's Cancer Research Program has information for patients and public, including cancer information, clinical trials, events and outreach, making a gift to the program, and survivorship. Susan Pappas-Varco also heads up a young survivor support group that meets either in Edina or at the U. Her e-mail to be added to the electronic invitations: spappas-varco@umphysicians.umn.edu.

Bikers Battling Breast Cancer Minnesota
http://bbbcmn.com/
If you like motorcycles, and you want to support breast cancer awareness, then this is the group for you! They host an annual ride/event (in 2011, it was in Stillwater, MN) to raise funds for the Breast Cancer Research Foundation. This is a link to their Facebook page:

http://www.facebook.com/pages/Bikers-Battling-Breast-Cancer-Minnesota-TM/121313137910562

Minnesota Breast Cancer Coalition
http://mnbcc.org/
Much like many of the other sites, this site includes links on advocacy, how to volunteer with the MNBCC, donating to their cause, and their contact information. However, there are some great new links! You can request a free book, "100 Questions & Answers about Breast Cancer." There is also a link on how to host a fundraiser OR to request a speaker to come to your event!

Minnesota Department of Health
Breast and Cervical Cancer Screening, Sage Program
http://www.health.state.mn.us/divs/hpcd/ccs/screening/sage/
For eligible women, Sage provides free office visits for breast and cervical exams, as well as a screening mammogram and Pap smears. You can call 1-888-6HEALTH to see if you are eligible. The site also offers information on breast and cervical cancer and Minnesota's Breast and Cervical Cancer Treatment Program.

Screening recommendations
http://www.health.state.mn.us/divs/hpcd/ccs/screening/sage/recommendations.htm

Services and eligibility
http://www.health.state.mn.us/divs/hpcd/ccs/screening/sage/services.html

List of participating clinics (by county)
http://www.health.state.mn.us/divs/hpcd/ccs/screening/sage/providers.htm

African American Breast Cancer Alliance
http://aabcainc.org/
This site educates and helps Black/African-American women, men, people

of color, families, and communities in the struggle with breast cancer. Under the AABCA Items link there is a "Sister 2 Sister" Directory for Black women diagnosed with breast cancer, posters, mugs, t-shirts, and bookmarks. Link to the Black Women's Health site:

http://www.blackwomenshealth.com/2006/index.php

Black Women's Health Imperative
http://www.healthyblackwomen.org/issues-and-resources/black-women-and-breast-cancer/

Link to Sisters Network, Inc.
http://www.sistersnetworkinc.org/

Office of Minority Health
http://minorityhealth.hhs.gov/
The OMH is dedicated to improving the health of racial and ethnic minority populations through the development of health policies and programs that will eliminate health disparities. They offer programs that address disease prevention, health promotion, risk reduction, healthier lifestyle choices, use of health care services, and barriers to health care. Specific populations (links provided) are African American, American Indians/Alaska Natives, Asian Americans, Latinos, and Native Hawaiians/Pacific Islanders. There are also links to data and statistics, on becoming culturally competent, and health topics.

Facing Our Risk of Cancer Empowered (FORCE)
http://www.facingourrisk.org/
FORCE is the only national nonprofit organization devoted to hereditary breast and ovarian cancer. Their mission is to provide support, education, advocacy, awareness, and research specific to hereditary breast and ovarian cancer. There are links to information and research, support for patients and survivors, how to help FORCE, how to be an advocate, and FORCE events.

National Breast Cancer Coalition
http://www.breastcancerdeadline2020.org/
Links to Give, Learn, Know, and Act. You can also sign a petition and tell The President to join us in ending breast cancer by the end of the decade. The fun links, picture mnemonic devices, answer questions like, "Why now?" "What if we fail?" "How will we do it?" "Who is behind us?" and "What are the leaders saying?"

Living Beyond Breast Cancer
http://www.lbbc.org/

The LBBC empowers all women affected by breast cancer to live as long as possible with the best quality of life. I appreciate the diversity in their links to include: Newly Diagnosed, Metastatic Breast Cancer, African-American, Latina, Young Women, and High Risk. Sometimes it is difficult to find direct links to these specific pieces of breast cancer.

LBBC Library Newly-Diagnosed
http://lbbc.org/Audiences/Newly-Diagnosed

Just poke around the site until you find the Newly-Diagnosed information in the LBBC Library. There are forty-six articles, twenty-two videos, fourteen events, nine "ask the expert," and five pages just for this population. Man, I wish that I had these links back when I needed them most. Being newly diagnosed is scary, and there are SO many choices you have to make within only a few days of diagnosis. These resources are helpful!

Alternative Cancer Therapies, Wellness Directory of Minnesota
http://www.mnwelldir.org/docs/cancer1/altthrpy.htm

I'm not a proponent of alternative therapies, though I can't say the thought behind them isn't intriguing. This is a site that gives information on specific alternatives.

The Cancer Information Network
http://www.cancerlinksusa.com/support/index.asp

On the left side of the home screen, there are great links geared toward the newly diagnosed again. Yay! I like the links to understanding your prognosis and finding a treatment center. There are links to all cancers, links to books recommended by their oncologists, a monthly newsletter you can subscribe to, and links to many support organizations.

Cancer Hope Network
http://www.cancerhopenetwork.org/

Patient Advocate Foundation
http://www.patientadvocate.org/

Cancer Wellness
http://cancerwellness.org/

Cancer Supportive Survivorship Care
http://www.cancersupportivecare.com/psychosocial.html

Anderson Network
http://www.mdanderson.org/patient-and-cancer-information/guide-to-md-anderson/patient-and-family-support/anderson-network/index.html

Link to a cancer caregivers support blog
http://health.groups.yahoo.com/group/Cancercaregiversrus/

CareGivers4Cancer
http://www.caregivers4cancer.com/
Site reads: "Caregivers4Cancer is here to educate and assure caregivers and oncology teams there are ways to ease the journey's relentless demands. You can emerge on the other end with less stress, more energy, and a feeling of accomplishment that you did all you could for your loved one." Includes the story behind the inception of this organization, links to support services, articles and resources, and a blog from the author.

Herceptin Information
http://www.herceptin.com
When I was her-2-neu positive, I had no idea what that meant or what Herceptin would do to help me with my cancer treatment. This website was phenomenal in describing all I needed to know about this.

Taxotere Information
http://www.taxotere.com
One of the drugs I was prescribed in my chemo cocktail, this website was very informational in finding out what Taxotere does.

Women's Health Magazine
http://www.womenshealthmag.com/
This is one of the best magazines for women's issues I've subscribed to. Not only does it have nutrition and exercise tips monthly, it also has sex/love, beauty, and style information. I loved this subscription and shared it always with my sisters.

Myriad Testing
http://www.myriadtests.com

This was the company that my genetic counselor sent my blood samples to. This site has great information on how/why/what the tests include, including my "favor polymorphism:"

http://www.myriadtests.com/result-coap2-nomut.htm

Pacem in Terris
http://www.paceminterris.org

This is the wonderful hermitage that I stayed in and talked about at the end of my book. Through the solitude, incredibly beautiful scenery, and the warmth of being surrounded by God's love and creation, I received just what I needed to regain inner strength through quiet reflection. The hermitage has many guest cottages, each named after a figure from the Bible, available for stays year-round. I recommend going on a Friday-Sunday trip; Friday there is a home-cooked dinner for all hermits at the main house that was incredible, and the rest of the weekend is yours. One night was enough for me at the time, but I sure would have enjoyed two!

BOOKS I READ OR THINK WOULD BE GOOD

Uplift: Secrets from the Sisterhood of Breast Cancer Survivors, by Barbara Delinsky

This was a nice one to read, though I wish I had saved it for during treatment. It was a lot to digest right after diagnosis.

Crazy Sexy Cancer Tips, by Kris Carr

Now THIS is what every young woman diagnosed with cancer should read! Not only did Kris tell about her own journey, she had the stories of many other young women to inspire me. She was funny and a gas to read. The laughter helped on more than one occasion!

Crazy Sexy Cancer Survivor: More Rebellion and Fire for Your Healing Journey, by Kris Carr

Again, what a fun book to read. I fell in love with her humorous style of writing and how she could make even the bleakest moments seem manageable.

Chicken Soup for the Surviving Soul: 101 Healing Stories About Those Who Have Survived Cancer, by Jack Canfield, et. al.
Yes, I am a big chicken-soup-for-the-soul fan. I have had more than fifteen of them at any given time. What better way to inspire me than with what has worked so often for me in the past. This was a gift from my mother.

Chicken Soup for the Breast Cancer Survivor's Soul: Stories to Inspire, Support, and Heal, by Jack Canfield, et. al.
Ironically, even with my love of the soup books, I never read this one!

Pretty is What Changes, by Jessica Queller
This was one of my inspirations for writing this book. Queller was also a young survivor in busy NYC, a successful business woman. However, what she didn't have to deal with was her husband leaving her (she was single). Sometimes I wished that I could have dealt with just one traumatizing event at a time, as she did.

A Spiritual Journey Through Breast Cancer, by Judy Asti
The first book I read after diagnosis. Judy combined her cancer treatment with her spiritual devotion, something I really needed to hear at the time.

I am Not My Breast Cancer: Women Talk Openly About Love and Sex, Hair Loss and Weight Gain, Mothers and Daughters, and Being a Woman With Breast Cancer, by Ruth A Peltason
I enjoyed this one not just for the information, but for the fact that finally a book on breast cancer addressed love, sex, and hair loss!

Fighting for Our Future: How Young Women Find Strength, Hope, and Courage While Taking Control of Breast Cancer, by Beth Murphy
I found out about this book from another member of the Young Survival Coalition; she was one of the women that contributed to this book! Her story about losing "all" her body hair was something I hadn't thought about before losing my hair, but it was funny and true!

The Victoria's Secret Catalog Never Stops Coming: And Other Lessons I Learned From Breast Cancer, by Jennie Nash
Can you tell that I preferred to read humorous cancer books? Here is another example!

Why I Wore Lipstick to My Mastectomy, by Geralyn Lucas
It was great to relate to another young survivor talking openly about what it was like to lose her breasts. This helped me deal with the body image issues that I knew I'd have for years.

Crazy Sexy Diet: Eat Your Veggies, Ignite your Spark, and Live Like You Mean It!, by Kris Carr

Just Get Me Through This!: A Practical Guide to Coping with Breast Cancer, by Deborah A. Cohen

The Breast Cancer Companion: A Guide for the Newly Diagnosed, by Nancy Sokolowski

Breast Cancer Husband: How to Help Your Wife (and Yourself) during Diagnosis, Treatment, and Beyond, by Marc Silver

Promise Me: How a Sister's Love Launched the Global Movement to End Breast Cancer, by Nancy G. Brinker (founder of Susan G. Komen)

You Can Do This!: Surviving Breast Cancer Without Losing Your Sanity or Your Style, by Elisha Daniels

Stand by Her: A Breast Cancer Guide for Men, by John W. Anderson
What I wish my ex had read and not returned to the library without my knowledge.

Eat Pray Love, by Elizabeth Gilbert
Now a major motion picture starring Julia Roberts, I felt instantly connected to Liz's quirky and beautiful writing style, not to mention that she was going through a painful divorce. I lived vicariously through her journey of finding herself through her travels. Loved the book, wasn't such a fan of the movie.

The Purpose Driven Life, by Rick Warren
One of the books I read to help me in my spiritual coming-of-age. It helped me realize that there is so much more out there than just me, that there is a reason for everything. Even if you aren't religious, the wisdom you gain from this book could be immeasurable.

The Last Lecture, by Randy Pausch

Though I didn't have children of my own, Randy talked about his own terminal journey and wanting to leave a legacy behind for his kids. In a way, I followed in his footsteps by writing my memoir, but I am lucky to get to verbally share my story with my daughter someday.

CPSIA information can be obtained at www.ICGtesting.com
Printed in the USA
BVOW03s0619030813

327577BV00003B/11/P